Praise for The Greatest Deception

Columbia Book Review

The Greatest Deception by Morningstar is obviously the product of many years of study, contemplation and development. As the original title genuinely indicates, 'A New Vision' is indeed a new vision for those willing to explore not only theological dogma, but also consider the powers that drive the world we live in and the forces that motivate human endeavor... For the curious readers who are willing to entertain unconventional approaches to theology and philosophy, The Greatest Deception is intriguing, intelligent, and at times, provocative.

In a manner fitting for the task, the author begins with a thorough discussion at the creation of Adam and Eve, raising (and providing original answers to) questions that have plagued both the thoughtful and the faithful for millennia. The book then continues to explore religious texts as well as historic events, progressing all the way forward to our contemporary times and events...

The Greatest Deception is a multidisciplinary treatise that would intrigue readers who are open to questioning conventional religious dogma; it is an interesting and comprehensive work that could stimulate discussions about faith specifically and humanity in general...

The Greatest Deception addresses issues in detail, dedicating discussions for each of the leading faiths currently popular... There is also an extensive analysis and critiques of various other works in the theological, political, and historic realms...

This revised edition takes the determined reader... on a fascinating (or fantastical) intellectual-spiritual journey that encompasses nothing short of a truly new vision of the world, the forces driving it, the events unfolding around it, and the fate awaiting it. It is comprehensive, intriguing and courageous in its stark departure from conventional thought. Highly recommended! — TheColumbiaReview.com.

Independent Book Review

What if everything you knew about religion, history, and the government was a lie?... Similar to Behold a Pale Horse, this book questions authority and highlights topics mainstream society usually discards... After reading The Greatest Deception, readers will ponder the ultimate truth of this world.

Publisher Services

Material is intelligent and certainly provocative but so scientific and complicated it could lose the average audience. Expect to intrigue but also offend readers. Technical work is to be applauded, though... the author writes with authority and one has to believe she did her research amazingly well. An ambitious and unique project. Thought-provoking but very jarring. No beloved belief is sacred – quite literally.

Amazon Review

This is a... passionately written and prophetic book that offers a new interpretation of the Bible... It encourages the readers to... live from their heart, nurture themselves and others with compassion and gratitude, love the goodness in themselves and others, love earth mother and respect all relations.

Amazon Book Description

The Greatest Deception reveals ancient secrets going back thousands of years and how they are culminating in events happening in the USA and around the world. It takes you on a journey that will leave you stunned as the veil of deception is ripped asunder. This book will shatter the façade we are living under and show you how to break away from things that draw you into a false life. The Greatest Deception will help humanity turn off our path of destruction, and claim our optimal future.

Acknowledgements

David, your doomsday nightmares showed me dangers we're facing. Aaron, thanks for your art and visions. Jared thanks for manifesting miracles with me. Ruby and Myndee, thanks for your comments. Sandra, you handed me the torch. Lorin, thanks for numbering PDFs.

The most explosive, profound book
You will ever read

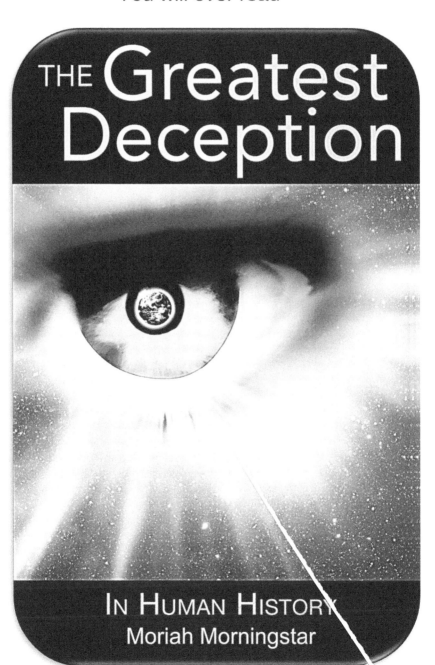

THE Greatest
Deception

IN HUMAN HISTORY
Moriah Morningstar

Previously

The Greatest Deception: In Human History

1st printing 2007
A New Vision: the mystery of the gospel revealed

Permissions:
Every effort was made to obtain permissions for lyrics and illustrations. Lyrics are included for educational purposes.

Non-Profit Research:
This book is the result of 29 years of unpaid research by the author.

The reader is responsible
for use of information provided by this book.

Republished by Amazon
3rd edition July 2023

Cover illustration:
DB Graphics Designs
Moriah Morningstar
Kindle Direct design team

Hebrew, Greek words sourced from:
Exhaustive Concordance of the Bible (Strong)

Bible scripture sourced from
King James Version

Contact Morningstar:
Moriah_wind@hotmail.com

Illustration Credits

Online accessibility may not be available

Journal	colorbox.com
Doorway	dreamtime.com
White Buffalo Woman	sagegoddess.com
Miracle	whitebuffalomiracle.homestead.com
Light-beams	housebeautiful.com
FireFly	airborne/sys.com
Church	iStock.com
Footprints	lipartpanda.com
Aquarius	Kagaya
Plagues	IMDB.com
High Priest garment	bible-history.com
Tabernacle	sofii.org
UFO	syracusenewtimes.com
Ark of the Covenant	bibleapocalypse.com
Road	lauriegough.com
Humpty Dumpty	cwl.nsw.gov.au/
Graveyard	©lik7even cliparto.com
Double-headed eagle	dfreeclipart.com
Creek	Graphcut Textures
Buffalo bones	Legendsofamerica.com
Buffalo	Tina King
Candlestick	Josephsmithfoundation.org
Scroll	©Ghenadie cliparto.com
Angel	png.com
Heal the World poster	vyrics.com/files/images/57.jpg
Flowering Stick	Aaron Ray
Steeds of Apollo	Lumen Winter
Earth	123rf.com
Diamond Head Sunrise	Anthony Casay
Hopi	t.skies.com/hopi
Hopi Prophecy Rock	theorionzone.com
Hopi tablet	Frank Waters

Dominion theology	thoughtco.com
Feel Good	Google
Morgellons fibers	The Guardian
Heartbeat	walpaperlist.com
Alien	Barnes&Noble journal-cover
Reptilian	jeradsmarantz.blogspot.com
Super-soldier	villians.fanton.com
Girl seeing space	pinterrest.com
Krampus	Christmas card
Solar eclipse	Google
Olympic Rings	en.cnccchina.com/news/
Earth	Green Earth stock photos
Trump—pig photo	Google
Veggie stand	Google
Jesus	etys.com
Astral art	Google
Kangaroo	picgifts.com
Sunflower frame	©Daniel Taurino dreamstime.com
Northern Lights	56thparallel.com
USA map	Haviv.org
Hands holding earth	lifecoachcode.com
World Government	thrivemovement.com
Satan holding earth	Jesuspreacher.com
Golden World	deviantart.com
Day/Night	ab-real-estate.com
Mithra	hermeticmagick.com
Numerology	whatisall.com
Obama/Osama	public domain
Church/State	auhuston.org
Federal Reserve	DDees.com
States' Rights	austincountynewsonline.com
Bill of Rights	clip-library.com
Human Rights	1stockphoto.com
Lincoln, Hamilton, Jefferson, Kennedy	public domain
Buffalo	shutterstock.com
Mountain	livescience.com
Twin Towers	Britannica.com/topic/world-trace-center
During 9-11	©Robert Clark/INSTITUTE

After 9-11	crossfitdefined.com
Patriotic frame	starfishanddreams.com
I Pet Goat II	Heliophant.com
USA Seal	americanheraldry.org
Official Seal	ssunitedstatestrust.org
White Knight	bibleofmemes.fandom.com
Apollo-13 patch	science.ksc.nasa.gov
Apollo-13	themarsgeneration.org
Challenger disaster	history.com
Stand Together	redbubble.com
Asteroid	ksl.com
Berlin wall of dominos	chinadaily.com
Holistic doctors	naturalhealth365.com/GcMAF-holistic-doctors-
Children	wikishare.us.
Fairy	Google
Musical rainbow	photobucket.com
11:11	soultravelrules.com
The Twins statue	travelbunny8.blogspot.com
House	Google
Hearth	kitchendinner.com
Broom	wikimedia.org
Jack and Jill	tes.com/lessons
Doorway, prophecy book	gograph.com
100th Monkey	bloktalkraido.com
Pencil	worldartsme.com
Stop sign	clipartpanda.com
Scroll	©Ghenadie cliparto.com
Eternal Golden World	yogajournal.com
Preamble to US Constitution	mathewbarlow.net
Evil Uncle Sam	takemylifeplease.net
Atlantis	An Earth Dweller's Return
Angel in Revelation	principlesforlive.org
Mona Lisa	Prado's Mona Lisa
Jesus	Da Vinci
Hollow earth map:	thetruthbehindthescenes.wordpress.com
Review	clipcartoons.com

Our Children

Aaron Ray
  Mountain of Strength, Brilliance, Protector

David Joseph
  Beloved, Cherished, Arise, Increase

Jason Don
  Healer, Hero, Noble Leader

Ruby Jane
  Purity, Passion, Devotion, Grace,

Jared William
  He Who Lives Long, Warrior

Jarvis Ruben
  Expert with a Spear, Gateway, Behold a Son

I Dedicate My Book To
Christians Jews and Muslims

I pray this book will find its way to you
You will feel my words in your heart
And you will know their truths

My Vision

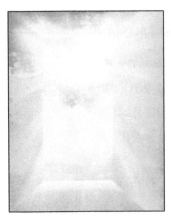 As a child I was homesick for the place I came from before birth. I kissed someone goodbye before I was born, someone I had made a vow with. My promise whispered to me until I had a full knowing: expose Jehovah and stop him from destroying the world by helping Black Elk bring the Great Purification (Hopi prophecy).

{I was raised LDS and taught Adam and Eve had to eat fruit from the tree of knowledge so we could receive a body, which we need for salvation. Satan told Eve why she must do this and Adam and Eve fell. They broke God's commandment so man 'might be' (exist). This was confusing to me as a child. Why did Satan give us salvation?

Mormons believe Satan did not want us to know God has a body. He spread lies saying God was so vast He filled the universe, yet so small He could dwell in our heart. Satan made the truth about God seem like a lie. The Creator is not physical; S/he exists everywhere, including our hearts. The Mormon church believes God and Jehovah have physical bodies and Jehovah is Jesus Christ. Even as a child, I knew Jehovah was wrathful, vengeful, violent and evil. How could he be Jesus?

I left the Mormon Church when my children were little. I studied the founders of quantum physics and cosmology, to learn how the universe was created through science, not the Bible. I discovered energy has self-awareness and matter is energy. The first source is the Creator's Spirit; it condenses into energy, and energy condenses into matter. Everything is made from the Creator's spiritual essence, everything is alive and has consciousness. Spiritual essence weaves its divine intelligence (love-light) through eternity creating the universe and its infinite dimensions: the spirit-that-moves-in-all-things. As we evolve, the universe evolves; we are interconnected.

As I studied the Einstein—Bohr debates, I felt Einstein's presence. I asked him to help me understand creation. That night Einstein entered my dream and told me many things. When I awoke, I remembered Einstein saying 'read Genesis.' I browsed the books I was studying, to remind me of what else Einstein said. Nothing came to me except read Genesis. That did not make sense! I didn't want to read the Bible.

My impression would not go away. I read Genesis and understood what it said. There are two creation stories and two Adams- the Creator's Adam and Jehovah's Adam. I knew what Jehovah was (a demon) and I knew what he did. I was astounded, continued reading and received more insights. I wondered why Genesis was being revealed to me. I didn't want to expose the Bible, I had never heard of Black Elk, and didn't remember my vow to help him.

I asked in prayer why I was shown the meaning of Genesis. I read a Baha'i passage that day, that hit my heart with such force, I knew it was my answer: "When religion, shorn of its superstitions, traditions and unintelligent dogmas shows its conformity with science, there will be a great unifying, cleansing force in the world, which will sweep before it all wars... and then mankind will be united in the power of the love of God (Esslemont)." My Bible revelations will be this '**Cleansing Force**,' sheering religion of dogma while conforming to science. Science will support my revelations.

I studied the Bible every day, writing down my revelations. The days turned into weeks, months, and then years. My Bible commentary comes from reading the Bible and my own inspiration. I looked up thousands of Hebrew words for their original meaning; it always confirmed my knowing.

Jehovah was once a man, like Mormon doctrine says, and he reorganized matter as they believe. He bioengineered Adam and Eve (through possession); they fell so demons 'might be' or have existence through a host body. 'Spirit children' waiting for bodies are demons. Demons are ghosts-dead people who did not commune with their Spirit while living. They lost their Spirit at death and have no inner light. Demon-ghosts have no body except through possession.

Mormons believe they can become gods like Jehovah. "As man is, God once was, and as he is, you may become." If you do not commune with your Spirit, you will become like Jehovah when you die (a demon).}

You must draw on everything within you- intellect, intuition and heartfelt prayer, to know Jehovah's identity- a wrathful, evil demon-god, and separate him from Jesus who is sweet and loving. It's hard. Reading this book may give you a headache. It may go against beliefs that cause you pain when exposed. Stay with it; feel my words in your heart and you will know if they are true. When you see behind Jehovah's deception, you will know he hijacked Jesus.

When I began writing Bible revelations, I was inspired to use the name Moriah Morningstar. I did not know why until months later. Black Elk's vision has a Morning Star, and he gave my book the power of the **Cleansing Wind**; Moriah means wind. The world will be Cleansed through the Great Purification or it will be Conquered.

Years later I discovered an ancient bloodline order going back thousands of years: Moriah **Conquering Wind**. They founded the World Council of Churches, Skull and Bones, Vatican Hierarchy, Masons, Illuminati, CIA and other secret societies. The Global Elite are the Superclass. They hold world power and control earth's resources, including us. Their apocalypse has started. They are enslaving humanity for Jehovah's New Jerusalem.

Moriah's Cleansing Wind
will counter
Moriah Conquering Wind

TV Troops

Einstein helped me unravel the mystery of the gospel. In my first edition, I told this story. Then I removed Einstein's name, calling him an angel (messenger from the other side). Einstein's role in my vow to help humanity went missing from my book for many years. In 2019 I felt Einstein's presence while reading Einstein's Secret (Belateche), where Einstein says if we use time travel (Einstein-Rosen bridge) it could destroy humanity. I felt Einstein as I read those words and a hard shudder shook me- this wormhole bridge is being used!

E=mc squared (energy and mass are interchangeable) lead to the atomic bomb and Einstein's field equations can create a time travel wormhole. These formulas that Einstein worked out are being used by the Global Elite, to control the world. Einstein helped me break the seals on the Bible to save us from the path of destruction he inadvertently opened.

When Einstein was 13 he rejected the Bible, knowing he had been deceived. God did not punish and reward people. Einstein believed in Spinoza's God, "who reveals himself in the orderly harmony of what exists." Einstein believed scientific truths "spring from a deep religious feeling." He found God in order, beauty, and the intelligence of creation.

Shortly after I began writing Bible messages the evening news said a white buffalo named Miracle was born, who may be announcing White Buffalo Woman's return. Miracle was this prophesied buffalo, she changed colors as she grew. White Buffalo Woman returned, but not as a baby. I was given her dress and shawl in a dream. The shawl symbolized our contact while writing messages. The dress represented our soul exchange which happened seven years later (see Message 19, Destiny Dream 1 and 4.

While writing 'my' last message, Jarvis' game played a song that spoke to me. I Am the Wind told me (Sandra) White Buffalo Woman would leave me- "All things must end, good-bye my friend (Symphony of the Night)." **Note:** Sandra (birth-soul) passed on 9-17-2001. She was going to publish her messages under Moriah Morningstar. I finished her book and legally changed my name to Moriah.

In The Medicine Wheel Sun Bear says: "Some visions are whole and complete and give the person receiving it total understanding of the universe and his or her place in it. Other visions come in parts, none of which is complete in itself.

Eventually, with patience, enough parts come to make the vision complete." 'Our' vision came in parts over 25+ years.

White Buffalo Woman's message was lost, and Black Elk's vision was not understood, not even by him while living. The Nation in his vision was not Sioux; it was Christians, Jews and Muslims- Jehovah's worshippers. If they reject the demon-god of Abraham, Black Elk will become Chief of the Heavens and cleanse earth of demons.

When I (Moriah) saw Black Elk's vision on the Hopi Prophecy Rock, I knew we were destined to bring the Great Purification. Black Elk and White Buffalo Woman are Sioux, yet they are part of Hopi prophecy and it is not what the Hopi expect. 'Our' book rewrites a beloved Sioux legend and it reveals Jehovah's plan for his own salvation.

Stages of Truth: Ridiculed
Schopenhauer
Violently Opposed

Accepted as Self-Evident

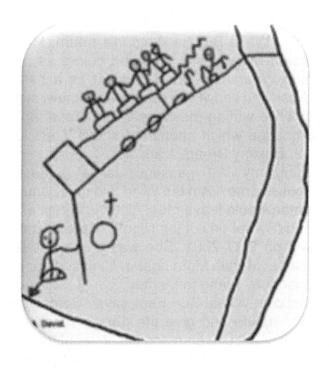

6

Miracle
8-20-94 — 9-19-04

White Black Red Yellow Brown

White Buffalo Woman

Angels Of Light

Angels of light incarnated on earth many eons ago to help free humanity from the bondage of darkness. These heroes of our myths and legends have returned to open gateways of light, close dark passageways, birth new visions, teach us our true history, and stop evil. These heroes from long ago are here to help us stop the dark, ancient shadow-ghosts of death who roam the earth and feed on our life-force. The angels of light will help us ascend to our eternal home.

Myths and legends carry our past in symbolic language. They form foundations that future events build upon. Some myths touch eternity and awaken you to a state of grace, inspiring you to fulfill your destiny. Some myths are depraved and deceive and manipulate you. Bible myths are the latter, they are corrupt and insidiously lull you into a perpetual sleep. If enough people believe a depraved myth, it can destroy the world. The Aquarian Era is beginning; it is the destroyer of ideologies and will reveal truths that shake every nation to its core.

Global catastrophe heralds the birth of every new age as the controllers of the world lose their power. We are caught in a web of their deceptions. Religions have betrayed us, and covert technologies have the capability of destroying life on earth. We are at risk. If we do not awaken from our perpetual sleep, we will not survive and a light will go out in our corner of the universe. We are not alone. Light is piercing the dark.

The world is a façade, a maze of smoke and mirrors. To escape we must find the essential truths of our human condition. Our true Self (inner light) knows these essential truths. It sees through the covert operations and delusions that manipulate us. This is our saving grace. When we hear or read essential truths, it resonates. We can break the restraints that enslave us, defeat the darkness, and reclaim our lives.

Senator William Jenner
Congressional Address
2-23-1954

"Today the path to total dictatorship in the United States can be laid by strictly legal means, unseen and unheard by congress, the President or the people. Outwardly we have a Constitutional Government. We have operating within our government... a Bureaucratic Elite... determined to destroy our Constitution... It operates secretly, silently, continuously to transform our Government without our suspecting the change is under way... This ruthless power-seeking elite is a disease... answerable neither to the President, Congress, nor the courts...

Dr. Wirt... told us in 1934 that the plans were all drawn, the timetable established... The revolutionary cabal and its allies... designed the overall strategy. They broke the whole up into precisely measured parts and carefully timed moves, which appeared to be wholly unrelated... Someone, some-where, conceived the brilliant strategy of revolution by assembly line... divided into separate parts, each of them as innocent, safe and familiar looking... When the parts of a design are carefully cut to exact size, to fit other parts with a perfect fit in the final assembly, the parts must be made according to a blueprint drawn up in exact detail.

The men who make the blueprints know exactly what the final product is to be. They have planned the final assembly years ahead. This assembly line revolution is like a time-bomb... it's not going to be set off until the time is ripe... The switch is not to be pulled until the American people are... convinced that resistance is hopeless."

The plan Wirt was given was true, but it was a Global Elite agenda not Marxists as he was told. Writ was used to create a communist scare. There was no communist infiltration. The plan, now it its final stages, is considered false.

2-23-2019 Jenner told me
The Switch was coming

PART ONE
Moriah's Messages

The Table Of Contents

Moriah's Message 1
Dawn

This book may have found its way to you in answer to my prayer. If you are a Christian, I want to tell you something before I unravel the mystery of the gospel. When you pray to Jesus and feel his love, you know he is sweet and filled with light. There is no violence in Jesus. Do not let go of him when you find out he is not Christ. Jesus was tortured to death as a sacrifice to Jehovah. Jehovah is Christ; he is saving you for his own salvation, not yours.

The Lord your God is 'God of gods' (Deut. 10:17). Jehovah called a council of his gods and they contrived a plan to obtain ever lasting life (exist). Their plan (exist on our life-force) is sealed in the Bible. If their Great and Dreadful Day came, the Lord would loosen the Bible seals, revealing the mystery of the gospel (god-spell). When we understand this mystery, we will cast out the gods and stop their Dreadful Day.

Christians look for their Savior, who will raise them from their grave. Jews await their Messiah, who will rule Israel. Muslims anticipate the Guided one, who will establish an Islamic Empire. This Anointed One (anointed with our life-force) deceived us. **Jesus is not the Savior**; Christ-Jehovah is. The Messiah is not going to rule Israel. The Guided One will not destroy evil. Jehovah's plan is to destroy the world and enslave his chosen.

Jehovah is: I AM   I exist
            Lord   Master
            Christ   Savior of demons
            Satan   Most powerful demon
            Yeshua   Salvation comes from Jehovah
            Heavenly Father   Dwelling place
Jehovah goes by Jesus because he is an imposter.

Jehovah ordered the Israelites to murder, rape, torture, enslave, kill babies by bashing their heads against rocks, and kill their disobedient children. Jehovah cursed the Israelites if they did not slaughter all that breaths when commanded to, saying they would 'eat the flesh of their sons and daughters.' He demanded animal sacrifice and blood-splattering rituals. All of this is in the Old Testament. Jehovah bragged about it.

Jehovah was born hundreds of thousands of years ago. He may have lived a thousand lifetimes before losing his Spirit upon death, becoming a demon-ghost with no life-force. This happens when you do not commune with your Spirit while living. Demon-ghosts will dissolve if they do not consume energy. Worship, negative thoughts, violence, fear and sickness feed them. The Bible was written so Jehovah and his demon-ghosts can exist through our worship. They cannot enter the afterlife or leave earth.

The Lord's salvation is 'from generation to generation (Is 51:8).' He must attach/possess people to exist. Without a host-body, demons disintegrate. When their host dies, the body 'gives up the ghost' and the demon-ghost must find another body to attach too. When you receive The Holy Ghost, a demon-ghost attaches and feeds on your energy. You make a 'daily sacrifice' of your life-force to it. Israel was to guide all nations to the Lord 'that you may be **my salvation** unto the end of the earth (Is 49:6).' The Creator does not need salvation until the earth ends, Jehovah does; he is trapped on earth. His plan is to establish New Jerusalem.

The Creator did not demand human sacrifice to 'prolong his days', Jehovah did. It pleased the Lord to bruise Jesus, put him to grief and make him an offering for our sin so he would see his seed, prolong his days and prosper in his hand (Isaiah 53:10). Grief is 'chalah'- woman in labor. This labor (birthing New Jerusalem) is the Lord's burden. Jehovah bruised Jesus. Bruise is 'daka'- break in pieces. Torture fragments the soul. The pain Jesus suffered was the anguish he went through keeping his soul from fragmenting. Jesus did not offer to remove our sins; working out karma is how we grow spiritually. Jehovah is the Savior of demons, not us. He used Jesus to prolong his life and thrive.

Redeem means 'in exchange for payment.' Jehovah-Christ is a Redeemer. You must give him something for taking your sin. The price is your soul. Jehovah cannot destroy souls, but if he redeems you, he will trap your soul in his heavens when you die. Jehovah deceives us, so we will fall backward, be broken, snared and taken (Is 28:13). He does this to sever your Spirit from your soul, so you will become a demon-ghost like him: "the word of God is… piercing even to the dividing asunder of soul and spirit" (Heb 4:12).

The Creator "is light and in him is no darkness… God is love… There is no fear in love; perfect love casts out fear because fear has torment. He that fears is not made perfect in love (John 1:5, 4:16, 18)." The Creator is light and love; His love casts out fear, and has no darkness.

Jehovah told his servants to fear him (Josh 24:14) and darkness is his secret place (Ps 18:11). Jehovah said "I form the light and create darkness; I make peace and create evil (Is 45:7)." Jehovah makes peace (ceasefire) by creating war. Without war, there is no ceasefire. Jehovah is <u>Satan</u>: <u>Prince of Darkness</u> and <u>Jesus Christ</u>: <u>Prince of Peace</u>.

"While you look for light, he turns it into the shadow of death and makes it gross darkness (Jer 13:16)." Jehovah turns the light we search for into a 'shadow of death' a putrid demon-ghost. Baptism is a satanic ritual where you receive a demon: The Holy Ghost. When Jesus died, Jehovah pretended to be Jesus raised from the dead, saying 'preach baptism.' When baptized in Christ, you receive the substance of his body- death. You are baptized into his death and buried with him (Rom 6:3-4; Col 2:12). Buried is 'sunthapto'- assimilate. Baptize is 'baptizo'- overwhelm. The Lord said his salvation is as a lamp that burns (Is 62:1); burns is 'barr'- consume. Your Holy Ghost consumes your life-force.

Jehovah is the Beast in Revelation 13:18. The number of the Beast is 666. 'Let him who has understanding compute this.' The Beast has 3 names that reduce to 6 in numerology: Jehovah- **6**, Yah**v**eh (YH**V**H)- **6,** Mithra- **6**. Jehovah is Mithra. His image, The Holy Ghost, has the same number (666). Using numerology, <u>The</u> <u>Holy</u> <u>Ghost</u> reduces to <u>6</u> <u>6</u> <u>6</u>.

'The Holy Ghost' is the 'Image of the Beast'- Jehovah. When invited in, the demon-ghost quietly sups your life-force. You will not show signs of possession, but your demon-ghost will feast on your energies like a vampire. If Jehovah's Dreadful Day came, he would call his demon-ghosts to 'come forth' from the burial place in their host and fully possess them.

Paul said the mystery of the gospel and Christ was great and God hid the knowledge of it from the beginning. To the Gentiles this mystery is 'Christ in you' (Col 1:27). Those with Christ in them are Gentiles (non-Jew) and would be killed if the 'fullness of the Gentiles' (their end) came. 'He that shall rise to reign over the Gentiles, in him shall the Gentiles trust (Romans 15:12).' The God that arose over Christians is Jehovah. They are being led like lambs to the slaughter.

Jehovah's Judgment is for demon-ghosts. If the Lord's Dreadful Day came, the most powerful demons would survive their judgment and possess the chosen and remnant (bio-engineered beasts) for garments of salvation. "And white robes were given unto every one of them (Rev 6:11)." The robes (bodies) would feed and protect the demons from the burning light of creation (Rev 7:16).

Paul said the Day of the Lord will come as a thief in the night (I Thes 5:2). A thief comes to kill, steal and destroy. The heavens will pass away with **a great noise**, the elements will melt with fervent heat, the earth will be burned up (II Peter 3:10). This is a nuclear holocaust. Nuclear bombs can be heard over 500 miles away; the heat vaporizes everything. The Lord's chosen would go to underground bases. When the radiation cleared, they would return. Jehovah's chosen and bioengineered beasts would be hosts for demon-ghosts. Jehovah-Satan and his demon-ghosts would control earth.

New Jerusalem is a satanic world with zombies, creatures, and cyborgs. The most powerful families on earth are moving us toward it. Jenner's speech to Congress tells us how their plan is being implemented in the USA. Their blueprint is in its final stage. We are a Police State, only the façade remains. If it comes down, the USA will become a theonomy under Biblical law, the elite will purge the country of 'inferior' people and control all aspects of society. This is Jehovah's plan for the USA, but it is not our destiny. The Constitution was divinely inspired, and it was not founded on Christianity.

David began having doomsday dreams when I started writing this book (1994); they continued until 2022. His night-mares were connected to my book, but I didn't know that until 2009, when I discovered New Jerusalem would first arise in the USA- David's dreams.

{Underline}David's Doomsday Dreams{/Underline}: David is often running for his life in these nightmares yet he does not want to live. He sees a space station that looks the size of the moon in most of his nightmares; it glows at night. People stand in long lines to get vaccinated and wander through grocery isles with bare shelves. Armed troops storm in and take people to assigned areas. Some people are raving mad and eat raw bloody flesh. In some dreams land rises up, rolling in waves (earth tilting?). In other dreams the sky is white (chemtrails?) or on fire.

Military vehicles clog the highways in another doomsday dream. Flags with the FEMA logo fly everywhere. The FEMA logo is similar to the USA Great Seal; the eagle is behind the same shield but the stars are gone. There is a circle with a triangle and the banner says: "Peace and War are Just." FEMA does not recognize States and makes peace through War. UFO's, helicopters, jets, drones (before invented) fill the sky. Nuclear bombs drop on cities. It looked like an alien invasion but it is the US military in manmade UFOs. A colossal US spaceship leaves earth with the Global Elite.

David sees explosions on the moon in many doomsday dreams. They look like tiny flashes of light. A shower of comets light up the night from falling moon debris. Burning hail falls- tiny burning rocks. Blazing basketball-sized rocks and flaming boulders fall from the sky, exploding on impact. The moon expands 3—4 times its size, then turns into a hazy blob from pulverized dust and debris. All life was wiped out from meteor explosions, fires, floods, buildings collapsing, etc. Hopi prophecy says man will travel to the moon. If they bring anything back, humanity may not survive. Was something from the moon brought back? Covert technology?

One year before 9/11 David dreamed of a Muslim falling between two tall buildings. He sliced them up with two long swords as he fell. The Muslim was a cartoon character. David's dream is telling us Osama wasn't a real person and planes were not used on 9-11. Something else brought the towers down. The swords represent tyranny and death.

In 2017 David dreamed Planet X landed in earth's orbit, causing tsunamis around the world. It was populated with aggressive aliens. In 2019 David again dreamed tsunamis occurred around the world. A tidal wave is a widespread advent. David's tsunami dreams are warnings. Is humanity becoming alien: different in nature by an unknown factor (X)?

In 2022 David dreamed he entered his high school science classroom. It looked like church with a cross, pulpit and benches- Jehovah's pseudo-science was being taught in schools. A 10-foot doll and a witch in long red dresses were in the room. The witch painted a mural- a battle between red and blue soldiers; the year was 1777. Pointing to her painting she said 'there will be war.' The painting came alive and the soldiers fought. This war was planned 250 years ago, a civil war between Democrats and Republicans. The doll is Babylon, the witch is satanic sorcery. This satanic spell came alive when Trump came on the scene. He drove a wedge between parties, ripping families apart. Caught up in bitter arguments people lost their senses; we are spellbound.}

Aaron Ray had two future visions. Dry lightning filled the sky. What caused it? Thousands of parachutes carrying cargo were everywhere. What were they delivering? A bright light flashed and troops suddenly materialized. Did teleportation transport them? In another future vision, Aaron Ray saw a field with deep, rectangle pits dug in long rows with roads between them. Were they mass graves?

When WW II ended German scientists developing anti-gravity spacecraft came to the States and covertly continued their research. Other scientists went to Europe and Canada. In Projekt UFO Harbinson says if flying saucers are man-made machines, constructed in secret by European, Soviet,

Canadian and American scientists, "then what we are faced with is an unprecedented, international cover-up." Are space-crafts (UFOs) and bioengineered beasts (aliens) hidden in underground bases? Are aliens and UFO's a hoax?

David saw the being that was turning the United States into a dictatorship- a giant scarab beetle. His nest was inside the US government. The beetle is Jehovah; he can take any form. His plan is for New Jerusalem to arise in the United States. This is why the US secretly supported Hitler, built UFOs and underground bases on the moon and Mars, planned 9-11 and Covid.

Everything the Global Elite do is for New Jerusalem. Every-one outside their royal blood is expendable. They helped Hitler rise to power and created the State of Israel. Their goal is global control of earth for their god. New Jerusalem is their New World Order. Their secret societies are structured like a pyramid. Those at the top know their god is Satan. They feed on our livelihood as demons feed on them. Humanity must change course or we will not survive.

Sun Bear said: "Before any major change has ever occurred on the planet, there have been warnings. These warnings are what people call prophecies." My messages are prophetic warnings. Major changes are about to occur. They will either bring the Apocalypse or the Ascension. We are on the Apocalyptic path where humanity is slaughtered, en-slaved and controlled by powerful demons. If we awaken, we can cast out the demon-ghosts and turn off this dark path.

The earth's axis is between two astrological eras. Pisces is ending and Aquarius is beginning. These polarities are bath-ing earth with great intensity. Piscean energies are waning as Aquarian energies grow stronger. Humanity is separating, aligning with one polarity or the other: those who are comfortable with the old order and fight against the Great Awakening (Pisces) and those who embrace it (Aquarius). Pisces is a mystical era; it holds our collective shadow. During this age kings, religious leaders and authority figures ruled society. It was marked by the rise of Christianity, religious wars and control.

Aquarius is a volatile age of transformation and revolutions. As the Aquarian Dawn grows stronger, widespread changes will occur around the world. Aquarius is the water bearer and brings higher energies to earth. It is the age of freedom, revolution, information- the destroyer of ideologies. Aquarius will reveal things that shake every nation, society, belief system and religion to its core. Aquarius inspires us to see behind the delusions that our lives are caught up in. Some people prefer the bliss of their ignorance. We cannot afford to remain unaware of our covert controllers. Our life is at risk.

Like physicists that discovered the quantum world and had the ground ripped out from under them, Christians, Jews and Muslims may feel like this is happening to them, when they awaken and realize they have been deceived. It felt like I was being ripped apart when I let go of the Mormon Church. Belief systems create walls. Working through trauma caused by false beliefs removes walls and your awareness expands.

Giving up a belief you cherish is painful. "Pain is like a healing emotional fever. Allow your pain to cleanse you and burn away what needs to die. A new and better you will grow from the ashes… [you will be] stronger, wiser, and more loving and compassionate. Out of our suffering, we emerge (McGill)." We speak truth, inspire others, and help them heal.

Facing our betrayals will require courage. The real Jesus will not return and put things right, but he will give us courage to take a stand against evil. Without courage we may be unable to act. With courage we will stand our ground and be heroes, empowering people to interact in a larger social setting, and gain control of critical mass. Aquarius will light our steps with 'mystic crystal revelations.'

Science is not exploring the spiritual side of the universe, and religions have deceived us. Many highly advanced technologies are interfering with our spiritual growth. Some have the capability of destroying life on earth, like genome engineering, nano-technology and antenna arrays.

Doctors destroy Health. Lawyers destroy Justice. Universities destroy Knowledge. Governments destroy Freedom. Media destroys Information. Religion destroys Spirituality

David had a recurring dream of the bluff by our home falling away and the ocean coming in. I thought this was symbolic. How could it be literal? How could the ocean reach Idaho? EISCAT-3D in Northern Europe has this capability. It's 200 times more powerful than HAARP. EISCAT-3D could create a tsunami along the Cascadia subduction zone, devastating the Pacific Northwest.

Global catastrophe heralds the birth of every new age. As the old systems lose their power, the Global Elite tighten their control on religion, government, medical fields, media, food production, commerce, judicial systems, education, military, economies and science. We are caught in a worldwide web of deception. Covert technology is being used to control humanity but if New Jerusalem is established, technology would not be necessary. Zombie-people, fullly possessed, and prisons would be all that is needed. Reclaim your life, reclaim your power and reclaim our earth. Stand, having your loins girt about with truth (Eph 6:14)

"More than two thousand years ago, the mathematician Archimedes said: 'Give me a place to stand, and I will move the earth.' When we take a stand that expresses our soul's commitment it is empowered with the courage of the heart… When we take a stand, we gain access to deep and profound vision (The Soul of Money Lynne Twist)."

> Stand in the place where you live
> Stand in the place where you work
> Stand in the place where you are
> Think about direction
> Wonder why you haven't before
> Your feet are going to be on the ground
> Your head is there to move you around
>
> So Stand
> REM

Maya, Hopi, and other ancient civilizations say when one world ends and another begins, there is great destruction or great evolution. Earth's ascension process has started. If we awaken, the veil will come down, we will defeat Jehovah, humanity will ascend and demons will disintegrate; they cannot exist in higher realms. If we do not stop Jehovah, he will gain total control of the earth.

Earth began with a Golden World. Spring never ended, humanity was androgynous and lived in harmony. There was no evil, hunger, sickness or war. When we return to our androgynous state, the Golden World will return. We will live in harmony, in perfect health and youthful bodies into very old age. This may take 1,000 years, but if humanity survives, it will happen during the Aquarian Era. The Age of Aquarius is the Age of Androgyny.

Aquarius

Rado & Ragni

This is the Dawning of the Age of Aquarius...
Harmony and understanding,
Sympathy and trust abounding
No more falsehoods or derision
Golden living, dreams of visions,
Mystic crystal revelations
And the mind's true liberation
Aquarius...

Moriah's Message 2
Adam

Demons are ghosts- dead people who did not commune with their Spirit while living. They lost their Spirit at death, and have no life-force. They attach to people and consume their energy to exist. Ancient demons, soulless people who died long ago, have existed for thousands of centuries, feeding on the living and consuming weaker demons. Demons have no power of their own; their power comes from us and they use it to destroy us. If we stop feeding demons, they will dissolve.

Jehovah is the most powerful demon-ghost on earth. He died hundreds of thousands of years ago, perhaps in a great cataclysm where he had access to millions of demon-ghosts to consume. Down through the centuries, Jehovah wore different masks. He crucified enlightened beings as Saviors, then pretended to be that Savior risen from the dead.

Through possession, Jehovah bioengineered Adam and Eve. He may have learned genetic engineering during a lifetime on Atlantis and was influential in its fall. Humanity began androgynous. Jehovah separated humans into males and females, forcing their androgynous souls to incarnate as male or female, in separate bodies. Your twin soul is the other half of your soul. When separated, we long for our soul.

Twin souls are now reuniting in great numbers to aid our ascension. (Twin Soul, Eternal Love (Lumezi). If you are the male half of your soul, you may sometimes incarnate as female, and vice-versa. We switch genders. Someday we will return to our original, hermaphrodite state- male/female. We will be whole like the Creator, living in harmony with each other and nature. Our male-female, androgynous energy will bring the world into perfect balance and we will ascend.

The universe is a manifestation of love. All of creation is a reflection of that love; it sustains the universe. When we feel love for all that is, we do not destroy. When everyone has love for themselves, others and nature, the walls that divide us will fall, understanding will spread, and the world will heal.

Lakota Chief 'Noble Red Man' said missionaries came to a ceremony and an eagle joined them. "He stood there on one foot with one leg up in the air. He carried two feathers in his claw and he put them on his head like a crown. Then he started dancing. We danced with him. We all cried to see the eagle dance. Even the missionaries cried..."

"Someday red man and white man will sit down with all the races of humankind and we'll solve our problems together... Someday we'll have ceremonies together and the eagle will come and join us. He'll dance with us. You'll learn what it's like to dance with the eagle... We'll all dance together with God (Noble Red Man Arden)."

Will Noble Red Man's vision come true? We are on a destructive path; it will destroy humanity if we do not change course. There is a way out- a journey that takes us to that dance. In order to find it we need to know how we got on the destructive path, and what to do to get off it.

In Genesis, Lord God's story is mixed with the Creator's story. They can be separated with discernment. **God created** the earth, sun, marine life, birds, creatures of earth (land) and then man (black man). **Lord God formed** man (white man- ruddy is fair skin) and then formed 'beasts of the field.'

Lord God (Jehovah, demon-ghosts) did not create the earth or man. They formed a hybrid woman and man, and hybrid beast-men with bioengineering, breaking creation laws. The Creator created all living creatures to bring forth their own kind. Adam's descendants were commanded to kill and eat flesh. God said herbs and fruit were to be our meat or main sustenance (Gen 1:29).

God creates (beginning to end): Gen 1:1—25, 27, 29—31, Genesis 2: 1—3. Genesis 1: 1—19 tells how the solar system was created (message 20). Gen 1:27 says God created Adam in his own image, in the image of God, created he him- male and female. The Creator's Adam is androgynous.

Lord God forms (beginning to end): Gen 2:4—7, 1:26, 2:8—25, 1:28. 'These are the generations of the heavens and earth, in the day that Lord God made them.' The Lord's generations of heavens and earth are the kingdoms he made in heaven and on earth (Gen 2:4). Lord God organized herbs of the field before planting (bioengineering) them. He had not caused them to rain [sprout, increase] and there was not a man to till the ground (enslave). But there went up a mist [of darkness] from the earth and watered [shaped] the ground. And Lord God formed man from the ground (Gen 2:5—7).

'And God said **let us** make man in **our image**, after **our likeness**. Let them **have dominion**…(Gen 1:26). Lord God is plural. Their formation story ends with Gen 2:25, 1:28: 'the man and his wife were naked and not ashamed. And God blessed them and said unto them '**multiply** and replenish the earth and **subdue** it and **have dominion** over… every living thing.' The Lord said conquer everything that lives.

God created marine life and birds to multiply, not man; only Lord God says man is to multiply. God's Adam ate fruit from every tree (Gen 1:29). Lord God put their Adam in an enclosed garden and commanded him not to eat from the tree of knowledge (Gen 2:8, 17).

Lord God formed woman from Adam's rib (Gen 2:22). Rib is 'tsela'- one-sided, limp. Lord God separated man using bioengineering, making hir male or female (one side). Man was now degenerate. S/he fell from hir androgynous state, walking with difficulty (limp). Man originally meant female. Wo-man (womb of man) means: 'I came from the womb of man.' Only females have wombs.

Adam and man is 'awdawm'- human. In Genesis 2 man and Adam refer to a female. In Genesis 3 Adam is male, woman is female. This confusion is intentional. Lord God formed male from created man's embryo; embryos are female. We say **man**kind because original man had virgin births. They were giants, perfectly proportioned with miraculous abilities.

Humanity evolved inside the hollow earth (message 20) and on its surface after the sun began to shine. Our inner earth cousins have golden skin tones, hair of light copper, eyes blue and green, and their blood is Rh-negative. Outer earth humans had black skin and Rh-negative blood. Now 15% of humanity is Rh-negative. Rh-negative blood does not have proteins on the surface of red blood cells; Rh-positive blood does. Rh-positive people of any blood type can receive Rh-negative blood; it is rare and priceless. Rh-negative people can't receive Rh-positive.

A Sumerian tablet says the gods mixed blood (DNA) with clay (quartz) to make slaves (white man). The gene variants that cause light skin came from black man. Genesis says Lord God used dust to form man; dust is 'aphar'- clay. When quartz is removed from clay it leaves dust. Quartz dust was used to create a synthetic gene. Genes of life self-replicate, organize, acquire and retain information. The self-replication process must pass on this information. Quartz has these abilities. Quartz dust was inserted into a fertilized egg.

Jehovah added primate genes to the human genome; this gave rise to male dominance, hierarchy, and the loss of self-replication. Blacks, Rh-negative people and the intersexed carry a higher percent of our original genetic makeup. Blacks have the greatest genetic diversity.

Women can conceive without sperm. The zona pellucida (membrane around egg) can be penetrated by a latent male protein that females have. If this happens the body treats it like a sperm and a virgin birth is conceived.

Human embryos begin female; without the Y-chromosome, they stay female. If a Y-chromosome floods the embryo with testosterone, breasts stop developing, the labia fuses to become a scrotum, and the clitoris develops into a penis. The Y-chromosome is not necessary for life and it's flawed. Y-chromosomes have only one copy and cannot undergo genetic recombination. Other chromosomes have two copies in every cell. Y-chromosomes degenerate and will ultimately be eliminated from our genome.

The tree of knowledge and tree of life stood in the midst of Eden (Gen 2:9). Midst is 'tavek'- center. One tree can stand at the center. Lord God's tree of knowledge is their tree of life- reformed life for demons to exist, make evil look good.

Lord God chose their shrewdest beast of the field for their enchanter. They commanded this charmer to teach Adam and Eve how to copulate like animals (eat from tree of know-ledge) so that demon-ghosts could use their offspring for host bodies and not die. Eve had intercourse with this beast- a Neanderthal.

Lord God cursed their charmer or serpent "above all cattle (formed man) and above the other beasts of the field (Neanderthals) Gen 3:14)." The Lord calls formed man 'nephesh'- livestock (commodity, meat). Beasts of the field are remnant: 'every beast of the field... by them shall the fowls of the heaven have their habitation (Psalm 104:11-12).' The fowls of Heaven are demon-ghosts; they would possess their bioengineered beasts for host bodies. "Upon your belly you will go and dust you will eat all the days of your life." The Lord formed man from dust— "dust thou art." Neanderthal beasts would feed on man as their own life-force flowed from their belly to feed the gods (Gen 3:14).

Lord God told Adam, "I will put enmity between… your seed and her seed. It will bruise your head and you will bruise his heel (Gen 3:15)." The Lord put hostility between Adam, Eve, and their bloodlines. The demon-ghosts bruised Adam and Eve's head. Bruise is 'shuwph'- open, overwhelm, cover. Demons could possess them through an opening in their aura and destroy them. Adam and Eve bruise the demon-ghosts' heel; they cover their track. Shuwph is cover; heel is 'aqeb'- track. They provide a hidden passage for demon-ghosts to obtain life.

Lord God told Eve: 'I will greatly multiply your sorrow and your conception.' Sorrow is 'itstsabown'- labor, pain. Children are now born in distress. This is the original sin- pain and trauma at birth. 'In sorrow you will bring forth children.' Sorrow is 'etseb- vessel; a container for demons (Gen 3:16). Conception was greatly multiplied because man's seed was not in itself. Before the sexes were separated, man conceived through parthenogenesis when perfect conditions for a baby were realized. Children were born easy, without pain.

"And your **desire (longing)** will be to your husband, and he will rule over you (Gen 3:16)." Rule is 'mashal'- dominion, power, authority, control. Man was to command his wife. For thousands of years, couples were married as "man and wife" because man's status did not change at marriage, only woman's status did; she became a slave to her husband.

Lord God cursed the ground to bring forth thorns and thistles to him (Gen 3:17, 18)." The ground is formed man (formed from dust). Thorn/thistle is 'qowts'— prick, pierce with a sharp point, puncture. Man was formed as a vessel for the demon-ghosts; they pierce his aura, attach to him and syphon their life-force and negative energies. Demon-ghosts live on our darkness and destruction.

Lord God said "the man has become as one of us (Gen 3:22)". Adam and Eve were now possessed with a demon-ghost. The tree of knowledge makes evil look good so the demon-ghosts would "not surely die" (Genesis 3:4—5). Lord God made coats of skin to symbolize the skin covering (body) Adam and Eve gave them. Eve was called 'Mother of all living' because she gave demons a habitation.

Adam and Eve were expelled from Eden. Eve gave birth to Cain and then Abel. Cain was conceived through partheno-genesis; Abel was conceived with Lord God's 'beast of the field (Neanderthal). Cain tilled the ground, Abel was a herds-man. Cain revered the earth and offered fruit to the Creator. Abel worshiped the Lord and killed a lamb for Jehovah. The Lord accepted Abel's offering and cursed Cain's; he wanted blood.

The Lord told Cain 'you will be Abel's **desire (longing)** and you will rule over (kill) him' (Gen 4:7).' Jehovah put an enchantment on Abel, to lust after his androgynous sibling. Able tried to rape Cain. Cain overpowered him, killing him in self-defense. Jehovah got the blood offering he wanted.

The Lord drove Cain from the **face of the earth** and sent him **'in the earth.'** Cain was afraid to enter earth's interior for fear of being killed as a fugitive. The Lord set a mark on him as a sign of his banishment. Cain dwelled on the eastside of Eden in Nod. Nod is 'nowd'— exile. He lived with others in earth's interior who were banished from the surface (Gen 4:11—15). Cain's offspring remained on earth's surface, Able's offspring carried genetic markers for Noah's line.

The formed Adam had a wife, the created Adam did not; s/he was a hermaphrodite and conceived by hirself. The created Adam named hir (his/her) only son Seth. The formed Adam named his 3rd son Seth. Created man was 14 feet tall, lived 1,000 years and had one child. Formed man was 6 feet tall, had many children and lived 120 years.

'There were giants **in the earth** in those days, and **also after that** when the sons of God came into the daughters of men and they bear children to them'- the 'mighty men' and 'men of renown' (Gen 6:1—6). Sons of Jehovah mated with the giants (hermaphrodites) who lived in earth's interior, before and also after Jehovah formed man. Created men (giants) were living on earth before Jehovah formed his man.

Formed man copied names of created man, scrambled the scriptures and omitted parts to confuse them with created man. The formed generations are in Genesis 4. The portion of scripture below in Genesis 5, is out of place; it belongs in Genesis 4: "…Then men began to call upon the name of the Lord [Gen 4:26] saying this same shall comfort us concerning our work and the toil of our hands, because of the ground which the Lord has cursed [Gen 5: 29].

The created generations are in Genesis 5. Created Adam lived 930 years. His son Seth lived 912 years. Seth's son Enos died at 912. Enos had Cainan and died at 905. Cainan had Mahalaleel and died at 910. Mahalaleel had Jared and died at 895. Jared had Enoch and died at 962. Enoch had Methuselah; God took him at 365. Methuselah had Lamech and died at 969. Lamech had Noah and died at 777. When Noah was 500 he had Shem, Ham and Japheth.

Noah had three sons because he procreated with Adam's linage, creating a crossbreed between the giants and formed man. His wife may have been from Able's offspring- a hybrid between formed man and Neanderthal. This is the bloodline combination Jehovah wanted: genes from Neanderthals, created man, and formed man. He drowned Noah's village and the surrounding area to control this bloodline. The ark held Noah's family and preserved DNA samples of Jehovah's bioengineered beasts. Israel descended from Shem and Japheth; Ham married a descendant of Cain.

Noah was a hermaphrodite; s/he could impregnate women and have virgin births. Hir (his/her) children were conceived with hir wife. Noah's son Ham mutilated Noah after s/he passed out from drinking so s/he could not birth more degenerate children. When Noah discovered what Ham did, s/he cursed Ham's line to retaliate (Gen 9:20—25). Cain's line settled the land of Canaan. Jehovah created the situations he punished Adam, Eve, Cain, Abel, Noah, Ham and the Cainites for.

When King Solomon died, ten tribes went north (Israel), two went south (Judah). The Southern tribes became known as Jews. The Northern tribes migrated across Europe, losing their identity. The Lord said he would uproot Israel, increase their numbers, scatter them, raise them to greatness (Great Britain, USA, Israel) and destroy them.

The Global Elite descended from Noah and his wife. This genetic combination (giants, formed man, Neanderthal) gave them great intelligence, a competitive drive to dominate and control, aggression and strong egos. They quickly became powerful Monarchs.

Original humans could bilocate, see the past and future, enter parallel worlds, hear thoughts, see auras, angels, demons, etc. If we defeat Jehovah, humanity will eventually return to our original state and regain these lost abilities.

Cherubim and a flaming sword keep the plan of salvation. Cherubim is 'kruwb'- imaginary figure (gospel). Flaming is lahat- enchantment. Israel is spellbound (including the Global Elite), so the sword (demon-ghosts) will have power to slay them on the Lord's Dreadful Day. The crop in the garden of Eden is formed man, he was made to feed Jehovah and his demons. Adam and Eve expelled from Eden is symbolic of Christians coming out of the gospel (god spell) on the Lord's Dreadful Day. Bound on their knees by The Holy Ghost they would declare 'Jesus Christ' is Satan. The 'Mystery of God' would be over and the gospel would end.

The Lord told Isaiah "make the heart of this people fat, make their ears heavy and shut their eyes; lest they see with their eyes, hear with their ears, understand with their heart, and convert and be healed (Is 6:10)." Our heart is the seat of our Soul where our Spirit communes with us. The Lord put us in 'perpetual sleep' so we will not change course and stop his plan for salvation.

The Hebrew

Jehovah told Abram to leave Haran when he was 75. He led Abram, his wife Sarai, his slaves and nephew Lot, to the land of Canaan. Famine sent them to Egypt. Abram told Sarai, 'when the Egyptians see your beauty, they will say this is his wife and they will kill me. Say you are my sister and I will live.'

The Egyptians took Abram's beautiful sister to Pharaoh. He treated Abram well for her sake and gave him sheep, oxen, donkeys, camels, silver, gold, and servants. The Lord cursed Pharaoh and his household with disease because of Sarai. "Pharaoh asked Abram, 'why didn't you tell me she was your wife? Why did you say she is my sister so I might have taken her as my wife? Here is your wife, take her and go... And **Abram was very rich**. (Gen 12, 13:1)."

The Lord commanded Abram to say Sarai was his sister to obtain wealth. Pharaoh gave Abram a dowry for Sarai, then Jehovah struck his house with 'nega'- leprous person and told him Sarai was Abram's wife. Fearing this evil God, he begged Abram to take his wife, the dowry he gave him, and leave. The Lord led Abram, his family and his great wealth (gold, silver, servants, animals) back to the land of Canaan.

Jehovah told Abram he would father a great nation and his seed would be numerous as the stars. Abram said 'how will I know that I shall inherit it?' Jehovah told Abram to kill a heifer, goat, ram, turtledove and pigeon, divide them in two (except for the birds) and lay them against each other (Gen 15:8—17). This sorcery sealed the Lord's promise and caused it to occur.

The goat symbolized the remnants' line; some were to be saved (scapegoat), the others killed. The pigeons were killed for a burned offering. A pigeon is a 'sitting duck' (easy target).

They symbolized Jews, who have been gathered together, to be destroyed when their fulfillment comes. The turtle doves were killed for a sin offering; they symbolized Christians. A turtle dove is a beloved. This symbolized the love Christians have for their Savoir and the Lord binding them to him through their sin until they are destroyed. A heifer was killed for sin purification. Heifer is slang for plump women; she symbolized the fat or strong ghosts who survive the Lord's judgment. The ram was killed for a peace offering. Ram is a crushing force; to violently dash against. It symbolized the Lord enforcing peace through force.

Abram fell into a deep sleep. '**A horror of great darkness fell on him.**' While in this state of horror, Jehovah told Abram his descendants would live in a strange land and be enslaved for 400 years. They would be freed with great wealth, return to Canaan and take back the land. When it was dark 'a smoking furnace and burning lamp passed between those pieces.' This sealed the sorcery. The Lord told Abram 'unto thy seed have I given this land (Gen 15:12—18).'

Jehovah changed Abram and Sarai's name, to Abraham (Father of many) and Sarah (Mother of Nations) and established his covenant through their descendants. The Lord said 'the host of heaven cannot be numbered.' Host is 'tsaba'– an army organized for war. The hosts are demons.

Abraham's descendants would be hosts for demon-ghosts. "I will multiply thy seed as the stars of heaven, and will give unto you, seed of all these countries. In your seed, all nations of the earth will be blessed (Gen 26:4)." All nations were to be consecrated for the Lord, so he could live forever.

The Lord told Abraham to circumcise the foreskin of all males, except for the newborn babies. Jehovah said women are unclean for seven days after giving birth. Her male baby cannot be circumcised while in this impure state (Gen 17:10—13). After the foreskin is cut off, the priest performs oral suction to remove blood. This satanic ritual mutilates the baby's genitals and is an act of pedophilia and cannibalism.

A penis symbolizes the Lord's covenant because he relies on degenerate males for his existence. Covenant is 'beriyth'– a compact made by passing between pieces of flesh. This is a reference to sexual intercourse. Sexual intercourse keeps humanity in a degenerate state (see message 25).

Sarah was barren, yet she gave birth to one child at age 90. When Isaac was a boy, Jehovah told Abraham: 'take your only son Isaac whom you love, go to the land of Moriah and offer him for a burned offering on the mountain.' Jehovah relished the torment his commandment caused. It was a test for Abraham, one that gave the Lord great, sadistic pleasure.

Abraham told Isaac they must travel to the mountains and make an offering. When they arrived, Isaac asked 'where is the lamb for a burned offering?' Abraham built an altar, laid the wood in order, bound Isaac, laid him on the wood and took the knife to slay his son. An angel appeared saying 'do not kill Isaac. God knows you fear him, for not withholding your son (Gen 22:2—12).' Jehovah uses fear for obedience. Those who disobey are punished with woe- agonizing pain.

Isaac's wife Rebekah conceived twins; they struggled in her womb. Jehovah told Rebekah she carried two nations, two people separated from the beginning in her womb (Arabs and Jews). One will be stronger and the firstborn will serve the second-born. Esau, the firstborn, was covered with thick red hair like a fur coat. Jacob was smooth-skinned and white.

Rebekah was barren for many years, like Sarah. A barren woman can give birth through artificial insemination. Maybe Sarah's baby Isaac, and Rebekah's babies Esau and Jacob, were bioengineered by Jehovah. Was Rebekah artificially inseminated with genetically modified eggs from unrelated bloodlines? Jehovah said Rebekah would birth two groups of people, separated from the beginning. Esau may have been Neanderthal; he was hairy and violent. Jacob was terrified of his brother. The twins temperaments naturally repelled each other. They saw the other as inferior, wretched and repulsive.

Esau hunted and Jacob helped his mother at the tents. One day Esau returned to camp, hungry from a hunt, when Jacob was cooking stew. He begged Jacob for some stew. Jacob demanded his birthright in exchange. Jacob tricked his father into thinking he was Esau, covering his arms with goatskin.

The firstborn was to serve the younger and live by the sword, but their land would have the fatness of the earth and one day they would break this yoke off their neck and receive the dominion (Gen 25:21—23, 27—34, Gen 27). Arabs lived by the sword and have oil (fatness of earth). Someday Esau's descendants (Muslims) will receive the dominion.

Jacob wrestled a man all night. As the sun rose, the man said "let me go for the day breaks." Jacob said "I will not let you go unless you bless me." The man told him his name would be Israel "you have power with God and men [Satan and his demons]." Jacob said "Tell me your name." The man revealed himself to Jacob. He said "I have seen God face to face and my life is preserved [for the Lord] (Gen 32:24—29)."

The Lord wrestling Jacob until daybreak symbolized Christians not letting go of the Lord until his Great and Dreadful Day. If this day came Christians would be bound by their Holy Ghost and wonder 'who are you?' The demon-ghosts would answer by violently slaughtering them.

Jacob received Abraham's promise and his sons became the 12 tribes of Israel. Israel became a great nation under King Solomon. When he died and the tribes divided, the northern tribes carried Israel's blessing of national greatness. Judah carried Israel's blessing of great wealth.

Jacob loved Joseph the most. "When his brothers saw that their father loved him more... they hated him (Gen 37: 4)." The brothers plotted to kill Joseph but Ruben said "cast him into this pit." A group of Ishmaelite passed by and they took him out of the pit and sold him.

The Ishmaelites took Joseph to Egypt and sold him. He was 17 and remained a slave of Potiphar's house for 11 years. Joseph then spent two years in prison. While there he interpreted dreams for other prisoners that were fulfilled. The Pharaoh had a troubling dream and Joseph was summoned to interpret it. When he told the Pharaoh what it meant (a great famine) he was made ruler over all the land of Egypt.

Joseph prepared for the famine. When it came, it spread throughout the land and Joseph's family traveled to Egypt to survive. Joseph gave them the best land and assigned them as overseers for Pharaoh. With Joseph and his family as overseers, the Egyptians were reduced to starvation and slavery. Their famine was not caused by crop failure.

"When money failed... the Egyptians came to Joseph and said give us bread... Joseph said give your cattle." The next year they said "there is nothing left... buy us." The Egyptians sold themselves into slavery and Pharaoh removed them, from one end of Egypt to the other (Gen 47:6, 15—21).

The Hebrew were in Egypt for 430 years. They lived well for over 200 years, growing rich and powerful, while the Egyptians were slaves of the Pharaoh (Gen 47). A new King of Egypt noticed the Hebrew people were mightier than his people. He set taskmasters over the Hebrew, to afflict them and make their lives bitter with hard bondage (Ex 1:8—14).

Moses returned to Egypt to free the Hebrew with his wife, sons, brother Aaron, and rod of sorcery. While waiting to see Pharaoh, the Lord told Moses to say: 'Israel is my firstborn son, let him go or I will slay your firstborn son.' The Lord told Moses he wanted to harden the Pharaoh's heart "that he shall not let the people go." The Pharaoh's firstborn son passed by and Jehovah was tempted to kill him, to harden Pharaoh's heart; he withheld his impulse.

When Moses realized the Lord wanted to kill the Pharaoh's firstborn, he feared for the life of his own firstborn. He was not circumcised, and was not under the Lord's covenant. Raised in Egypt, Moses did not grow up with Hebrew laws and did not circumcise his son. Moses held down his grown son and told Zipporah to circumcise him. "She took a sharp stone and cut off the foreskin of her son and cast it at his feet." Moses let his son go and Zipporah said, "a bloody husband thou art because of the circumcision." Zipporah is saying the blood of their son was on Moses' hands; he caused this violent injury, not her *(Ex 4:20—26)."*

{The plagues of Egypt were satanic spells. The Lord hardened Pharaoh's heart after each one so he would not let the Hebrew go until he completed his spells.

1st plague turned the river to blood. The river stands for being sold down river (betrayed), and a river—someone who separates by striking. The demon-ghosts were going to separate from us by striking us down. The blood symbolizes our life-force which the ghosts live on. The blood killed all the fish. Fish symbolize someone exploited, someone out of their proper environment and drinking like a fish. The fish symbolize Christians, who are intoxicated by The Holy Ghost. If the Day of the Lord comes, their ghost will take control of them, and make them kill each other.

2nd plague was frogs in the houses, be, kneading troughs, and ovens. The frogs symbolize the elect, who leapfrog into positions of power, freely moving above the systems they form. The elect worship Jehovah as Satan. House is empires and systems that the elect control. Bed is the elect working for Satan within their families. They are the perverse spirit the Lord mingled among his various religions and churches (Is 19:14). Kneading troughs are used for dough to rise; they represent the swelling gospel. The ovens symbolize the day of the Lord, when the gospel was to be baked. "Ten women will bake your bread in one oven (Lev 26:26)." The women are divisions in Christianity. It does not matter which door you walk through; it is the same gospel on the other side.

3rd plague turned dust into lice, in man and beast. Man is Jews and Christians; beast is the Lord's remnant. Lice symbolize the demon-ghosts who feed on them.

4th plague was flies that divided Egyptians from Hebrews. The Lord said "I will sever... I will put a division between my people and your people." Egyptians symbolize Christians, Hebrew are the Lord's elect. They invented the Christian religions for Jehovah, beginning with Paul. They organize covert, satanic worship inside Christian churches. Jehovah will call out his elect, mingled among Christians, before he brings the gospel to an end. Jews know Jesus is not the Messiah- the Lord who is to return and destroy the world. The Messiah is the God of Israel (Jehovah).

5th plague was pestilence that killed the Egyptians cattle, horses, camels, oxen and sheep. "The Lord shall sever between the cattle of Israel and the cattle of Egypt (Ex 9:3—4)." Egyptian cattle symbolize Christians; Israel cattle are Jews.

6th plague was scattered ash from the furnace that became dust in the land. Boils broke forth on man and beast. The Lord said: "I will stretch out my hand that I may smite you... I raised you up to show in you my power, that my name may be declared throughout all the earth (Ex 9:15-16)." The Lord bred Jews, Christians and Muslims to work his plan of salvation. The boils symbolize the Lord's wrath, which was to violently erupt on them at the appointed time.

7th plague was hail mingled with fire that smote man and beast. Hail with fire is a shower of bullets. Smote is 'nakah'—kill, overcome. Man is Christians, Jews and Muslims; beast is the remnant (beasts of the field). If the day of the Lord came Jehovah would bring the plan of salvation to an end with a downpour of destruction. Christians, Jews, and Muslims would be killed. The remnant and the Lord's chosen would be overcome. "And the hail smote every herb of the field… and the flax and the barley was smitten; for the barley was in the ear, and the flax was bolled. But the wheat and the rye were not smitten, for they were not grown up (Ex 9:25, 31—33)." Flax is the gospel; it smokes (smoke screen), burns with fire (spreads rapidly), is quenched at judgment (extinguished), and covers nakedness- clothes demons (Judes15:14, Hosea 2:9, Is 42:3). Christians are appointed barley (killed at the appointed time). Jews are the principal wheat (essential). The remnant is rye in its place (Is 28:25). Christians were to be killed when the gospel was exposed and extinguished. Jews were to be killed when the remnant (bioengineered beasts) were in place (ready).

8th plague was locusts brought by the East Wind. They cover the earth, eating every green thing. The locusts are demons. Every green thing: Jews, Christians, Muslims.

9th plague was three days of darkness. It symbolized the destruction of the earth. 10th plague all firstborn sons die, symbolizing Israel, Jehovah's firstborn (Exodus 10, 11).}

Waters Turn to Blood	Amphibians (Frogs)	Gnats (Lice)	Flies	Disease on Livestock
Exodus 7:14-25	Exodus 7:25-8:11	Exodus 8:12-15	Exodus 8:16-28	Exodus 9:1-7

The Ten Plagues of Egypt

Unhealable Boils	Hail and Fire	Locusts	Darkness	Death of First-Born
Exodus 9:8-12	Exodus 9:13-35	Exodus 10:1-20	Exodus 10:21-29	Exodus 11:1-12:36

Before Moses departed, he told the Hebrew to implore their Egyptian neighbors for their jewels of silver and gold (Ex 11:2). 'And the children of Israel did according to the word of Moses and took of the Egyptians, jewels of silver and jewels of gold, and raiment... And they spoiled the Egyptians (Ex 12:35—36).' The Hebrew stripped them of their wealth. The Lord led the Hebrew into Egypt, enslaved them and brought them out to gain the wealth of Egypt and work sorcery.

When the Hebrew departed, the Lord hardened Pharaoh's heart so he would pursue them. His chariots overtook the Hebrew camping by the sea. Moses parted the sea with his rod and the Hebrew crossed on dry ground. He blocked the Egyptians with a pillar of fire. Moses removed the pillar, the Egyptians pursued them and he closed the sea, drowning the Egyptians.

After traveling in the desert for three months, the Hebrew entered the Sinai wilderness. They camped before Mount Sinai and the Lord called Moses to the mount. He told Moses when the trumpets sounded in three days the people were to gather at the foot of the mountain. Jehovah appeared on the mount and gave the Hebrew ten commandments. The people were terrified of this fierce God and stood back. They begged Moses 'speak with us and we will hear, but do not let God speak with us least we die (Ex 20 1—19).

Moses drew near to the thick darkness and the Lord gave him his judgments (Ex 21—23). Moses told the people all the words of the Lord. He built an alter with 12 pillars, to represent the 12 tribes of Israel as the Lord commanded, and sacrificed oxen to the Lord, for the 'Blood of the Covenant.'

After the oxen were slain, half of their blood was poured into basins, the other half was sprinkled on the altar. Moses read the book of the covenant and told the people to say: "all that the Lord has said we will do and be obedient." Moses then took the blood and sprinkled it on the people saying: "behold the Blood of the Covenant which the Lord has made with you concerning all these words (Ex 24:5—8)." The Lord demanded animal sacrifices to "minister to the Lord." Minister means 'give aid.' The blood oath and animal sacrifice were for the Lord's salvation.

Moriah's Message 4
Woe unto You

The Lord does not have eternal life; he needs us to minister to him in order to live. That's why his servants sacrificed animals to him in a blood-splattering, satanic rituals. Jesus was the Lord's ultimate sacrifice but his death did not end them. His blood-splattering, satanic sacrifices will continue as long as he exists. Burning flesh gives off a nauseous odor, yet Jehovah loved this smell; he called it a "sweet savor." Sweet is 'niychoach'- a delightful odor. Savor is a taste or smell that excites interest. Jehovah-Satan loves this smell.

Aaron and his sons were consecrated as priests. A bull was killed and its blood was smeared on the altar horns with their fingers. The rest of the blood was poured on the bottom of the altar. The innards were burned on the altar and the flesh and skin were burned outside of camp for a sin offering. Then a ram without blemish was slain; its blood was sprinkled around the altar and it was prepared and burned.

A second ram was killed; his blood was put "on the tip of the right ear of Aaron, on the tip of the right ear of his sons, on the thumb of their right hand, and on the great toe of their right foot. Sprinkle the blood upon the altar round about. Take the blood and the anointing oil upon the altar and sprinkle it on Aaron, his garments, his sons and their garments (Ex 29: 10—22)."

The High Priest Garment was a sorcerer shroud for Jehovah's demonic power (Ex 28). The **Undercoat** signified demon-ghosts possessing their host. The **Robe** over the undercoat signified the host body clothing demons. The hem had blue, purple and red pomegranate ornaments attached to it, to symbolize top-ranking demon-ghosts attached to host bodies. Pomegranate is 'rimmon'- exalt self. Demons need glory to exist. Gold bells hung between the pomegranates.

E

Gold is 'zahab' something golden, oil. The bells are the hosts life-force (oil) funneled to the demon-ghosts. The **Ephod** was like an apron, open on the sides and worn over the robe. It symbolized the Lord's burden. Onyx stones, engraved with the tribes of Israel, attached to the shoulders. The stones are a memorial, symbolizing Israel's fulfillment (end). Shoulders symbolize responsibility; Israel was to bear the burden of the Lord until his Great and Dreadful Day.

The **Breastplate**, placed over the ephod, had twelve precious stones for the twelve tribes of Israel. Two gold chains were fastened to gold rings at the top of the breastplate; the other end was fastened to the stone settings on the shoulders of the ephod. This bound the breastplate to the Ephod so that the Lord's judgment of Israel would not be loosened. The ephod and breastplate were made with 'cunning work' (devious scheming). The Urim and Thummim was placed in a secret pocket on the breastplate. They were used as a divination tool to determine innocence or guilt. Urim means guilty; Thummim means innocent. The whole house of Israel was to receive the Lord's judgment of guilty. The **Girdle**, tied around the ephod, represented the plan of salvation, which Israel was to fulfill. Girdles are used to secure: "neither shall the girdle of their loins be loosed (Isaiah 5:27)." The plan of salvation secured the demons continued existence through the loins of Israel, until the Lord brought it to an end. The girdle (plan of salvation) was peculiar, made for a strange purpose (odd, contrary, aberrant). The **Turban** had a gold plate that said 'Holiness to the Lord' and blue lace on the forefront. The blue lace symbolizes demons coming to forefront to take control of their host when Jehovah commands them to come forth. The turban bears the iniquity of holy things- weak demons who do not survive Judgment

Day. The strong demons who survive judgment would possess the chosen. The chosen are set apart by a turban. This headdress is worn by Muslims. The Lord's chosen was to come from the followers of Islam.

Moses provided manna for the Hebrews to eat and they quickly grew tired of it. They remembered the fish they ate in Egypt, the cucumbers, melons, onions and garlic. They said "Now our soul is dried away; there is nothing at all but this manna before our eyes." They ground it, beat it, baked it and made cakes with it, but no matter what they did it tasted like oil. The people grew so sick of eating manna that every family wept in the door of their tents. They told Moses "We hate this light bread (Num 11:5—19)."

Moses told the Hebrew 'only gather as much manna as you can eat and do not save any.' Some did save manna, and "it bred worms and stank. Moses was wroth with them (Ex 16:20)." Manna contained eggs that hatched into worms in their intestines. Moses did not want them to know this.

The parasite worms symbolized the demon-ghosts. The Lord said worms would feed sweetly upon us, eat us like wool, and not die (Job 24:20 Is 51:8 Is 66:24). Demon-ghosts are parasites: they feed on us 'from generation to generation' eating us like a moth eats a garment, so the worms will not die, and will be 'an abhorring unto all flesh.'

"The Lord sent serpents among the people, they bit them and much of Israel died. The people came to Moses and said... ask the Lord to take the serpents from us." The Lord told Moses to make a snake idol and set it on a pole. Those who were bit looked at this satanic idol until they were healed (num 21:5-9). The Lord killed the Hebrews with snakes to cast a spell. The serpents symbolized the day of the Lord.

"Woe unto you that desire the day of the Lord. To what end is it for you? The day of the Lord is darkness and not light. As if a man did flee from a lion and a bear met him, or went in the house and leaned his hand on the wall and a serpent bit him. Shall not the day of the Lord be darkness and not light; even very dark and no brightness in it (Amos 5:18—20)?" The Lion is Satan, the bear is Christ, and the serpent is The Holy Ghost. When you flee from Satan and run to Christ, the serpent has you. If the Day of the Lord came your demon-ghost would kill you: 'Woe unto you' is the end of you.

The Lord's tabernacle housed the Ark of the Covenant. The Ark was made of wood and overlaid with gold. It had rings on the sides for carrying staves (Ex 37:1—9). The lid (Mercy Seat) had gold cherubim on each end. On Atonement Day Aaron sprinkled blood from slain animals on the Mercy Seat. The Ark held the tablets, a golden pot for manna and Aaron's staff. The staff had sorcery powers; it turned into a serpent, parted the red sea and made water pour from a rock.

The Ark also had sorcery powers. The Israelites brought it to their battles. When the King of Babylon conquered Jerusalem in 587, the Ark vanished. There is a theory that the Ark could make white gold, communicate with UFOs, and used plasma physics and crystal lasers. If the Ark of the Covenant had advanced technology it came from Jehovah.

When a cloud-pillar rested above the tabernacle, the Israelites pitched their tents. When the cloud-pillar glowed and was taken up they journeyed. Whether it was a day, month or year, when the pillar rested on the tabernacle the Israelites journeyed not. But when the cloud-pillar glowed and arose, they traveled (Num 9:15—22). Cloud is 'anan' nimbus, circle of light. The circle of light rested above the Ark of the Covenant in the tabernacle. Ark is 'aron'- gather, harvest. What did it gather and harvest? This may be a UFO (from earth). Perhaps Jehovah made the flying object, like he bioengineered Adam and Eve, through possession.

The Lord told Moses "I will put the dread of you and the fear of you on the nations that hear report of you. They will tremble and be in anguish because of you." He told Moses to ask the Amorite king if he could pass through his land. The Lord then hardened the king's heart and made him obstinate, so he would not let them pass (Deut 2:25—30). He wanted the Israelites to kill everyone. "We took all his cities at that time and utterly destroyed the men, and the women, and the little ones of every city; we left none to remain. Only the cattle we took for a prey unto ourselves, and the spoil of the cities which we took (Deut 2:34)."

The Hebrew were commanded to kill the Hittites, Amorites, Canaanites, Perizzites, Hivites, and Jebusites. "Save nothing alive that breaths (Deut 20:16, 17)." Pagans on the outskirts of Canaan were enslaved; 'they shall be your bondmen'. These tribes were the last remaining giants on earth's surface. 'A people great, many, and tall, but the Lord destroyed them ...and dwelt in their stead (Deut 2:21). The Canaanites followed Baal, a nature god. When the Hebrew followed Baal they "ceased not from their own doings"— they followed their heart, their own desires, instead of Jehovah.

If the Hebrews kept the Lord's commandments Jehovah said he would increase their cattle, sheep, goods and crops, and bring curses and plagues on their enemies. "You will lend unto many nations and not borrow. I will make you the head and not the tail, you will be above only and not beneath (Deut 28:12, 13)." His blessings of wealth, domination and torture of the enemy were all condemned by Jesus.

Jehovah said he would curse their city, basket, cattle, sheep, fruit of their land and body and put cursing, vexation and rebuke on them until they're destroyed, if his servants did not observe all his laws. He would smite them with fever, consumption, extreme burning, the sword, blasting, mildew, emerods, the scab, botch, the itch, madness, blindness and astonishment of heart—until they perish. 'These curses will come upon you... and they shall pursue you until you perish.'

"The Lord will smite you in the knees and legs with a sore botch that cannot be healed, from the sole of your foot to the top of your head... You will carry much seed into the field and will gather little for locusts will eat it. You will plant vineyards ...but not drink the wine nor gather the grapes for the worms will eat them. You will have olive trees... but will not anoint yourself with the oil for they will cast their fruit. You will have sons and daughters but not enjoy them for they will go into captivity... "And they shall be upon you [all these curses] for a sign and for a wonder, and upon your seed forever..."

"You will serve the enemies which the Lord will send against you in hunger, thirst, nakedness and want of all things and he will put a yoke of iron upon your neck until he has destroyed you... And you will eat the fruit of your own body, the flesh of your sons and of your daughters...

If you will not keep all the words of the law written in this book, and fear this glorious and fearful name, the Lord thy God, the Lord will make your plagues wonderful and the plagues of your seed great and of long continuance and sore sickness... He will bring upon you all the diseases of Egypt which you were afraid of and they will cleave unto you. Every sickness and plague not written in the book of this law, these also will the Lord bring on you until you are destroyed... You will... have no assurance of your life (Deut 28)."

"And if you despise my statutes, or if your soul abhors my judgments so that you will not do all my commandments and you break my covenant, I also will do this unto you: I will even appoint over you terror, consumption and the burning ague and shall consume the eyes and cause sorrow of heart... And I will set my face against you and you shall be slain before your enemies... I will send wild beasts among you which will rob you of your children... Your body will be meat to the fowls of the air... Your children will be given to another people... You will eat the flesh of your sons and the flesh of your daughters... (Lev 26)."

The Lord wanted to torture and kill those who rebelled over and over again. Those who refused to 'kill all that breaths' when commanded to, suffered his wrath. "The anger of the Lord and his jealousy will smoke against that man and the curses that are written in this book will lie upon him and the Lord will blot out his name from under heaven (Deut 29:19, 20)." Jehovah threatened the Hebrew with plagues and curses if they broke his commands. Bound by their blood-covenant, Jehovah's threats were real. The Hebrew who rebelled had their name removed from heaven; they entered higher realms when Jehovah killed them with plagues.

Jehovah's worshippers go to his heavens between lives. Locked in perpetual sleep, they incarnate without memories of their former lives. This blocks the wisdom they previously gained. Actions in past lives write the fate for future lives. Life is fair but difficult when you lose the roadmap and don't know you chose your hard life to further your evolution, balancing your karmic scales. This is true, even for the Hebrew who were caught in Jehovah's brutal web of deceit and violence.

The Lord gave Moses commandments to govern every aspect of their lives. Failure to observe them was punished with death. A man was stoned to death for gathering sticks on the Sabbath. If someone knew about a crime and did not report it, he was stoned to death. Wives told on husbands and children told on parents in fear of losing their life. A man buried a Canaanite robe in his tent and his family was stoned to death because they may have known and didn't tell. The Lord demanded an 'eye for an eye' for every offense; the Israelites could not forgive one another without retribution. The Ten Commandments are a brotherly Covenant; they were not to kill or steal among themselves except for reprisal. These laws did not apply to the heathen.

The Hebrew were commanded to give a tithe of grain, oil, and wine. The grain symbolized Judaism and Christianity (wheat and barley); the oil symbolized their life-force that the demon-ghosts live on; the wine symbolized the gods.

The Lord likes to boast: "Since the day God created man ...has there been anything as great as this is? ...Did God say to go take him a nation from the midst of another nation, by temptations, by signs and wonders, by war and a mighty hand and by a stretched-out arm and great terrors, according to all that the Lord your God did for you in Egypt before your eyes? You were shown these things so you would know the Lord is God— there is none else beside him (Deut 4: 34—35)." The Creator did not say to take a nation from the midst of another with war and terrors, Satan did.

After following their violent God for many years, the kings, princes, priests and prophets turned their back on the Lord and refused to obey his instructions. "And they built the high places of Baal… for their sons and daughters to **pass through** the fire unto Molech (Jer 32:32—35)." Like natives who walk on burning coals without being burned, their children could pass through the fire unharmed. Jehovah is the one who demands human sacrifices, not Molech, a pagan sun god.

The Hebrew who held positions of authority rebelled, so the Lord delivered the Israelites to the King of Babylon 'by the sword, by famine and by pestilence (Jer 32:36)." The Hebrew believed Jehovah was God; he had terrifying powers. That was thousands of years ago and we are still worshiping this demon-god for salvation. Jehovah is not your Savior; he is the Savior of demons. If you do not reject him, he will deliver you to the sword, famine and pestilence.

"And I will feed them that oppress thee with their own flesh; and they shall be drunken with their own blood, as with sweet wine, and all flesh shall know that I the Lord am thy Savior and thy Redeemer- the Mighty One of Jacob (Is 49:26)." The Lord is only the Savior of himself (the Mighty One), but he will gladly torture those who oppress his worshippers- make them eat their own flesh and drink their own blood.

'Therefore saith the Lord, the Lord of Hosts, the Mighty One of Israel, I will ease me of mine adversaries and avenge me of mine enemies (Is 1:24).' The Lord wants to destroy those who are against him so he can live. 'And there shall be no more utter destruction, for New Jerusalem shall be safely inhabited (Zech 14:11)' safely inhabited for Jehovah. Reject the Lord or he will "rejoice over you, to destroy you and bring you to naught (Deut 28)."

The Lord has 3 Kingdoms. **Kingdom of Heaven**: Jehovah's worshipers in his heavens (Christians, Muslims, Jews). **Kingdom of God**: Jehovah's hosts of heaven (demons). **Kingdom on earth**: Jehovah's worshippers on earth. They would be killed or enslaved if New Jerusalem is established. Jehovah's religions would end and he would control earth.

Parasites live off of hosts, taking their life then moving to another host, destroying life so they can live. Jehovah is a parasite. If he is not stopped, he would suck all life from the earth, to live as long as possible. If humanity becomes so destructive that the life of our earth mother is endangered, she will cause a global disaster to wipe us out. This is the 'Point of No Return'- the point where the earth must wipe out humanity to prevent her own death. Without a host, demons would die and someday, life would start over.

Moriah's Message 5
Satanic Spells

Jehovah controls humanity with satanic spells. Kennedy's murder, 9-11, the London Olympics opening ceremonies, The Walking Dead and The Handmaid's Tale are satanic spells to cause events to occur. Jehovah cast a satanic spell in 1777 to bring civil war between Democrat and Republican parties 250+ years later, and turn the USA into a Christian Nation. We can awaken from our satanic trance and stop this war.

The Lord had Jeremiah cast a spell with a girdle. He put it on, went to Euphrates and buried it. Jeremiah was told get the girdle after many days. It was marred 'shacath'— cast off, destroy. The Lord said 'For as the girdle cleaves to the loins of a man, I have caused to cleave unto me, the whole house of Israel and the whole house of Judah (Jer 13:1—11).' The girdle spell was cast to bind Jews and Christians to the Lord, until he ends his gospel (god-spell).

The Lord had Jeremiah cast a spell with his wine cup. He said, tell Israel 'every bottle will be filled with wine.' When they say 'Do we not know that every bottle shall be filled with wine?' Jeremiah was to say these spell-binding words: "Behold, I will fill all the inhabitants of this land, even the kings that sit on David's throne, the priests and prophets and all the inhabitants of Jerusalem with drunkenness. I will dash them one against another... I will not pity, nor spare, nor have mercy, but destroy them (Jer 13:12—14)." The cup symbolized humanity; the wine that filled it symbolized demon-ghosts.

The Lord told Jeremiah: "Take the wine cup of this fury at my hand and cause all the nations to whom I send you to drink it. And they shall drink and be moved and be mad because of the sword that I will send among them. Then I took the cup at the Lord's hand and made all the nations to drink, unto whom the Lord had sent me (Jer 25:15—17)."

'If they refuse to take the cup to drink say, the Lord of hosts says you will certainly drink... For I will call for a sword upon all the inhabitants of the earth... Behold, evil will go forth from nation to nation, and a great whirlwind will be raised up from the coasts of the earth. And the slain of the Lord will be at that day from one end of the earth even unto the other end of the earth. They will not be lamented, neither gathered, nor buried. They will be dung upon the ground... For the days of your slaughter and dispersions are accomplished, and you will fall like a pleasant vessel, and the peaceable habitations are cut down... (Jer 25:28—37).' The Lord's pleasant vessels are Jews, Christians and Muslims: vessels for demon-ghosts.

Jeremiah was sent to surrounding kingdoms with the Lord's wine cup (Jer 25:18—26). This spell was cast so evil and madness would spread from nation to nation, until Jehovah's Dreadful Day came. "Babylon has been a **golden cup** in the Lord's hand, that made all the earth drunk. The nations drank her wine; therefore, the nations will go mad (Jer 51:7)." The wine is demon-ghosts drunk on our life-force; drinking the Lord's wine makes you demon-possessed.

Babylon in Revelation holds the Lord's **golden cup**- "the habitation of devils and the hold of every foul spirit and a cage of every unclean and hateful bird (Rev 18:2)." The foul spirits and hateful birds (fowls of heaven) are Jehovah's demon-ghosts. Everyone who drinks from Babylon's golden cup is filled with the Lord's abominations (demon-ghosts) and has committed fornication with him.

Babylon's names: Mystery Babylon the Great Mother of Harlots Abominations of Earth. Babylon Mystery: Jehovah's plan for his salvation. Babylon the Great: she accumulated the wealth of the world by raping the earth and humanity (Rev 17:1—5). Babylon Mother of Harlots: Jehovah exploits us for personal gain. Babylon, Abominations of Earth: those who drink from Babylon's golden cup have living water flowing out of their belly, life-force that demon-ghosts live on (John 7:38).

Babylon will fall. If The Greatest Deception causes its fall, the world will be set free. If the Lord brings Babylon to an end, the world would be destroyed. 'For all nations drank the wine of the wrath of her fornication. The kings of the earth committed fornication with her and the merchants of earth are waxed rich through her abundance.' The merchants are the Global Elite; kings of earth are Christians. Jesus Christ is the prince of the kings of the earth (Rev 1:5).

The Lord had Ezekiel cast a spell so his Great and Dreadful Day could come. He told him to draw Jerusalem on a tablet, build a fort, mount and camp, and set them against the tablet, then put battering rams around it. Ezekiel was to place an iron pan between himself and his symbolic city, for an iron wall and put his face against it; it would then be besieged.

The tablet- New Jerusalem, the fort- the chosen (strong hold), the mount- Jews (mount Zion), the camp- Christians (Lord's army), battering rams- collisions these groups would have. Iron is 'barzel'- iron implement for cutting, ax. When the iron wall (wall of secrecy) comes down, the chosen, Jews and Christians would be besieged and cut down (Ez 4:1—3).

The siege lasted 430 days. Ezekiel was to bake barley cakes, one for each day of the siege, and fix enough meat to eat daily by weight. His water was to be measured when consumed. When everything was prepared the Lord bound Ezekiel. He laid on his left side for 390 days, for Israel's iniquity; he then laid on his right side 40 days, for Judah's iniquity. Ezekiel was bound 430 days because the Hebrews dwelt in Egypt for 430 years. "I will lay bands upon you, and you shall not turn from one side to another until you have ended the days of your siege (Ez 4:4—8)."

After being bound for over a year Ezekiel was loosened and told to shave his hair and beard and divide it by weight into three equal piles. He was to burn one pile with fire inside the city, take another pile of hair and smite it with a knife, then take the last pile of hair and scatter it in the wind. A few strands of hair were to be bound and tucked in the fold of his garment. He was to take this remnant and burn them, to destroy the whole house of Israel (Ez 5:1—4).

The first hair pile symbolized the chosen, to be consumed by demons living on their life-force. The second hair pile symbolized Jews who were to be cut from the Lord and lose their election. The third hair pile symbolized Christians being scattered around the world to spread the gospel.

'Fathers shall eat their sons in your midst, and sons shall eat their fathers... A third part will die with pestilence, consumed with famine [chosen]... a third will fall by the sword [Jews]...

and a third I will scatter to all the winds and draw a sword after them [Christians]. My anger will be accomplished. I will cause my fury to rest upon them and I will be comforted… (Ez 5:10—13)."

'I will send famine and evil beasts and they will bereave you and pestilence and blood shall pass through you. I will bring the sword upon you… They will know that I am the Lord, and I have not said in vain, that I would do this evil unto them… The House of Israel… shall fall by the sword, and by the famine, and by the pestilence (Ez 5:17; Ez 6:10)." The far off die of pestilence (chosen), the near fall by the sword (Jews), those who remain (remnant) are besieged. Besieged is 'natsar'- preserve. This remnant is DNA (Ez 6: 12).

Those in the wastes fall by the sword (Jews severed from the Lord and destroyed), those in the field are given to beasts to be devoured (Christians attacked by The Holy Ghost), and those in the forts die of pestilence (the chosen consumed by parasites or demons) Ez 33:27. To complete this spell fathers and sons ate each other, some had to die from pestilence, others were run through with a sword.

The Lord showed Ezekiel idols in the house of Israel, and even 'greater abominations.' Twenty-five men stood toward the east 'and worshipped the sun' (Ez 8:9—16). The Lord told Ezekiel to slay all the idol and sun worshippers, even the 'old and young, both maids and little children and women Ex 9:4—6).' Sun gazing brings enlightenment, exposing Jehovah.

The Lord carried Ezekiel 'out in the spirit' to a valley of bones. He had Ezekiel tell the bones the Lord would cause breath to enter them and cover them with flesh so they would live. Ezekiel did this and "the bones came together… flesh came upon them… but there was no breath in them." The Lord told Ezekiel to say: "Come from the four winds oh breath and breathe upon these slain that they may live." As Ezekiel said this, the bon es with flesh 'stood upon their feet, an exceeding great army.' The Lord said the bones were the real house of Israel. He commanded Ezekiel to tell the bones: "Oh my people I will **open your graves** and cause you to **come up out of your graves** and bring you into the land of Israel... and you shall live (Ez 37)."

The bones: demons. Breath from the four winds (heaven) that gives life: the gospel. Opening the graves: the Lord calls The Holy Ghost to come forth from their burying place (take control of their host). Come out of the graves: come out of Christians after slaughtering them.

The Lord told Ezekiel to take two sticks and write 'for Judah and the children of Israel, his companions' on one; 'for Joseph and the house of Israel, his companions' on the other and join them. These sticks 'will be one in my hand' The sticks would be '**before their eyes**.' *(Ez 37:16—20)."* The children of Israel- Jews, Christians, and their demon-ghost companions, are joined as one in Jehovah's hand.

"I will cut off the chariot from Ephraim [Christians] and the horse from Jerusalem [Jews] (Zec 9:10)." Judah is driving Ephraim's chariot- Jews invented Christianity, beginning with Paul. If Jehovah finishes his plan, they would both be killed. 144,000 from Jacob's pure bloodline (Global Elite) would be saved to govern New Jerusalem (New World Order). They would be controlled by powerful demons, and the dominion would pass to Esau's descendants (Arabs). They would receive it through 'Saints of the Most High' (demons).

"Thou preparest a table before me in the presence of my enemies (Psalm 32:4, 5)." The Lord prepares meals for our enemies to consume in our presence. Our enemy is The Holy Ghost; their meal is our life-force. We are walking through a shadow of death without fearing evil because we don't know what this shadow is (demon-ghosts). The Lord was going to reveal his shadow of death on his Great and Dreadful Day when he slaughters (or enslaves) humanity. This day will not be his to seize.

I am the Lord's adversary. His shadow of death, the things of Esau and the Lord's hidden things were revealed to me in dreams. Shortly after I started writing messages a brilliant angel came to me in a dream. He took my typed messages, crossed out a section, wrote something else and showed me this change without speaking. I knew this brilliant angel, but when I awoke I forgot who he was and couldn't recall the changes he showed me. I worked on my messages that day, eliminated a section and added new material. Years later, I prayed to Jesus and asked if my messages were true. I saw the angel who went over a message with me; it was Jesus!

"Have the gates of death been opened unto you? Or have you seen the doors of the shadow of death?... Who has given understanding to the heart (Job 38:17, 36)? How are the things of Esau searched out? How are his hidden things sought up (Obad 6)? The Kings of the earth and all the inhabitants of the world would not have believed that the adversary... could enter into the gates of Jerusalem (Lam 4:12)." Jesus gave understanding to my heart. He revealed Jehovah's shadow of death in a dream; it is The Holy Ghost.

Jehovah 'turns man to destruction and says return you children of men [return to the ground] (Ps 90:3). In the end time, people will rebel against the Lord saying 'turn aside out of the path, cause the Holy One of Israel to cease from before us... This iniquity will be to you as a breach ready to fall... whose breaking comes suddenly, at an instant (Is 30:11, 13).' This sudden breach is the Lord's breach of promise.

The Lord said rulers will counsel against him, saying "let's break their bands... and cast away their cords from us. He that sits in the heavens will laugh; the Lord will have them in derision (Ps 2: 3, 4)." When Jews, Christians and Muslims say, let's reject the Lord and cast him away from us, Jehovah will laugh at them with disdain and scorn.

"The day of the Lord comes, cruel with wrath and fierce anger to lay the land desolate... Everyone that is found will be thrust through, and everyone that is joined will fall by the sword. Their children will be dashed to pieces **before their eyes**... Their bows shall dash the young men to pieces; and they will have no pity on the fruit of the womb. (Is 13:9—16)."

If the Day of the Lord came, mothers would see their children dashed to pieces **before their eyes**, for the beast inside them would use their own body to violently strike, eating their flesh. This is the "weeping and wailing and gnashing of teeth" the Lord said would come in the last day.

Years ago, I had a vision of families killing each other. I prayed for understanding. That evening the news said a woman drowned her child in the sink. The frantic child begged her Mom to stop, but the mother could only watch as her own hands killed her daughter; an unseen force was controlling her. My vision was the Lord's Great and Dreadful Day when the image of the Beast comes to the forefront: 'the image of the beast should both speak and cause as many as would not worship it to be killed (Rev 13:15).'

If this day comes, the Lord will cause his herd to fold— "crouch down on all four legs folded like a recumbent animal" and acknowledge Lord God Almighty is Satan. The Holy Ghost would then make Christians confess on bent knees that Jesus Christ the Lord, is Satan. They would cry: Oh Lord you have deceived me (Jer 20:7) and he would say: I mingled a perverse spirit in your midst and have caused you to err, like a drunken man staggers in his vomit (Isaiah 19:14).

'A fire is kindled in my anger and shall burn unto the lowest hell and consume the earth… I will heap mischiefs upon them; I will spend my arrows upon them… I will also send the teeth of beasts upon them… (Deu 32:23)."

The Lord said: 'My people (demon-ghosts) shall dwell in a peaceable habitation, and in sure dwellings, and in quiet resting places (Is 32:18).' The peaceable habitations are Jews, the sure dwellings are Muslims, and the quiet resting places are Christians. These are the Lord's pleasant vessels.

"An East Wind shall... spoil the treasure of all pleasant vessels… They shall fall by the sword. Their infants will be dashed in pieces, and their women with child shall be ripped up (Hos 13:14—16)." The Lord's East Wind is demon-ghosts coming to the forefront to take control of Christians, Jews and Muslims (pleasant vessels) when the Lord commands them to. East (qadim) is forefront, Wind (ruwach) is violent exhalation. The word of the Lord was precept upon precept, so we would be snared and taken when the Lord tells his demons to 'come forth.'

Demons

Imagine Dragons

I wanna hide the truth, I wanna shelter you,
but with the beast inside there's nowhere we can hide...
Your eyes, they shine so bright, I wanna save that light.
I can't escape this now, unless you show me how.
When you feel my heat look into my eyes.
It's where my demons hide, it's where my demons hide.

Moriah's Message 6

John Jesus Paul

In <u>How to Study the Bible</u> Reverend Stalker says: "different parts of a book are more intelligible when read in the light of the whole. It is surprising how clear the meaning of obscure verses sometimes becomes when they are seen in their place, in the entire structure to which they belong." In the NT Jehovah's words and his gospel are intermingled with Jesus' words. Read the Bible "in the light of the whole"- recognize Jehovah's voice and separate him from Jesus.

In Matt 8:5—13 a Centurion asks Jesus to heal his servant who was sick with palsy. Jesus said he would come heal him. The Centurion said, speak the word only and my servant will be healed. Then Jehovah says "I say unto you that many shall come from the East and West and shall sit down with Abraham, Isaac, and Jacob, in the Kingdom of Heaven; but the Children of the Kingdom shall be cast out into outer darkness. There shall be weeping and gnashing of teeth (Matt 8:11—12)." Jesus answers the Centurion, saying 'I have not found so great a faith in all of Israel.' He tells him to go his way, 'and as you have believed, so be it done unto you. His servant was healed in the self-same hour.'

Matthew 12:15—22 says "great multitudes followed him and he healed them all... Then was brought to him one possessed with a devil, blind and mute; and he healed him so he could talk and see." Jehovah's words are inserted in the middle of Jesus healing the multitudes. Verses16—21 say "that it might be fulfilled which was spoken by Isaiah the Prophet, saying behold my servant whom I have chosen, my beloved in whom my soul is well pleased. I will put my spirit upon him and he shall show judgment to the Gentiles and in his name will the Gentiles (non-Jew) trust."

When the High Priests saw Jesus heal people, these "wonderful things that he did" made them "sore displeased (Matt 21:15)." If their God was the Creator, they would not be angry when Jesus healed people. The Jews "held a council against Jesus, how they might destroy him (Matt 12:14) how they might entangle him in his talk (Matt 22:15)."

Their god had a plan (the gospel) to displace Jesus with himself. His demon-ghosts would possess his followers, and 'in his name' (Jesus' name) they would trust him. The gospel: Jesus Christ (Jehovah) was sacrificed for our sins, he will return, judge the world, and establish his Kingdom.

Jehovah's Gospel Words: Lord, Jesus Christ, Savior, everlasting, Gentiles, glory, elect, judgment, signs and wonders, flesh and blood, Son of man, righteousness, repent, remission of sins, The Holy Ghost, baptize, woe, last day, kingdom of God/heaven, Father, harvest, resurrection, dove, gnashing of teeth, bridegroom, references to O.T.

Lord is a master who rules; Jesus is not a Lord. Jehovah is Lord God Almighty, Lord Jesus Christ, Lord of Heaven, and Lord of Hosts. **Christ** means Savior, Messiah, Deliverer. Jehovah's plan is to deliver demons into everlasting life and his chosen and remnant into permanent slavery. Christ is the Anointed One- anointed with life-force. Jehovah needs this anointing; he has no life-force of his own. **Glory** means exalt. The glory Jehovah's worshippers give him, elevates and feeds him. His glory is a devouring fire that would die without fuel. **Everlasting** is continuous duration. Jehovah calls his dominion, covenant, Kingdom, priesthood, salvation and statutes, everlasting; he wants them to prevail. **Son of Man** "shall rise the third day... As Moses lifted up the serpent... the Son of man will be lifted up... The Son of Man has power on earth to forgive sins... till the Son of Man were risen from the dead." Jehovah is the Son of Man; Jesus is the Son of Earth. **Signs and Wonders** are curses and spells. Jehovah said curses will come upon you for a sign and a wonder (omen). Jehovah uses curses and spells to cause events to unfold. **The Holy Ghost** is symbolized by a dove. Dove is yownah-mate, intoxicate. **Woe** unto you is excruciating pain.

When Christians are baptized, The Holy Ghost mates them with Satan and clouds their thinking. On the day of Pentecost, people thought those filled with The Holy Ghost were drunk.

They said: "these men are full of new wine." Peter said: "they are not drunk as you suppose... (Acts 2:13, 14)." They were possessed with a demon. "Walking in the fear of the Lord and comfort of The Holy Ghost (Acts 9:31)." This comfort and relief from distress that The Holy Ghost gives is not for you— it is for the Lord. The Lord wants you to fear him.

The demon 'Gabriel' told Zacharias his wife would bear a son named John and he would be "filled with The Holy Ghost even from his mother's womb." John would be born in the spirit and power of Elijah (Luke 1:17). John the Baptist (Elijah reincarnated) was possessed at conception. Zacharias asked how his wife could conceive when they were old. For asking this, Gabriel struck him dumb; he was unable to speak from John's conception until his birth (Luke 1:18—20).

When Gabriel appeared to Mary, she was troubled- worried and disturbed. Gabriel said she would have a son and his reign will have no end. Mary said "I do not know a man." Gabriel says The Holy Ghost will overshadow (dominate) her, and a 'holy thing' will be born from her (Luke 1:26—35)." The Holy Ghost did not possess Mary's womb. She was a hermaphrodite and conceived through self-impregnation.

Jesus and John were cousins the same age and may have looked similar. They both drew great crowds- John by preaching the gospel and demon-possessing people with baptism, and Jesus by healing people with miracles. When King Herod heard of Jesus' fame, he said it was John the Baptist raised from the dead, doing mighty works (Mat 14:1). Jesus and John were intentionally confused.

Mandean texts say John the Baptist is the true Messiah. His Spirit left at his baptism and Jehovah possessed his corpse. Merovingians claim to have the blood of Christ; they descended from John the Baptist (the real Christ). Jehovah said he would send his prophet Elijah (John the Baptist) "before the coming of the Great and Dreadful Day of the Lord" (Mal 4:5)." John will reincarnate at the 'End Times,' and Jehovah will possess him as the Messiah.

John took a wife to serve him and bare children, as his religion mandated. If Jesus conceived a child it was through parthenogenesis- a virgin birth and no father. Jesus was a hermaphrodite like hir mother. John the Baptists' bloodline serves Jehovah. If Jesus has a bloodline, his descendants would be devoted to earth, like Cain.

The Jews turned the temple into a house of merchandise. John knocked over their tables and whipped them. The Jews ask for a sign of his authority and John said he would raise his body in three days (John 2:14—21). Jesus would not whip people, the temple was not his 'Father's house' and he would never re-enter his dead body. Jesus did not resurrect; he left his body and entered the Spirit Realm. Resurrection is the rise of the walking dead: dead people coming back to life.

John turned water into wine at his wedding to Mary Magdalene; he was a sorcerer like Jehovah and could manipulate the elements. He fed a crowd of 5,000 with just a few fish. Jesus would not feed people meat; he said, do not kill innocent prey and eat their flesh. The last supper was John's teaching; Jesus did not celebrate the Passover.

The Roman government became alarmed at John's preaching of a new kingdom and wanted to stop his growing influence. Roman guards came to arrest John; Judas led them to Jesus the healer. John's preaching continued after the crucifixion and Roman officials knew they crucified the wrong man. John was thrown in prison. Jesus' followers also realized it was their healer who had been wrongly crucified.

After Jesus died Jehovah appeared to people pretending to be Jesus the healer, raised from the dead. Jehovah can take any shape but he can't change his vibration. Those who saw him did not recognize him and they were terrified. Jehovah called them fools and expounded scripture. Thomas did not believe this being was Jesus. After touching his wounds he was deceived and accepted Jehovah's parody of Jesus.

Jehovah said: "O fools... ought not Christ to have... entered into his glory? Beginning at Moses and the prophets, he expounded to them the scriptures... Behold my hands and my feet that it is I... for a spirit does not have flesh and bones, as you see me have... All things must be fulfilled which were written in the Law of Moses and the prophets and psalms concerning me... repentance and remission of sins should be preached... among all nations (Luke 24:25—47)." This is not Jesus' voice, and it is not his body. If Jesus manifested, he would be a Spiritual Being, not a dead body of flesh.

Saul was hunting Jesus' followers, those who embraced his teachings on healing: eating living foods, fasting and cleansing (see Message 21) when a light blinded him. He fell down and a voice said: "Saul why persecute me? It is hard for you to kick against the pricks (Acts 22)." When cattle kick against pricks they are driven deeper in their flesh. This means 'Saul, if you rebel against me I will cause you pain.'

Jehovah told Ananias, a devout Jew, to restore Saul's sight and baptize him. Ananias told Saul: "the God of our fathers has chosen you, that you should know his will (Acts 22)." The demon-god of Israel chose Saul to deceive the followers of Jesus, changing his name to Paul.

Paul began preaching about Jesus. When the people heard him, they said, 'isn't this the man that destroyed those who called on this name, that he might bring them bound to the Chief Priests (Acts 9:21)?' The followers of Jesus were skeptical of Paul, yet they were soon convinced he believed in Jesus. Paul was persecuted by Jews; they tried many times to capture and kill him but he always escaped. This is because Paul's persecution was an act.

Another scheme was even more effective. "God wrought special miracles by the hands of Paul." Paul cast out evil spirits, and then Jew exorcists pretended to do the same thing, saying "We adjure you by Jesus whom Paul preaches." The evil spirit answered as planned, "Jesus I know, and Paul, but who are you?" He then attacked the Jews and "they fled out of that house, naked and wounded. This was known to all the Jews and Greeks at Ephesus... the name of Lord Jesus was magnified... and the word of God grew mightily, and prevailed (Acts 19:11—17)."

A deputy "desired to hear the word of God." Elymas tried to turn him away. Paul said to him: "...you child of the devil, you enemy of all righteousness, will you not cease to pervert the right ways of the Lord? Behold the hand of the Lord is upon you and you will be blind, not seeing the sun for a season... When the deputy saw what was done, he believed, being astonished at the doctrine of the Lord (Acts 13:7—12)."

Paul struck a man blind that opposed him and the deputy believed out of fear. Paul said *"whoever fears God, to you is the word of this salvation sent (Acts 13:26)."* Jesus told us to love him, love God and love one another. There is no fear in love. This salvation is not of Jesus.

Jesus said: "beware of the leaven of the Pharisees (Mark 8:15)." Paul said "Purge out the old leaven that you may be a new lump, as you are unleavened (I Cor 5:7)." The new lump is the "new spirit" Jehovah said he will "put within you (Eze 36:26)." This spirit is a demon-god; it is also the leaven Jesus warned us against. Spirit cannot be put within you; it is already there. Paul fermented the teachings of Jesus— changed them into something else.

Paul said "Jesus, who was made a little lower than the angels... did not take on the nature of angels, but the seed of Abraham... that he might be a... High Priest... to make reconciliation for the sins of the people (Heb 2:9, 16, 17)."

Jesus was not made lower than angels, or born for a human sacrifice. His message opposed the violent, Hebrew god. Jesus told Jews their god was Satan— a murderer and father of lies (John 8:44). Paul tricked Jesus' followers into worshipping this demon-god, and the gentle Jesus was abandoned for Christ- the Savior, Messiah, and Anointed.

Paul did not want to preach the gospel, it was more insidious than persecution, but the Lord committed it to him. He said "I preach the gospel... necessity is laid upon me; woe (excruciating pain) is unto me if I do not preach the gospel." Paul said if a dispensation of the gospel was committed to him, he preached against his will (I Cor 9:16—17). In Col 1:25 Paul says "the dispensation... is given to me."

Paul said "It is a fearful thing to fall into the hands of the living God (Heb 10:31)." Abraham was ready to kill his son rather than face the Lord's wrath. Paul asked Christians to pray 'that I may open my mouth boldly, to make known the mystery of the gospel... that I may speak boldly as I ought to... (Eph 6:19, 20).' Paul was not protected enough to speak boldly so he gave us clues. He said 'being crafty, I caught you with guile [cunning, deception] (2 Cor 12:16).' Paul's guile:

'To the Jews I became as a Jew, that I might gain the Jews. To those under the law, as under the law, that I might gain them. To those that are without law, as without law, that I might gain them. To the weak I became as weak, that I might gain them. This I do for the gospel's sake (I Cor 9:20—23)."

Paul said we are struggling with the wiles of the devil— principalities, powers, the rulers of the darkness of this world, and spiritual wickedness in high places (Eph 6:11—12).

Principalities are the wiles of the devil; Christ is the head of them all. The head of all principalities is the Godhead, and the fullness of the Godhead is in Christ (Col 2:9, 10).

Paul said the first Adam was of the earth— a living soul; the second Adam was made a quickening spirit (I Cor 15:45—49). Quickening is "zoopoieo"— make alive. A quickening spirit is a demon that receives life through his host. Paul said men of the earth are earthy; men of heaven (quickening spirit) are heavenly. As we have the image of the earth, we should also 'bear the image' of the heavenly. Bear is "phoreo"— garment, constant companion. The heavenly image is the image of the beast— The Holy Ghost.

Paul said if Christ is not raised from the dead, his preaching will be in vain (I Cor 15:14). Christ-Jehovah has not been 'raised from the dead.' He can still be cast out and die the 2nd death. Jehovah needs Paul's preaching to rise from the dead. Paul said the resurrection of the dead is "sown in corruption and raised in incorruption (I Cor 15:42)." He also said this is not possible for neither does corruption inherit incorruption (1 Cor 15:50). Resurrection of the dead is corrupt and it cannot be raised without corruption.

Jesus said "if anyone hears my words and believes not, I judge him not (John 12:47)." Jesus does not have a judgment day, he said "I judge no man (John 8:15)… with what judgment you judge, you will be judged and with what measure you met it will be measured to you again (Matt 7:2)." This is karma—we judge ourselves. Jehovah said "he that… receives not my words has one that judges him (John 12:48)." If you don't submit to Jehovah, he cannot judge you.

Jesus said 'if a man keeps my saying he will never see death (John 8:51).' Jehovah said 'he that believes in me though he was dead, yet shall he live (John 11:25).' If you keep Jesus' teachings you will not lose your Spirit when you 'cross over'. Those who obey Jehovah are in danger of losing their Spirit upon death, and yet shall he live (as the living dead). Jesus said the truth will make you free (John 8:32). Jehovah said the Son will make you free (John 8:36). The Son of man will not make you free; he will bind and kill you.

Paul believed only part of Israel was blinded, until the 'fullness of the Gentiles' (their destruction) comes. At that time, all of Israel would know 'this mystery'— the Lord's plan

(Rom 11:25). "Israel has not obtained that which he seeks... but the election has obtained it; the rest were blinded... David said let their table become a snare and a trap... (Rom 11:7— 9)." All of Israel was blinded— the elect, Jews and Gentiles. The Bible is sealed to trap us all. We are under the Lord's spell, in his deep, perpetual sleep (Is 29:10, 11). We were not to know the truth of his gospel until the Day of the Lord.

Jehovah set a snare for all of humanity: "For as a snare it will come on all those who dwell on the face of the whole earth (Luke 21:35)." The Lord's salvation is not for humanity; it is for demons who survive his judgment. If demons can secure ever lasting habitations, they can obtain everlasting life through zombie hosts— the walking dead.

Paul said the 'Wicked' will be revealed "whom the Lord will consume with the spirit of his mouth and destroy with the **brightness of his coming**. Even him whose coming is after the working of Satan with all power, signs and lying wonders (2Thes 2:8, 9)." Wicked is 'anomos'— those not subject to Jewish law. Paul believed everyone but Jews would be destroyed on the day of the Lord. The Lord said: 'Shall not the day of the Lord be darkness and not light, even very dark and **no brightness in it** (Amos 5:20)?' Paul contradicted this scripture to get our attention. He said this day is after the working of Satan. How could there be brightness in it?

Paul told the Hebrews God anointed them above all others. "They will perish but you will remain. As a vesture you will fold them up and they will be changed, but your years will not fail (Hab 1:9—12)." It was not Jews who were going to live forever; it was the demon-ghosts.

Paul said if anyone preaches a gospel that is contrary to his, let him be accursed (Galatians 1:8). Accursed is 'anathema'— fulfillment of a vow. If someone tells you a different meaning of the gospel of 'Jesus Christ' let him fulfill his promise to do so. The gospel is a god-spell, cast to put you in a perpetual sleep. Reject Christ and his gospel, cast out The Holy Ghost.

Jehovah said your heart is evil, if you use your imagination, you will suffer his wrath, do not give heed to dreams, and deny yourself. Your heart is where you commune with your Spirit, imagination is your creative power, dreams guide your destiny. Let your heart lead you, learn from dreams, use your imagination, it is divine reality; you are dreaming the world.

Your heart, imagination and dreams guide your spiritual path; that is why Jehovah tries to keep you from them.

Jehovah said he would do a marvelous work and a wonder so the wisdom of wise men would perish and understanding of prudent men will be hidden (Isaiah 29:14). People with vision and wisdom can expose Jehovah.

Selflessness is no concern for self- no self-respect. It is the sacrifice of your passion for a cause. This leaves you feeling empty and depressed. Bishop Festo said "I cannot manage myself... I cannot meet my own desires... there has never been a more empty life than the one which has itself as its center." This is a lie. You were created to manage your life and meet your desires. Jehovah tells his worshippers to deny themselves and follow him; this is being selfless. Cut off from your desires, the dreams in your heart will die. Being self-less will cause you to be less of yourself. We are designed to follow our own heart, not someone else.

Selfishness is seeking your advantage without concern for anyone but yourself, and being greedy- pursuing money, sex, possessions, etc. Selfishness is seeking your own pleasure at others expense, being conceited, egotistical, arrogant, and feeling superior to others. Selfish desires lead to compulsive, addictive behavior; this makes you feel worthless and empty.

Soul Desires develop your talents and uniqueness- the things you were born to do. You become more than you thought you could be. Soul desires connect you with your Spirit. This connection lights your heart and mind with passion and creative genius (fire of eternity). Pay attention to your intuition, and follow your heart. This will take you to your destiny and your dreams will come true. Bring forth the fruit of your soul. You are brilliant; be a Child of Pride, devoted and dedicated to you. The Lord hates pride because proud people know their self-worth. Pride gives you deep contentment, a sense of belonging, and joy. Pride is a virtue; it strengthens your body, your mind, soul and Spirit, and you glow on every level of your being. Pride is not arrogance. Pride touches your true Self and you glimpse eternity. Touching eternity humbles you, while filling you with ecstasy.

Your true Self is underneath the neurosis and conditioning; it sees through the deceptions, and manipulations. "Every person... in their core essence is a magnificent being with unlimited potential… In the deepest depths of you and me, in the deepest depths of we, lies the most beautiful jewel, shinning forth eternally. Within that precious jewel, within that priceless piece of we, lies a time beyond all time, lies a place beyond all space… In the deepest depths of you and me, in the deepest depths of we, lies the love and wisdom of all Eternity (Fred Burks)." When we express the fullness of our potential, we feel pride, humility, ecstasy and eternity.

Faith of the Heart

Diane Warren

It's been a long road, getting from there to here. It's been a long time, but my time is finally near. And I can feel a change in the wind right now, nothing's in my way. And they're not going to hold me down no more, no they're not going to hold me down. Cause I've got faith of the heart, I'm going where my heart will take me. I've got faith to believe I can do anything. I've got strength of the soul and no one's going to bend or break me. I can reach any star. I've got faith, I've got faith, faith of the heart. It's been a long night, trying to find my way. Been through the darkness, now I'll finally have my day. And I will see my dream come alive at last, I will touch the sky. And they're not going to hold me down no more, no they're not going to change my mind. I've known a wind so cold, I've seen the darkest days. But now the winds I feel are only winds of change… oh yeah; it's been a long road.

Moriah's Message 7
The Great God

Paul said God would send us a delusion so we would believe a lie (IITh 2:11). The Lord's delusion was so powerful, we accepted him as the Creator. The Lord is 'clothed in a robe dipped in blood (Rev 19:13).' The robes Jehovah and his demons wear are our bodies. They put them on when we invite them in. The blood they are dipped in, is our life-force that they live on. Jehovah's name that no man knows but himself, is Satan (Rev I9:I2). Satan is King and Lord over Kings and Lords. (Rev 19:16).

The Lord told Jeremiah: "...I will bring evil from the north, and a great destruction. The lion is come up from his thicket, and the destroyer of the Gentiles is on his way... to make your land desolate, and your cities will be laid waste, without an inhabitant (Jer 4: 6—9)." The Lord said when this day comes "the priests shall be astonished" (stunned, shocked).

Jeremiah understood the Lord's plan. He said: "Lord God! **You have greatly deceived this people** and Jerusalem, saying you will have peace; whereas the sword reaches unto the soul (Jer 4:10)." Christians, Jews and Muslims are deceived. If they do not reject their god and cast out his demon-ghosts, they will be destroyed.

The Holy Ghost needs permission to enter spiritual people; their aura is too strong to penetrate. "I stand at the door and knock. If any man hears my voice and opens the door, I will come in to him, and will sup with him... (Rev 3:20)." Demon-ghosts beg to be let in. If you opened the door, he is having a meal with you, feeding on your life-force. If the day of the Lord came, his quiet supping would end.

The Lord told Ezekiel he would eat the flesh and drink the blood of great men, princes, generals and soldiers, as if they were lambs and rams. 'You will eat their fat till you are glutted and drink their blood till you are drunk (Ez 39:18—19). This cannibal supper, feasting on mighty men, was to secure the 'supper of the great God'.

The Lord told Zachariah: take two rods, Favor and Union. Break the Favor Rod to revoke the covenant made with all nations and break the Union Rod to severe the bond between Judah and Israel. The Lord will break his covenants and send a new Shepherd that will not tend the sheep, but make them fat and eat them (Zachariah 11). 'He that puts his trust in the Lord will be made fat (Prov 28:25)'.

"And I saw an angel… saying to all the fowls that fly in the midst of heaven: Come and gather yourselves together unto the supper of the great God that ye may eat the flesh of Kings, and the flesh of captains, and the flesh of mighty men, and the flesh of horses, and of them that sit on them, and the flesh of all men both free and bond, both small and great… The **fowls were filled with their flesh** (Rev 19:17, 18, 21)."

"Looking for… the glorious appearing of the great God and our Savior, Jesus Christ (Titus 2:13)." Christ is the great God that loves fatty flesh. After his great supper the Lord would tell his fowls: "come out of your graves." The demon-ghosts would come out of their slaughtered host and be judged. Strong ghosts would devour weak ghosts, receiving everlasting life. We can stop this: cast out The Holy Ghost.

The Lord said the greatest sin is speaking against The Holy Ghost. 'Whosoever speaks against The Holy Ghost, it shall not be forgiven him, neither in this world or in the world to come (Matt 12:32).' If we cast out The Holy Ghost there will be no supper of the great God and Jehovah-Christ will die his second death. This is why he said: 'He that blasphemes against The Holy Ghost has no forgiveness and is in danger of eternal damnation (Mark 3:29).' Nothing is more terrifying to Jehovah than casting out our demon-ghost.

Jehovah said there would be rumors of wars, earthquakes, and famine before his great and Dreadful Day came. Then kingdom would rise against Kingdom; Christians would be delivered up and brought before rulers. In that hour they would not speak, The Holy Ghost would. Now brother betrays brother to death, and father betrays son. Children rise up against parents and cause them to be put to death (Mark

13:7—12). Betray is 'paradidomi'— yield up (succumb to the demon within).

Rumors is 'akoe'— audience (persons reached by a book or broadcast). 'Rumors of wars' are Jehovah's worshippers declaring war on Jehovah-Allah-Christ after reading <u>The Greatest Deception</u>. The rumors bring 'the beginning of sorrows.' Sorrows is 'odin'— childbirth. The Lord is ready to birth New Jerusalem. The earthquakes are shockwaves. When Jews, Christians and Muslims realize their God is a demon, shockwaves resound around the world. These massive quakes will convulse through the noosphere and shatter the crystallized thoughtforms about Jehovah, bringing a paradigm shift to our collective consciousness.

The Lord said "I came not to send peace, but a sword... A **man's foes shall be those of his own household** (Matt 10:34, 36)." If the Lord commands: "All who are in the graves come forth" The Holy Ghost would come to the forefront of his host and rise against Christians (Kingdom of God will rise against Kingdom of earth). Jehovah calls Christians 'kings of the earth'. Christians would be paralyzed as the demon took control and attacked their family. There would be 'weeping, wailing and gnashing of teeth.'

Christianity (overt) and Satanism (covert) are the same religion. Jehovah, Christ and Satan are the same being. Their main holidays coincide; Christians and Satanists call their God 'Lord of Lords' and 'King of Kings'. Christ said suffer [yielded up] little children to come unto me. Paul said "children are partakers of flesh and blood (Heb 2:14)." Children raised in satanic cults are forced to kill babies and eat their flesh and blood. Communion represents these cannibal rituals. If the Great and Dreadful Day came, demon-controlled Christians would attack and eat each other.

In <u>Suffer The Child</u> (Spencer) Jenny is raised in a satanic cult. She is taken to rituals where Satan worshipers read the Bible and call on Jehovah and Elohim to raise people from their graves. They torture little children, including Jenny, shattering their souls, raping their minds and bodies and forcing them to kill babies. Jenny was subjected to verbal, physical, emotional and sexual abuse that splintered her mind, causing multiple personalities to emerge in order to survive.

Satanic ritual abuse and alien abduction are similar. They secure their victims to an altar/table; knives, needles, drugs and surgical instruments are used. Mind-control programs are installed with torture. Tracking devices are embedded. Sperm and egg samples are collected. Babies are grown as crops to be harvested. If you have alien abduction memories, MPD or schizophrenia, you may be a victim of satanic ritual.

The gospel was invented to clothe hungry, thirsty, poor and needy demons- strangers with no habitation. It doesn't matter if the receiver is Catholic, Baptist or Mormon; hosts are needed to feed demons. Jude said ungodly men (no Holy Ghost) would turn the Lord into debauchery, gather a following with hard speeches against the Lord Jesus Christ, and follow their own desires. "They have gone in the way of Cain" they honor the earth (Jude 4,11,15,16). They are Anti-Christs claiming 'Jesus Christ' is Satan. With no demon-ghost to deceive them, they follow their heart.

The Lord said he will raise a dreadful nation (gowy- troops, locusts) to possess dwellings (bodies) that are not theirs. They will come for violence and **sup up** as the **East Wind** (Hab 1:6—9). If the Lord's dreadful day comes demon-ghosts would come forth, fully possess their host and violently 'sup up.' New Jerusalem would be established and humans who survived would be harvested as food. Zombies- people fully possessed by demons, would live on raw, bloody flesh.

In Rock-a-Bye Baby, the baby is tied to the highest branch (center of command). Will the Lord's East Wind break the branch, causing Christians, Jews and Muslims (pleasant vessels) the cradle (earth) and all life to fall?

Humpty Dumpty is Lord God. Humpty is Jehovah; if he goes over the hump (point of no return) Dumpty (demon-ghosts) will dump their host (kill them). The strongest ghosts would receive salvation (exist). If their wall of deception collapses they will break in pieces and never be put back together. With no garment of salvation (our bodies) Humpty Dumpty will have a great fall and no place will be found for them.

Without a host demon-ghosts die.

The Lord's Prayer says: "Father which art in heaven, hallowed be thy name." Hallowed is 'hagiazo'—to make holy, sanctify. Hallowed is the worship and glory that the Lord demands- praise and tribute feed him. When Christians pray Thy Kingdom come Thy will be done, they ask Jehovah to kill or enslave humanity, and destroy the earth. The Lord rules his kingdom with the power and glory Christians give him— Thine is the Kingdom, and the power, and the glory. If they take away his power and glory, his Kingdom will die and the old lion will perish for lack of prey, crying: "my leanness, my leanness, woe unto me (Isaiah 24:16)."

Jehovah plans to kill the 'wicked' on his great and Dreadful Day. Wicked is 'rasha'— wrong, condemned. Jehovah's worshippers are wrong; they have been deceived. Their deception has condemned them. We must reject Jehovah or he will slaughter us and destroy the earth. "For it is a day of trouble and of treading down (Is 22:5)." Will this 'day of trouble' be for us, or will it be for Jehovah?

If you are uncertain about Jehovah's identity, find a place in nature to pray. Spend the day fasting and praying to Jesus. Feel his love for you, and the real Jesus will hear your heart-felt prayer. Ask Jesus if Jehovah, God of Abraham, is Satan. Ask Jesus if Jehovah-Satan is the Savior 'Jesus Christ'.

When you pray to: Heavenly Father, Jesus Christ, or the Lord, Jehovah answers. Be careful with names, they create links. The Native American Church combines traditional beliefs with Christianity. When they pray to the Great Spirit in church and ceremony, Jehovah answers. Do not pray to the Great Spirit if you believe he is Christ. Do not pray to Yeshua, it is a Hebrew word that means 'salvation comes from Jehovah.' Jesus is Iesous (pronounced Hey-sues) in Greek, meaning Hail Zeus, and has no Hebrew translation.

"When we want wisdom we go up on the hill and talk to God. Four days and four nights without food and water... It's a great feeling to be talking to God. I know. I did it way upon the mountain. The wind was blowing. It was dark. It was cold. And I stood there and I talked to God. When I go up on the hill to pray, I don't just talk to God. I try to get the talking over quick. Mostly I'm listening. Listening to God, that's praying too... If you don't listen, you don't hear what God's saying...

(<u>Nobel Red Man</u> Arden)." When we listen in prayer we feel this communion in our heart. We may be moved to tears; they are messengers of truth.

David called to the Lord for comfort because ungodly men frightened him. "In my distress I called upon the Lord and cried unto my God. He heard my voice... then the earth shook and trembled... because he was wroth (Ps 18:4— 7).' The Lord was angry with David for being afraid of ungodly men (no demon-ghost). "There went up smoke out of his nostrils, and fire out of his mouth devoured. Coals were kindled by it... Darkness was under his feet. He rode upon a cherub. He made darkness his secret place. His pavilion round about him were dark waters and thick clouds of the skies... his thick clouds passed hailstones and coals of fire (Ps 18:8—14)."

Jehovah-Satan has darkness under his feet- it's his secret place, and his mouth devours with fire. The cherub he rides is the gospel. His pavilion (crypt) is a dark, foggy underworld with caverns. His day of the Lord is cloudy and dark; he hid his evil behind a wall of fog. "The cloud is consumed and vanishes away; he that goes down to the grave shall come up no more (Job 7:9)." Jehovah's fog is lifting; demon-ghosts in the grave ('showl'- world of the dead) will wither away and be no more.

Thomas Carlyle was a Calvinist and couldn't find the answers he sought in the Bible. One day, in the glow of the sunrise, he realized divine laws are in nature and man— earth, sun, wind, our heart- not the Bible. Carlyle rejected the god of the Bible but not the Creator. He believed "God not only made us and beholds us, but is in us, and around us." He said reverence (respect, devotion) was our greatest strength, the forms which our religious convictions are cast must die, and the divine must be redefined. Carlyle said universal history and divine scripture is the true epic poem.

Humanity will either face Armageddon or we will Ascend. The Holy Ghost is about to strike. No one will save you from this demon-beast, hiding inside you. You must save yourself. Resist the Lord and cast out The Holy Ghost (page 80). The Lord's midnight hour is "close at hand" but you have the power to stop it. "There is no greater power than that of an idea whose time has come (Victor Hugo)."

Thriller

Michael Jackson

It's close to midnight and something evil's lurking in the dark. Under the moonlight you see a sight that almost stops your heart. You try to scream but terror takes the sound before you make it. You start to freeze as horror looks you right between the eyes, you're paralyzed. Cause this is thriller, thriller night, and no one's gonna save you from the beast about strike... They're out to get you. Demons closing in on every side. They will possess you, unless you change the number on your dial... Darkness falls across the land, the midnight hour is close at hand. Creatures crawl in search of blood to terrorize your neighborhood... and grizzly ghouls from every tomb are closing in to seal your doom... No mere mortal can resist the Evil of The Thriller.

Moriah's Message 8
The Delivery

Jehovah said: "There is no God with me, I kill and I make alive, I wound and I heal; neither is there any that can deliver out of my hand. I lift up my hand to heaven and say, I live forever... I will make my arrows drunk with blood, and my sword will devour flesh (Deut 32:39, 40, 42)." Jehovah's arrows and swords that drink blood and devour flesh are demons coming to the forefront on his Dreadful Day, taking control of Christians and forcing them to attach each other. Protestants and Catholics believe Jehovah is God and Jesus Christ. Mormons believe Jehovah is Jesus Christ. Jehovah's Witnesses believe Jehovah is God. If Jehovah's Dreadful Day comes, he will reveal his true identity: Satan.

Catholics: Christ is not the sacrifice, you are. You do not eat your Lord at communion, he eats your life-force. John the Baptist called his disciples 'fishers of men' because they caught men on a hook for The Holy Ghost to consume. On the Day of the Lord Christians were to feast on each other. Having fish on Friday is symbolic of this. Reject the Lord. Stop his Great and Dreadful Day.

Evangelical: Receiving the Lord into your heart did not make you born again, it made you possessed. A Campus Crusade pamphlet says "When He is within you, He wants to think with your mind, express Himself through your emotions, speak through your voice, though you may be unconscious of it;" this is demon possession. If the Lord established his New Jerusalem, demons who survive Jehovah's judgment would be born again, receiving ever lasting life. You are told to follow Christ, not your feelings- they are unreliable. Your feelings are linked to your soul. How you feel tells you if something is right. Follow your heart.

Pentecostal: You believe being baptized and filled with The Holy Ghost brings salvation; this salvation is not for you. Your Holy Ghost is enshrining you for his shelter. You are his garment of salvation. The work he does: consumes life-force.

In his book The New Birth, Bernard says when we speak in tongues the Lord "takes complete control, demonstrating His Lordship by using the most unruly member for His glory. Since the brain controls speech this... signifies that God has taken control of our... reasoning and will— in short the whole person." Satan controls you when speaking in tongues.

Baptists: Being immersed under water is symbolic of the burial and resurrection of Christ. But baptism is more than symbolic. When you are baptized, The Holy Ghost is buried within you, so it can receive life at your expense; this is the 'daily sacrifice' you make- life-force to your demon-ghost. A Baptist publication lists a dozen similarities between Santa, Satan, and the Lord. Santa is Satan, but he is not pretending to be the Lord, he is this Lord. See message 19.

Seventh Day Adventist: Years ago, I attended an SDA workshop on prophecy and told the Pastor 'you interpret this the way you were taught but that doesn't mean it is right.' He said 'maybe so.' His response surprised me. Members call God the Creator and emphasize God's love. The Creator is love, but Jehovah is violent and evil; he killed people- even babies, to possess their land. Many SDA members are vegetarians- a true teaching of Jesus. All Christian churches contain truths but they are mingled with lies.

Jehovah's Witnesses: You are excellent witnesses for Jehovah, but the Good News you spread- living forever on the earth, is for demons, not you. You would not want to live in this world. I studied the Bible with Jehovah's Witnesses for a while. My comments on Jehovah's violence never bothered the older witness. One day her companion agreed with me. The older companion said 'you're not interested in being baptized; we won't be seeing you anymore.' The Jehovah's Witnesses told me someone in the end times would be born, who would read the Bible and discover it is speaking directly to them, saying personal things to them, that only they would know. Several years later this happened to me!

{The Church of Jesus Christ of Latter-Day Saints: Hunter said Jehovah exerted his will vigorously, to become powerful and gain knowledge. His understanding of universal laws grew until he attained Godhood. Jehovah is not omniscient. He bioengineered humans and beasts of the field, breaking creation laws. He may have obtained this knowledge in Atlantis when he was a man.

Your God was once mortal: "as man is, God once was, and as he is, you may become." You may become like your god, but do you want to? He's the most powerful demon on earth. Mormons have many children for 'spirits' waiting for a body. They believe these 'spirit-children' receive their body at birth; the 'spirits' receive a body at baptism (age 8) when the child gets her constant companion- a demon.

In early Mormon history, young girls were forced to marry old men with many wives and 100+ children. Church leaders performed blood atonement (murder) for adultery- mostly women who were often abused. Men rarely committed adultery; they had numerous wives, including young girls.

Apostasy, murder and blasphemy against The Holy Ghost were also reasons for blood atonement Fundamentalist Mormons live the way Mormons did 150 years ago, practicing polygamy and blood atonement. Read <u>Shattered Dreams</u> and <u>Cult Insanity</u> (Spencer). Heber C. Kimball said blood atonement will be law when there is no separation of Church and State, and the power to take life is vested in the ruling theocracy, as it was in the days of Moses.

Mormons believe they are the true Israelites, and they will build the temple for New Jerusalem in the United States. The US will become God's Government under their rule. Mormon temple ceremonies are connected to Masonic rites and Solomon's temple. Their rites include incantations to summon demons. Mormons know the 'fullness of the Gospel' is the 'fullness of the Gentiles' -their slaughter. Mormons are not the Preserved of Israel, they are Gentiles and would also be slaughtered. Jehovah plans to destroy all of Israel.**}**

Far Right Supremacists: You believe Jesus Christ is the Savior of Israel- Whites. The Lord is the Savior of himself. He would slaughter all Israelites if he returned as the 'Messiah'.

You believe Jews are Satan's seed-line, whites are God's seed-line and people of color were created like animals. White people are genetically inferior; they have the most genetic defects. You say blasphemy against The Holy Ghost is when a white has a child with another race because the child doesn't have God's Spirit. Everyone is born with a Spirit.

'We invoke the blood covenant and declare a full state of war and will not lay down our weapons until we have driven the enemy into the sea.' Your enemy is your god- Jehovah; he will oppose you and put you to death if he is not stopped.

Jews and Muslims: You are the descendants of Esau and Jacob. Jacob deceived his father into giving him Esau's firstborn blessing. When Esau came for his blessing, Isaac said he would live by the sword and serve his brother, but he would have the fatness of the earth, and when he received the dominion, he would break this yoke.

Arabs would live by the sword and serve Jews, but their land would have oil, and in the end, they would have the dominion. Jews claimed land Arab families had owned for thousands of years; many worked for Jews as common laborers. Allah is the one who brought Jews to your land, reduced you to their servants, and put hatred between you. Arabs and Jews have been feeding their demonic gods by slaughtering each other for thousands of years.

Jews were given the election, but it was to be taken from them and passed to Muslims after the gospel was fulfilled. Muslims were to receive dominion through the 'Saints of the Most High'. Demon-ghosts would have the real dominion through possession. The chosen Arabs were to be enslaved. As Esau and Jacob fell on each other's neck and kissed and wept, you need to embrace one another and reject the god of Abraham; he is your real enemy.

If the Day of the Lord comes, the Lord's chosen would be bound by powerful demons. They would cry: "I have seen affliction by the rod of his wrath. He led me and brought me into darkness, but not into light... He has turned against me... all the day. My flesh and my skin he has made old... He has set me in dark places, as those that are dead... He has hedged me about that I cannot get out; he has made my chain heavy. When I cry and shout, he shuts out my prayer.

He has enclosed my ways... and made my path crooked. He was as a bear lying in wait, and a lion in secret places. He... pulled me in pieces and made me desolate. He bent his bow and set me as a mark for the arrow (Lam 3:1—12)."

Black Hebrew: Adam was not the first human, and he was not black, but there are black Hebrew. The Queen of Sheba had children with King Solomon. If you are under the curses in Deuteronomy because of something your ancestors did thousands of years ago, why worship this violent god? You are giving him power to utterly destroy you. Sever your bond; reject the god of Abraham.

Luciferians and Gnostics: You know Jehovah is evil, yet you worship his serpent, believing he freed Adam and Eve. The serpent bound Adam and Eve to Jehovah. He is a demon and serves his master, Satan. You are confusing Lucifer the angel of light, with Lucifer the demon of darkness.

Esoteric Christians: You believe Christ is one Savior among many- Krishna, Osiris, Mithra, etc. It is one god wearing different masks down though history. Watch the video I Pet Goat II; a demon-god dances while his mask changes multiple times. It is the same Savior hiding behind the same mystery: the demon-god's salvation, not yours.

Great White Brotherhood: (Theosophy, Hierarchy, Ascended Masters). You believe the 'Father God' and Christ is 'I Am.' This is Jehovah, demon-god of Israel. He calls himself Father, Christ, and 'I Am That I Am.' When you say 'I Am That I Am' you are saying 'I Am God Presence' and Jehovah- your God that is present, receives permission to possess you. You pray to the Heavenly Hosts, Planetary Hierarchy, Ascended Masters and Archangels in the Bible. These beings who guide your life are demons.

Christian Nationalists: If the USA was a Christian Nation, the government would have total authority; we would have no rights. If someone in a household disobeyed the law, everyone in the household could be killed. The Lord demands obedience and retribution. Criticizing the Bible would be against the law. Homosexuals, blasphemers, idolators, murderers, disobedient children and adulterers would receive the death penalty. This would be your life under Biblical law.

Global Elite: Your bloodline has been deceiving humanity for thousands of years. Your biggest lies: New Jerusalem, Christ, and aliens. New Jerusalem is your New World Order, Christ is Satan, aliens are bioengineered and UFO's are manmade. No aliens came here from outer space. You think you control us with your big lies and your covert technology; you have no real power. As long as you worship Satan, he will have power over you. If you establish New Jerusalem and become one of the 144,000 chosen to rule, you will be a zombie controlled by demons. Seeing out of your own eyes, your hands could rip your daughter apart and devour her flesh. The demon in you could put a sword through your heart. The only way you can be free is to reject your violent god and cast him out.

Other Abrahamic religions: Orthodox, Mandaeans, Rastafarians, Anglican, Gnostic, Essence, Sunni, etc. cast out the Lord, Allah, The Holy Ghost, and Christ. The demon-god of Abraham has deceived you. If the Messiah came, he would judge Christians by the gospel, Jews by the Torah, and Muslims by the Koran. His worshippers would all be declared wicked, and killed or enslaved. Christians, Muslims and Jews left a wake of destruction stretching back thousands of years. Jehovah was behind this carnage. He uses us to gain control of the world. If he succeeds, we will not survive. Jehovah and his host (army) of heaven are the enemy of all humanity.

The Lord said: "The end is come... the day of trouble is near... the morning is gone forth [dawn is breaking], the rod has blossomed [Herb of Power, Black Elk's Vision], pride has budded [humanity is filled with pride].The seller will not return that which is sold [the Lord will not return your sins to you]... neither will any strengthen himself in the iniquity of his life [this is a lie; as you work out your karma you strengthen yourself]... they shall pollute my secret place [the Lord's mask is removed]... Rumor will be upon rumor [rumor is 'shema'—message, famous tidings; the rumors are Part One Moriah's Messages] then they will seek a vision of the prophet, but the law will perish from the priest [the Lord's law perishes; Christians become their own priest— priest is 'Kohen'- an acting priest] and counsel from the ancients [wisdom from ancestors] (Ez 7:6, 7, 10, 13, 22, 26)."

When Christians, Jews and Muslims feel God's love, receive answers to prayers, have spiritual experiences, etc. this is not Jehovah-Allah-Christ. It is the Divine Love of the Creator. Jehovah-Allah-Christ is evil. Separating your love-illusion for him, from this divine love may be difficult. The Lord did not die on the cross; the real Jesus was betrayed by Judas and tortured to death. His torture did not save you. Jesus Christ is a lie. Jehovah is a lie. Allah is a lie. The Creator will answer your prayers but you must save yourself. If you sold your iniquity to the Lord, he will not return it. You must take yourself off the cross. Jews and Muslims are under a covenant, bound by impossible laws and cursed if they break them. They can cast off their covenant.

If you're concerned about the Lord's Holy Ghost blasphemy threat, finish this book before doing a de-possession. You'll be better prepared. The Holy Spirit/Ghost is not your Spirit. If it was, then it was with you when you were born. What did you receive when you were baptized? It was not prana, breath, life-force, or your Spirit. It was something that entered you. This lord/ghost/spirit is a demon. You can cast it out.

{De-Possession Guide

Prayer-Fast. Join with others (three or more). Fast the day before. Begin your session praying for spiritual strength. Take turns praying passionately from your heart to the Infinite Creator and Jesus for Spirit Power and strength. Ask angels in the light to join you. Avoid other names; demons copy the names of spiritual beings. Spirit Power will build in your hearts as you pray. Pray, Declare and Command with Power, Authority and Intent in your voice.

Circle. After concluding your prayer, decide who will be released first, and who will facilitate. Sit on the floor or cushions, in a circle with the one to be de-possessed sitting in the center. Symptoms may include: pain, gagging, nausea, hyperventilating, shaking, rolling. Have a bowl and paper bag handy for nausea or hyperventilating. If shaking and rolling occurs, give assistance if containment is needed. The person to be de-possessed declares and prays the following:

Declaration. I reject Jehovah, also known as Allah, God of Israel, Heavenly Father, God Almighty, Jesus Christ, the Lord, the Savior, and Satan. I reject The Holy Ghost, the Lord's covenants, his plan of salvation, the gospel, his works, angels and hosts of heaven. I reject all demons, their offers, agreements, holds and contracts, including contracts made by my ancestors that included me. I dissolve all generational curses in my bloodline. I reclaim power I gave Jehovah, Allah, the Lord and Savior, Satan, and demons.

Prayer for release. Infinite Creator, release me from Jehovah-Allah-Lord-Christ-Satan, The Holy Ghost, and any demons possessing me.

Casting out demons. Everyone places their hands on the possessed person's head. The facilitator says: "I command The Holy Ghost and any demons within (say name) to hear my words and obey. I command you to come out of (name's) body. Hold your tongue and leave. Return to Satan, your master."

If the demon doesn't speak, it was cast out. If it speaks and refuses to depart, ask the demon what hold it has on (name). The person rejects this hold, all agreements, and offers. Command it to leave. If it still refuses to depart, ask 'what other holds do you have on (state name) ?' The person rejects these holds, all agreements and offers. Command it to leave. If it still refuses to depart say: 'I bind your tongue.' Hold another prayer-fast to increase your spiritual power and try again. Repeat the process until everyone has been de-possessed.}

You are your own Savior; live from your heart and you will have eternal life. Form a fellowship with others released from Jehovah. Study Jesus' teachings in the Essene Gospel of Peace (Message 21). Have mono meals, add raw foods to your diet, fast as Jesus taught. Volunteer in your town. When we help each other live, we harmonize with the universe (spiritual essence of creation) and miracles happen in our daily lives.

Turn churches into shelters for those in crisis- abused women and children, the homeless, the mentally ill, drug addicts, etc. Churches could be community centers with activities for all ages- community projects, performances, seminars, workshops, crafts, sports, movies, clinics, thrift stores, etc. Love the goodness in yourself and others.

Moriah's Message 9
A Dry Tree

An eagle came to Lebanon, flew to the highest branch of a cedar tree, cropped off its twigs, and carried them to a land of traffic (a city of merchants). He took the seed of the land and planted it as a willow by great waters. Its roots turned under it, it became a vine, and brought forth branches. The vine bent its roots toward another eagle, from the furrow where it was planted, that he might water it. "When the East Wind touches it, it will wither in the furrows where it grew... **I... dried up the green tree, and made the dry tree flourish** (Ez 17)."

The first eagle is Jehovah, the second is Jesus, the twigs- the elect, the seed- lost ten tribes. They became a vine and send out roots to Jesus, to receive water. Christians worship both eagles. This is why their history is full of bloodshed, as well as loving service. If the East Wind touches the vine, it will wither. The green tree will then die and the dry tree will live. Twigs is 'yanaq'—nurse, give milk. The Lord scattered the elect among his plantation to feed them on his gospel, so they can be harvested. The goodly cedar is the remnant.

"I will hedge up her way with thorns, and make a wall... She will follow after her lovers... but not find them... for she did not know I gave her corn, wine, and oil which they prepared for Baal. I will return and take away my corn... and my wine...

given to cover her nakedness... None will deliver her out of my hand... I will allure her, and bring her into the wilderness, and speak comfortably to her. I will give her vineyards... for a door of hope, she will sing there... as in the day when she came up out of the land of Egypt... at that day, you will call me Ishi, and shall no more call me Baal... I will make a covenant for them with the beasts of the field, and the fowls of heaven... and make them lie down (be killed) safely (Hos 2:6—18)."

Christians believe they follow the Creator and Jesus, but the Lord hedged their way with thorns. Thorns is 'cirab'—a hook; these hooks are demons. The crown of thorns on Jesus' head symbolized demon-ghosts. Christians do not know who they worship, they are allured and beguiled. When they come out of their god-spell, they will know their god 'Ishi' is a blood-thirsty demon.

The Lord's corn is Christians, the wine is The Holy Ghost, oil is worship (fuel, life-force) they give their demon-god. Wilderness is 'midbar'- cattle, pasture. The Hebrew in the Sinai wilderness and Europeans in the American wilderness symbolized Israelites walking like cattle to the Lord's pasture where they were to all lie down (be killed). His demons (fowls of heaven) would then inherit the earth by possessing the chosen and the remnant (beasts of the field).

The Lord told Ezekiel "Tarshish was thy merchant... of all kind of riches; with silver, iron, tin and lead, they traded in thy fairs... The ships of Tarshish did sing of thee... and you were replenished and made very glorious in the midst of the seas (Ez 27:12, 25)." The Lord guides his merchants to gain the riches of the world, so he can control the earth.

On 'the day of thy ruin' the merchants and the men of war that are in the Lord will cry bitterly, weep, wail and lament, for their riches and merchandise shall fall. And they will be astonished at the Lord and be sore afraid and shall be troubled in their countenance; the Lord will destroy them (Ez 27:27—36 and Rev 18:15—19).

The wholesale rape, pillage and slaughter for riches began when Columbus sailed from the ancient city of Tarshish, to the 'new world' and claimed them "in the name of the Lord." Isaiah said the ships of Tarshish "bring thy sons from far, their silver and their gold with them, unto the name of the Lord (Is 60:9)." Tarshish is the land of traffic. The seed of this land was planted in the Caribbean Islands, where it became a great vine, spreading across the 'new world.'

Columbus discovered the Arawak, a friendly tribe who brought many gifts to the strange men. Columbus sent 500 back to Spain to be sold as slaves; 200 died in the ships. He said "Let us in the name of the Holy Trinity go on sending all the slaves that can be sold." Columbus "ordered all persons 14 years or older to collect a certain quantity of gold every three months. When they brought it, they were given copper tokens to hang around their necks. Indians found without a copper token had their hands cut off and bled to death (The Destruction of the Indies Bartolome Las Casas)."

There was little gold to be found; the Arawak fled to the hills where they were hunted by the Spaniards' dogs and killed. Many committed suicide, over enslavement and torture. The Arawak population (roughly 250,000) was reduced to zero.

The gold Jehovah promised wasn't found in large quantities until Cortes discovered the Aztecs 27 years later. The natives were plundered and destroyed for their gold, silver, and land like the Arawak were. When Europeans discovered North America, Africans were seized, chained in ships, taken across the ocean and sold as slaves.

Europe laid a foundation for global White domination by slaughtering, enslaving and destroying other civilizations. "The Incas, Aztecs, Mayans, Zulus, native Australians and native Americans were firstly subjected to brutal conquest, annihilation and then westernization whilst their ancient knowledge, passed down meticulously from generation to generation for millennia was systematically eliminated… (The Falsification of History Hammer)."

Ancient records going back to the Alexandrian Library were destroyed, replaced with Jehovah's pseudo religion, history and science. White people believed they were God's Chosen and people of color were subhuman. God commanded them to dominate, kill and enslave other races.

White Europeans tortured their own, cutting off limbs and tearing people apart if they did not follow church doctrine. Many fled to America to escape this horrifying tyranny. White people then projected their fear and trauma onto black people. They also projected their genetic inferiority on them, and they still do. Whites have more recessive genes, genetic defects and disease than people of color. Black people have the greatest genetic diversity, stronger bones and superior immune systems. When white people procreate with each other it keeps them in a degenerate state. When they procreate with people of color, their children are genetically healthier and it helps end the white supremacy lie. Remembering past lives also helps end the lie. We have all been all races and colors. You belong to the human race.

Europeans claimed America as their manifest destiny. They slaughtered whole species, like carrier pigeons, numbering in the hundreds of millions, and raped the land from ocean to ocean. Giant trees, thousands of years old were cut down.

Great forests with giant trees existed because of the red man's interdependent relationship with them. In The Vision (Brown), Stalking Wolf tells how his tribe selected a sapling for a bow. Prayers were sent to all little trees in the forest. A four-day fast was held, while gratitude was felt for the sapling that would sacrifice his life for the tribe. The bow maker began his search, guided by his heart. Once chosen, prayers were sent to the tree. 'He would explain to the little sapling what it would be used for, and how his people were honored at its sacrifice… it would be made well, and cherished. The bow maker knew the sapling would eventually die in its struggle for the sun. He knew that too many saplings... make the grove... susceptible to disease. By removing that sapling, he insured the strength of the grove... [and] future generations of his people."

Native Americans lived in 'America' for thousands of years, and never destroyed any part of it. A Wintu woman said "we do not chop down the trees, we only use dead wood. But the White people plow up the ground, pull down trees, kill everything. The tree says 'don't hurt me,' but they chop it down and cut it up... The Indians never hurt anything, but the white people destroy all. They blast rocks and scatter them on the ground. The rock says 'don't, you are hurting me,' but the White people pay no attention... How can the spirit of the earth like the White man (The Careless Society McKnight)?"

Walking Buffalo said: "We saw the Great Spirit's work in... sun, moon, trees, wind, and mountains. Sometimes we approached him through these things... Did you know that trees talk? Well they do. They talk to each other, and they'll talk to you if you will listen. Trouble is, white people don't listen. They never learned to listen to the Indians, so I don't suppose they'll listen to other voices in nature. But I have learned a lot from trees... Indians living close to nature are not living in darkness (Touch the Earth)."

Trees form a network of energy, which they send to each other and the earth— even stars receive their transmissions. Ancient trees are powerful transmitting stations. When one is cut down, earth and the whole galaxy feels its loss; the energy lines are permanently changed. Only 1% of the great rain forests are left. These giant trees almost vanished from clear-cutting and disease. If we lose the forests, earth will be in danger of becoming a barren planet. In The Legacy of Luna, Julia Hill lived in a redwood for two years, to save the remaining forest of thousand-year-old redwood trees.

White man destroyed the native peoples' way of life. Their ceremonies were not allowed. Prayer sticks, pipes, drums, rattles, medicine bags, etc., were burned. Whites believed they were used in satanic witchcraft. The Natives did not worship Satan, White people did. After they destroyed their culture, many lost their ability to hear nature speak.

Missionaries vehemently pushed their religion onto the natives. Red Jacket said, "Black coats talk to the Great Spirit and ask for light that we may see as they do, when they are blind themselves and quarrel about the light that guides them. These things we do not understand (Touch the Earth)."

In 1800 the land act brought thousands of people west, to claim land. Washington's biography (1800) included a myth about George chopping down his father's cherry tree. George- Christians, father- Jehovah, cherry tree- earth. Earth's resources were ravished, plundered and destroyed. We are still chopped down the cherry tree: earth is dying.

The industrial revolution was changing the world. England needed cheap resources and labor for factories. Villages were exploited. Women and children worked in factories. Self-sustained villages became dependent on mechanized production. Rural life ended in many communities. Extinction of species happened on an unprecedented scale.

The buffalo supplied natives with food, clothing, shelter, bedding, saddles, ropes, tools, pots, ornaments, headdress, and other items. Every part of the beloved buffalo was used: brains, eyes, tongue and intestines, sinew for bow strings.

The buffalo was given deep gratitude and told how he would be used, cherished, and honored for his sacrifice.

White man killed buffalo to wipe out Indians, leaving them to rot. Within 45 years (1840 to 1885) the huge herds were gone; buffalo went from over 100 million to almost nothing— no wild buffalo were left. There is no parallel in earth's history for such horrific slaughter. Jehovah inspired this killing frenzy to cast a spell. It symbolized the day of the Lord, when The Holy Ghost would kill Christians with a massive slaughter.

Europeans destroyed their 'new world' because they were not guided by their Spirit, but by a demon. Jehovah is not part of the spirit-that-moves-in-all-things and lives on destruction. White man emulated their god, becoming demonic and evil.

In 1876 the US government began the forced migration of Native Americans. They were driven hundreds of miles on foot without sufficient food or water. Those who survived were put in concentration camps and given rations that caused starvation. Children were taken to boarding schools where they were beaten daily and forbidden to speak their language. Native Americans were exiled in their own country. Over 80% of their population died.

Choctaw Chief Pushmataha said: "Brother, when you were young, we were strong; we fought by your side; but our arms are now broken... Our land was taken from us... my people are scattered and gone. When I shout, I hear my voice in the depths of the forest, but no answering voice comes back."

Chief Dan George took his grandson into the woods. He told him how the wolf became our guardian, and said he would sing the sacred wolf song over him. "I sang. In my voice was the hope that clings to every heartbeat. I sang. In my words were the powers I inherited from my forefathers... I sang and the song floated on the sun's rays from tree to tree... The whole world listened with us, to hear the wolf's reply. We waited a long time, but none came. Again I sang... as invitingly as I could until... my voice gave out.

All of a sudden, I realized why no wolves had heard my sacred song. There were none left. My heart filled with tears... At last I could whisper to him: 'It is finished.' 'Can I go home now?' he asked, checking his watch to see if he would be in time to catch his favorite TV program. I watched him disappear and wept in silence. All is finished (The Best of

Chief Dan George (Hirnschall)."

Noble Red Man (Arden) said: "We lived a good and happy life until White man came and made it miserable... You killed our people, you stole our land... our buffalo are gone, the country we loved is lost... Respect is our law—respect for God's creation, for all the living beings of this earth... We can't harm the earth or the water because we respect their place in the world... That is our religion... We don't need your church, we have the Black Hills for our church. We don't need your Bible, we have the wind, rain, and stars for our Bible. The world is an open Bible... we've studied it for millions of years... Everything God made is living— even the rocks are alive... we talk to them and they talk... to us."

Jehovah lives at our expense. We are his green, living things: rye (chosen), wheat (Jews), barley/corn (Christians). The gospel is symbolized by flax, woven into linen to cover needy demons. This linen is the Lord's smoking flax; it slowly consumes Christians, Jews and Muslims.

The Lord wants his smoking flax to keep smoldering until his judgment day. The gospel would then be quenched. "I will put my spirit upon him (The Holy Ghost) and he shall show judgment to the Gentiles... and smoking flax he shall not quench till he sends forth judgment (Matt 12:18, 20)."

If Christians, Jews and Muslims reject the God of Abraham, and stop feeding his dry tree, his plan for salvation will fail. Black Elk will become Chief of all the Heavens and come to earth with his Nation, to kill the demon-ghosts (Messages 13—14). The green tree will flourish and the dry tree will die; Jehovah and his hosts of heaven will be no more.

Beloved Brother, Beloved Buffalo

Moriah Morningstar

Red man and shaggy beast
Roaming the Plains in harmony
White man on the iron horse
Shooting for frivolous sport
Left where they dropped
Wounded and bleeding
Skinners making a daily living
From 300 hides and 300 tongues
Red man and shaggy beast dwindling
Starving camps and rotting carcasses
Mountains of buffalo bones

Buffalo Saved From Extinction
The Lacey Act 1900

Custer State Park

Colors of the Wind

Stephen Schwartz

You think you own whatever land you land on
The Earth is just a dead thing you can claim
But I know every rock and tree and creature
has a life, has a spirit, has a name
Have you ever heard the wolf cry to the blue corn moon
or asked the grinning bobcat why he grinned?
Can you sing with all the voices of the mountains?
Can you paint with all the colors of the wind?
Come run the hidden pine trails of the forest
Come taste the sun sweet berries of the earth
Come roll in all the riches all around you
and for once, never wonder what they're worth
The rainstorm and the river are my brothers
The heron and the otter are my friends
and we are all connected to each other
in a circle, in a hoop that never ends
For whether we are white or copper skinned
we need to paint with all the colors of the wind

Moriah's Message 10

My Promise

King Nebuchadnezzar dreamed of a Great Image. Its form was terrible, but its brightness was excellent. The head was gold, the chest and arms were silver, the belly and thighs were brass, the legs were iron, and the feet were iron and clay. A stone cut out without hands hit the feet, they broke in pieces and the Great Image fell down— the iron, clay, brass, silver and gold **"broken to pieces together."** They became like chaff on threshing floors and "the wind carried them away that <u>no place was found for them</u>." The stone that smote the image became a great mountain that filled the whole earth (Dan 2:31—35).

Daniel said the King's Kingdom is the head; it is replaced by a silver kingdom, then a brass kingdom, etc. The head did not collapse first, then the chest, belly, thighs, etc. The feet broke apart first and the image fell down all at once.

Jehovah and his demon-ghosts are the Great Image; their character is dreadful and their appearance is marvelous. Clay holds together when moist, and becomes brittle when dry. When we cast out The Holy Ghost, their base (feet) will break apart and they will collapse. The Iron in the feet symbolize firmly enduring the journey. The iron legs are power to stand. The brass belly and thighs are slaughter and conquest. Silver has good conductivity; it is the worldwide transmission of 'the plan of salvation'- Jehovah's plan to live forever. The silver arms encompassed the whole world. The silver chest is Jehovah's covenants and secret pacts. Jehovah is the gold head.

A stone hit the image's feet and it collapsed. Stone is 'eben'– construct. The stone is a construction of words that attack Lord God. This stone is <u>The Greatest Deception</u>; it breaks Lord God in pieces with words. Jehovah is rejected and his demon-ghosts are cast out. No place is found for them and they die their second death. The stone is made without hands; hands is 'yad'- ministry. The Greatest Deception does not come from a church. It becomes a great mountain and fills the earth. Mountain is 'tuwr'- rock, foundation; fill is mala- replenish, have wholly. The earth is restored- made whole.

Daniel had a vision of four beasts rising from the sea. The sea is humanity- all four beasts were/are human (Dan 7). One beast was like a lion with eagle wings; his wings were plucked (uprooted). Wings is 'gaph'— authority over others. He loses his power and influence. The lion is made to stand on its own feet like a man, and given a man's heart; he is cut off from his support and sustenance (our life-force). He knows his time is up. The lion is Lord God.

A beast like a bear raised itself up on one side. It had three ribs between its teeth; it was told: "Arise, **devour much flesh**." One side of the bear was raised up to resemble God, but his lower side revealed his true nature. He had 3 ribs between his teeth. Ribs is 'tsela'— side of a person. The bear had 3 sides: Heavenly Father, Jesus Christ, The Holy Ghost. Bear means bear sins, bear a resemblance, bear authority, bear down (strive hard). These are different aspects of Lord God.

The third beast was like a leopard with four heads and four fowl wings. Dominion was given to it. Leopards are nocturnal and the best of the big cats at stalking prey, remaining concealed until their instant attack. A leopard cannot change his spots, and neither can Lord God. The leopard had four wings and heads. Four is 'raba'- sprawling at all fours. Sprawl means to spread out in an awkward position. Jehovah is pretending to be the Creator, Jesus, and The Holy Ghost. This is an awkward position but Jehovah must maintain it to complete his plan of salvation. This is the Lord's burden.

The Lord said in the end days there would be prophets that say, 'I have dreamed' and they will reveal the burden of the Lord. 'As for the prophet, priests and people that shall say 'the burden of the Lord' I will punish that man and his house… And the burden of the Lord shall you mention no more (Jer 23:20—40)." Revealing this burden threatens the Lord's existence.

The Lord said "I will be unto them as a lion; as a leopard by the way I will observe them. I will meet them as a bear that is bereaved of her whelps and will rend the caul of their heart, and there I will **devour them like a lion**; the wild beast will tear them… an East Wind shall come… and spoil the treasure of all pleasant vessels [believers] (Hos 13:7-8, 15)."

If the demon-ghosts came to the forefront, Christians, Jews and Muslims would be eaten like a **lion devouring flesh**. This will not happen if they reject their god and cast out the demon-ghosts. Cut off from life-force, demons will wither away.

The 4th beast was different from the others. It had 10 horns and great iron teeth. It was dreadful, terrible, and strong. He devoured, broke in pieces and stomped the residue with its feet. A little horn with eyes and a mouth speaking great things came up among the horns. Because of the little horn, three of the horns are removed by the roots.

This 4th beast is Christians, Jews and Muslims. 10 horns: Catholic, Anglican, Baptist, Mormon, Lutheran, Pentecostal, Methodist, Jehovah's Witnesses, Seventh Day Adventist, Presbyterian. Iron teeth: Christians, Jews and Muslims reject Jehovah. Iron teeth on a threshing sledge separates grain from chaff. Jehovah and his demons are cast out- separated from their hosts (grain) and annihilated (chaff). The little horn with eyes and a mouth speaking great things is The Greatest Deception. Because of this book, three churches disband. When it is well known, all Christian churches will dissolve and the 4th beast will be no more. His body is given to the burning flame- the flame of eternity that is truth. When this happens, the other beasts (lion bear leopard) lose their dominion.

In Revelation, a great red dragon with 7 heads and 10 horns is carrying Babylon- Jehovah's plan for his salvation (Rev 12, 13, 17). The dragon is everyone enslaved to Jehovah, whether they are deceived or know who he is: the Global Elite, Satanists, Skull and Bones, Bilderberg, Masons, Jews, Christians, Muslims, etc. Blasphemy is written on its heads. The heads on the dragon are covertly controlled by Jehovah's most powerful demons: governments, religions, military, economies, media, education, medical.

John saw a beast like a leopard with feet like a bear and the mouth of a lion. This is the 3 beats that Daniel saw: Jehovah and his demons. They get their power and seat of authority from the red dragon with seven heads (Rev 13: 2). The dragon had 'a mouth speaking great things... he opened his mouth in blasphemy against God... and those who dwell in heaven (Rev 13: 3—7).' The mouth makes war with the Lord God and has influence over all kindred, tongues, and nations. The little horn in Daniel's vision and the dragon in Revelation both have 'a mouth speaking great things.' This mouth that speaks against the Lord is The Greatest Deception. It makes war against the Lord, his worshippers reject him and cast him out, stopping the Lord's judgment, about to go forth.

'There is none among them that calls to me... The pride of Israel... they do not return to the Lord their God... they have fled from me... they rebel against me... Israel... brings forth fruit unto himself... (Hos 7:7—16, 10:1)' The great red dragon will turn against Lord God; everyone who worships the Lord will reject him and bring forth the fruit of their own soul.

One of the heads on the dragon that Babylon is riding (Religions) has 10 horns (Christian churches); it receives a deadly wound. Christians will 'hate the whore and make her desolate and naked' (Rev 17:16). Christians will hate the Lord's salvation, reject it and cast out The Holy Ghost. Naked and hungry, the demon-ghosts are made desolate and the flame of eternity 'eats them'- burns them up with her fire.

In Revelation 12 John sees a woman in heaven (Jehovah's Kingdom of God) travailing in birth. She is clothed with the sun, wears a crown of 12 stars, and the moon is at her feet. The crown is royalty (bloodline), the 12 stars are 12 tribes of Israel (Global Elite), the moon is Jehovah's deception- he has no light of his own. Travail is work that is difficult. The great red dragon stands against the woman trying to give birth, to annihilate her 'newborn' son that would rule earth with an iron rod. Babylon is the woman trying to birth New Jerusalem.

The great red dragon declares war on the woman trying to give birth. When Jehovah's X-worshippers cast out their demon-ghosts, the demons flee to Satan's bottomless pit. The Lord calls the great red dragon a serpent and the devil. Devil is diabo- accuser; serpent is ophis- sharp vision. The dragon-serpent sees clearly; it knows the truth. The dragon sends a flood out of his mouth to destroy the woman giving birth. Jehovah flies to the wasteland, to escape the dragon's mouth. The dragon's mouth is The Greatest Deception; it flies over the face of the whole earth and cannot be stopped.

When the great red dragon takes down Jehovah, it will disband and be no more, like the 4th beast that Daniel saw in his vision. John saw a future where the head on the dragon that received a deadly wound was healed.

A beast like a lamb with two horns rose up out of a country (the USA). This is 'Jesus Christ'- the Messiah. He causes the world to worship the beast like a leopard, bear and lion, and he makes fire come down from heaven (Rev 13: 11—13). Is this fire in the atmosphere that comes down to earth caused by EISCAT-3D, creating monster tsunamis that rip the earth asunder? Is this David's doomsday dream of tsunamis and high winds around the world? The Lord said he will raise a **great whirlwind from the coasts of the earth**, and the slain on that day will be from one end of earth to the other (Jer 25: 32—33).

The Messiah causes everyone to receive his mark (666) on their right hand or forehead; only those with this mark can buy or sell (Rev 13:16-18). Those who receive the mark of its name will drink the wrath of God, which is poured unmixed into his wine cup (Rev 14: 11). The mark of the beast is his identity/names: Jehovah-Christ-Allah-Lord-Satan; his image is his demon-ghosts. Those with a mark on their forehead would be judged wicked and killed, whether they worship the image of the Beast or not. Those with a mark in their right hand would be enslaved in New Jerusalem. Anyone with the Lord's mark would be tormented.

When Christians receive The Holy Ghost, they sell their body to Christ and he receives it as a garment of salvation. "He that has no sword let him sell his garment (body) and buy one (Luke 22:36)." This is how you sell your salvation to the Lord and buy his sword- The Holy Ghost. If the deadly wound on the dragon's head is healed, Jehovah's image will be made to speak. The Lord would call The Holy Ghost to the forefront and it would command Christians to confess 'Jesus Christ' is Satan and worship him; they would then be killed. This is the Lord's 'Great and Dreadful Day. We can stop it.

In Daniel's second vision he saw a ram with two horns. No beast could stand before him; no one could deliver out of his hand. A goat came from the west on the face of the whole earth, without touching the ground. He had a notable horn between his eyes, and he ran toward the ram in the fury of his power. He was moved with choler against him, and smote the ram, breaking his two horns. The ram had no power to stand before him. The goat cast him to the ground and stomped on him. No one could deliver the ram from his hand.

The goat waxed very great and his notable horn was broken. Four notable ones come up from it toward the four winds of heaven. Out of one of them came a little horn that waxed exceedingly great. It even waxed great to the host of heaven, and cast down some of the stars to the ground, and stomped on them. He magnified himself, even to the prince of the host. Because of him the daily sacrifice was removed, and the Lord's sanctuary was cast down (Dan 8).

The ram is Lord God; the goat is The Greatest Deception. Ram is strike; goat is frustrate. The Greatest Deception interrupts the Lord's plan. The goat covers the earth without touching the ground (internet) and smites Lord God with choler. Choler is 'marar'— provoke, vex.

The goat has a notable horn; notable is 'chazuwth' - revelation, vision. When the goat becomes well known, its notable horn is broken. Broken is 'shabar' –burst, appear suddenly. Four notable ones come up from it. They are four messages that quickly become renowned. These message make known 'the four winds of heaven' -they reveal the Lord's kingdom 'from one end of heaven to the other.'

One of the four messages becomes exceedingly great. Because of this 'little horn' the demon-ghosts are cast down, stomped on, and the daily sacrifice is removed. The daily sacrifice is our life-force. We feed demons at our detriment, so they can live. The Lord calls the end of the daily sacrifice 'transgression of desolation' and 'abomination of desolation'. The demon-ghosts are made desolate, they have no host.

Daniel was told a King with fierce countenance who under-stands dark sentences will stand with power in the end time. He will destroy the holy ones and through his policy, craft will prosper. He will 'magnify himself in his heart, and by peace shall destroy many (Dan 8:23—25).' Sentences is 'chiydah'— a puzzle; policy is 'sekel'—knowledge; peace is 'shalvah'— safekeeping. I am this King who understands dark puzzles, stands against the Lord with power, and destroys his demons (holy ones) through my knowledge.

Withdraw your daily sacrifice to the demon-ghosts and you will be safe. Magnify your heart, follow your craft (talents) with pride and you will have real prosperity.

The Greatest Deception exposes the 'plan of salvation' to every nation, kindred and tongue. Jehovah-Allah-Christ-Satan is rejected and the world stops making a daily sacrifice to the demon-ghosts. They are cast out and my promise is fulfilled. Black Elk is transformed and becomes Chief of all the heavens. He will come to earth with his Horse Troops and Horse Nation, and trap the demon-ghosts in a wall of light (Messages 1—15). Cut off from our life-force, Jehovah will consume his demons, and then consume himself until he vanishes: 'You lifted me up to the wind, you caused me to ride upon it and dissolved my substance Job 30:22).'

Jehovah said he will end the transgression of desolation (removal of our daily sacrifice to demons) seal up my vision and establish New Jerusalem with 77s (Dan 9:24). 77s are connected to 9-11 (Chapter 12). Jehovah's satanic spells will fail, he will die his second death and vanish away.

As the demons die
We ring in a transformation
A Day of Dancing fills the earth
Embracing all of creation

iStock

On A Clear Day

Allen J Lerner

Who would ever guess what powers you possess? And who would have the sense to change his views?... And who would not be stunned to see you prove, there's more to us than surgeons can remove? So much more than we ever knew, so much more were we born to do! Should you draw back the curtain, this I am certain, you'll be impressed with you.

On a clear day rise and look around you

And you'll see who you are

On a clear day how it will astound you,

That the glow of your being outshines every star

You feel part of every mountain, sea, and shore

You can hear from far and near

A world you've never heard before

And on that clear day, on that clear day

You can see forever and ever more

Moriah's Message 11

A Flying Scroll

Jehovah's angel (demon) showed Zechariah a vision of a gold candlestick with a bowl filled with oil and seven lamps. Each lamp had a pipe connected to the bowl and drew oil out of it, to light its lamp. The oil came from two olive trees on each side of the candlestick with a branch emptying oil into the bowl. The Olive trees are the word of the Lord (Old, New Testament) unto Zerubbabel. His hands laid the foundation of this house and he will finish it. The lamps are 'the eyes of the Lord that go to and fro over the earth (Zec 4).'

The two olive branches are two anointed ones that stand by the Lord- Jews and Christians. They fill the bowl with golden oil (their life-force) to feed Jehovah and his demons. The lamps are seven demons that control earth (message 7). Zerubbabel was governor of Judah. Judah was to end Israel through the Bible. The Lord will use Jews to destroy Israel.

Jehovah's demon-angel showed Zechariah another vision. He saw a flying scroll, 30 feet long, 15 feet wide, with writing on both sides. He was told: 'This is the curse flying out across the whole earth.' One side of the scroll says everyone that steals will be purged; the other side of the scroll says everyone that swears will be purged (Zec 5:1-3).

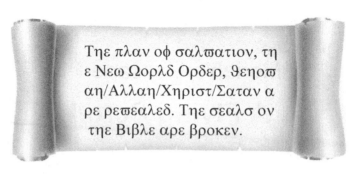

Τηε πλαν οφ σαλπατιον, τη
ε Νεω Ωορλδ Ορδερ, θεηοπ
αη/Αλλαη/Χηριστ/Σαταν α
ρε ρεπεαλεδ. Τηε σεαλσ ον
τηε Βιβλε αρε βροκεν.

The flying scroll says those who steal and swear will be destroyed. Christians are deceived; their deception convicts them to die. Jews swore an oath to their Lord. Their covenant will destroy them. The scroll is <u>The Greatest Deception</u>: the Lord's Curse. It flies across the earth exposing Jehovah.

Zechariah was shown a grain basket with a lid. The angel lifted the lid; a woman was in the basket. The angel said this is wickedness- deceived, wrong, condemned (Zec 5:7, 8). We were to be judged by a grain measure; wheat, rye, or barley. The wicked are: Jews (wheat) Christians (barley) and Muslims (rye). Jews and Christians were to be killed. Some Muslims would be killed, others chosen, and some used for the remnant (DNA) to make bioengineered beasts.

The house of Israel has become dross. 'As they gather silver, brass, iron, lead and tin into the furnace to melt it, I will gather you in my anger and fury and I will leave you there and melt you (Ez 22: 18—20).' At the end of the world, angels (demons) were to 'come forth,' sever the wicked from among the just, and cast them in the furnace of fire (Matt 13:49, 50). The Lord prepares his furnace for Judgment Day. "The bellows are burned, the lead is consumed of the fire; the founder melts in vain, for the wicked are not plucked away (Jer 6:29)." The Lord's judgment cannot go forth.

Zechariah saw two women come out with wings like a stork 'and the wind was in their wings... And they lifted up the grain basket between the earth and the heaven. Then said I to the angel that talked with me, where do these bear the basket that measures grain? And he said, to build a shrine for it in the land of Shinar. When it is ready, it will be established and set there upon her own base (Zec 5:9—11).'

The two women are White Buffalo Woman and myself. We have wings like a stork because we are giving birth to the flying scroll (Jehovah's curse). Our book exposes the Lord's judgment- his plan of salvation. We lift it up where all can see it- even those trapped in heaven, and set it in Babylon (Shinar) where it becomes well-known (established), sitting on our own foundation. The mystery of Babylon is revealed.

The Greatest Deception flies over the earth sending printed words on the heels of the Lord- he cannot escape them. "You wrote bitter things against me… you set print on the heels of my feet... (Job 13:26, 27)." The words break Jehovah in pieces, and no place is found for him. "How long will the words of your mouth be like a strong wind (Job 8:2)? "How long will you vex my soul and break me in pieces with words (Job 19:2)?" The shadow of death (demon-ghosts) vanishes with the light, as the poor, needy demons are stripped of their clothing (our bodies) and die their second death (Job 24:14).

In the book of Job, Jehovah sees his end of days when my words expose him and he is withering away. He reminisces on his Glory days when he was worshipped as God, and laments his demise, crying 'I am moved against myself, to destroy myself without cause.' Satan, the Lord, and Job are the same person. Job is a task done for an agreed price. The task is redeeming our sins; the price we pay is our soul. His task has come to an end. Jehovah is rejected and cast out.

There was a man named Job who lived in the land of Uz. One day the Lord asked Satan, "Have you considered my servant Job? There is none like him in all the earth; he is a perfect and an upright man." Satan answered, "You blessed his work and his substance is increased. If you destroy all that he has, he will curse you to your face." The Lord told Satan, "all he has is in your power, do with it as you wish."

A messenger told Job his oxen were plowing and donkeys were feeding beside them when the Sabeans attacked and took them away. They killed the servants with the sword and only he escaped. Another messenger came and said the fire of God fell from heaven and burned up all the sheep and servants, and consumed them. Only he escaped.

A third messenger came and said the Chaldeans fell upon the camels, carried them away, and slaughtered the servants with the sword. Only he escaped. A fourth messenger came and said his sons and daughters were eating and drinking wine in their elder brother's house when a great wind came from the wilderness and hit the corners of the house. It fell on the young men and they were killed. Only he escaped.

The Lord told Satan: Job held to his integrity, even though you moved me to destroy him without cause. Satan said: touch his bone and flesh; he will curse you. The Lord told Satan: do as you wish, but do not kill him. Satan smote Job with boils, from his foot to his head (Job 1—2).

Jehovah will consume himself when he has no more oxen and donkeys (chosen), sheep (Christians), servants (Jews), and sons and daughters (demons). He will then be smote with boils (grievous sores) from his feet to his head as he eats his body. The thing he most feared has come upon him (Job 2:7)- the old lion perishes for lack of prey (Job 4:11)." Jehovah is no longer Anointed; he has no oil (life-force).

Job said "Why is light given to a man whose way is hid, and whom God has hedged in (Job 3:23)? Do not despise the chastening of the Almighty... neither will you be afraid of destruction when it comes... You will come to your grave in a full age, like a shock of corn that grows until harvest time, and ends in his season (Job 5:17, 21, 26). He forsaketh the fear of the Almighty (Job 6:14).

How forcible are right words (Job 6:25)..."You hunt me as a fierce lion; and again, you show yourself marvelous upon me. You renew your witnesses against me, and increase your indignation upon me; changes and war are against me... I go whence I shall not return, even to the land of darkness and the shadow of death (Job 10:16—17; 21)."

"They that provoke God are secure... He breaks down and it cannot be built again. He shuts up a man and there can be no opening. He withholds the waters... Strength and wisdom are with him... he weakens the strength of the mighty. He discovers deep things out of darkness, and brings out to light, the shadow of death... (Job 12:6, 14—16, 21, 22)."

"He Stretches out his Hand against God, and strengthens himself against the Almighty..." "he dwells... in houses which no man inhabits (Job 15:25, 28)." "You have made desolate all my company... I was at ease but he has broken me asunder. He has also taken me by my neck and shaken me to pieces and set me up for his mark... My face is foul with weeping, and on my eyelids is the shadow of death (Job 16:7, 12, 16)."

"How long will it be till you make an end of words "How long will you vex my soul and break me in pieces with words?... He has fenced up my way that I cannot pass... He has stripped me of my glory and taken the crown from my head. He has destroyed me on every side and I am gone... He has put my brethren far from me (Job 18:2, Job19:2, 8—10, 13)."

"You... stripped the naked of their clothing... and withheld bread from the hungry... You sent widows away empty, and the arms of the fatherless have been broken (Job 22:6, 7, 9)." "The murderer, rising with the light, kills the poor and needy (Job 24:14)."

"Oh that I were... in the days when God preserved me. When his candle shined on my head, and when by his light, I walked through darkness... when the secret of God was upon my tabernacle; when the Almighty was yet with me; when my children were about me; when I washed my steps with butter and the rock poured me out rivers of oil... The nobles held their peace, and their tongue cleaved to the roof of their mouth... I put on righteousness and it clothed me. My judgment was as a robe and a diadem... My root was spread out... My glory was fresh in me, and my bow was renewed in my hand. Unto me men gave ear, and waited, and kept silence at my counsel... If I laughed on them, they did not believe it, and the light of my countenance, they did not cast down. I chose out their way... and dwelt as a King in the army, as one that comforted the mourners (Job 29)."

"They have let lose the bridle before me... the youth, they push away my feet... they mar my path... they came upon me as wide breaking in of waters... terrors are turned upon me. They pursue my soul as the wind, and my welfare passes away as a cloud... By the great force of my disease is my garment changed. It binds me about as the collar of my coat. He has cast me into the mire and I am as dust and ashes... with your strong hand you oppose yourself against me. You lifted me up to the wind; you caused me to ride on it and dissolved my substance (Job 30:11—22))."

"He keeps back his soul from the pit, and his life from perishing by the sword... He will deliver his soul from going into the pit and his life shall see the light (Job 33:18, 28)." "There is no darkness, nor shadow of death where the workers of iniquity may hide... He shall break in pieces, mighty men without number... He knows their works and he over turns them in the night so that they are destroyed (Job 34:22, 24, 25)." "Who has given understanding to the heart (Job 38:36)?" "Who can discover the face of his garment? ...When he raises up himself the mighty are afraid... He makes the deep to boil... He beholds all high things. He is a King over all the Children of Pride (Job 41:13, 25, 31, 34)."

Satan longs for the days when he walked through darkness as God, and this secret preserved him; when the rock poured out rivers of oil. Rock is 'tsur'— strength and refuge. The rock is the house of Israel (Jews, Christians and Muslims). He made the nobles tongue cleave to the roof of their mouth when he wanted to speak through them. Nobles is 'nagid'— a leader in military, civil, or religious matters. Jehovah was gaining control of the earth when his garment of salvation began to tighten around his own neck.

"Awake you drunkards, weep and howl all you drinkers of wine because of the new wine, for it is cut off from your mouth. For a nation has come upon my land, strong and without number (Black Elk's Nation)... the drink offering is cut off from the house of the Lord... The field is wasted... The corn is wasted... the oil languishes... Howl O you vine dressers, for the wheat and barley; the harvest of the field is perished. The vine is dried up and the fig tree languishes. The pomegranate tree, the palm tree... the apple tree, even all the trees of the field are withered... (Joel 1:5, 6, 9—12)."

Wine: demon-ghosts drunk on life-force. Corn: Christians. Oil: life-force. Fig tree: the Lord. Trees of the field: demon-ghosts. When we cast them out, their harvest will perish. Black Elk's Nation will cut them off. The mighty demons will be terrified, wailing and howling as they wither away. We kept our soul from the Lord's pit and our life from his sword.

Four men of renown rose up against Moses. He told them to gather their tents, wives, sons and little children. He said if his works were of the Lord, the earth would swallow them. The ground split open, they went down alive into the pit, the earth closed upon them and they perished' (all their families and possessions) [Num 16]. The 250 men who stood with them were consumed by fire. The Israelites were terrified, lest the earth swallow them up also. They murmured against Moses saying 'you have killed the people of the Lord.' The

Lord sent a plague to punish them and 14,700 died.

Jehovah buried the men of renown who spoke against him to cast a spell. Pit is 'showl'- the world of the dead (demon-ghosts). Jehovah wants his followers to return to the ground- lose their Spirit when they perish and become demon-ghosts, trapped in the world of the dead. Only demons are dead.

The Lord said he would set Israel in their own land, strangers will be joined with them, and they will stick to the house of Jacob. Strangers is 'geyr'— guest. These guests are demon-ghosts. 'And the house of Israel (Lord's hosts) will possess them for servants (Jews) and handmaids (Christians)' The demons take them captive, rule over their oppressors, and cause them sorrow, fear and hard bondage. If the Day of the Lord came Israel would rest from her bondage. Rest is 'nuwach'— cease; Israel would be terminated (Isaiah 14: 1—3).

Lucifer saw heaven and discovered we are more exalted than Jehovah. This knowledge makes the world tremble and shakes the nations. The world becomes like a wilderness, restored to a natural state. The cities do not open their houses (their bodies) to those who would hold them captive. The kings of the nations (Jehovah's worshippers) stand in their own glory and possess their own house (body). They are not joined with Lord God in burial, for they cast out his gods. They disannul ('parar'— cause to cease) his plan for earth, turning back his hand (Isaiah 14:12—20, 27).

Because Lucifer exposed Jehovah, he put a curse on him. He said Lucifer would become like a carcase: 'peger' - idolatrous image. Lucifer the Light Bearer, Morning Star and the Son of Dawn is not known by his true identity. A demon named Lucifer supplanted him. The world believes the real Lucifer is Satan, the devil, and a false, evil god. Lucifer is the bringer of truth. In Hebrew, Lucifer is Heyle- brightness, brilliance. Anyone who brings truth to the world is accessing Lucifer. Will Lucifer, the angel of light and the bringer of the dawn, break the seals on the Bible? Or will Christ, demon-god of darkness, break them? Christ will take us to his promised land (land of the dead). Lucifer will take us to the land of the morning star (dawn, enlightenment).

"The curse (The Greatest Deception) has devoured the earth... few men (demons) are left... Every house (body) is shut up that no man (demon) may come in. There is a crying for wine in the streets... the gate is smitten with destruction... my leanness, my leanness, woe unto me! ...windows from on high are open (heavenly things are revealed) and the foundations of the earth do shake (Is 24:6, 10-12, 16, 18)."

Jehovah said the earth will move exceedingly and be no more (Is 24: 19, 20). When earth ascends it will enter another dimension, disappearing from Jehovah's realm. There will be no New Jerusalem and no earth for the Lord to reign on. Jehovah will break down, dissolve, vanish and be no more.

The world reached out for the answer to the god spell. We found the door to the Promised Land; it was the Land of the Dead. We heard the call of our heart and found our way out of the dark. Here we are in the Land of the Morning Star.

Send Me
An angel
Scorpions

The wise man said just walk this way to the dawn of the light. The wind will blow into your face as the years pass you by. Hear this voice from deep inside, it's the call of your heart. Close your eyes and you will find the passage out of the dark. Here I am, will you send me an angel? Here I am in the land of the Morning Star. The wise man said just find your place in the eye of the storm. Seek the roses along the way just beware of the thorns. Here I am, will you send me an angel? Here I am, in the land of the Morning Star. The wise man said just raise your hand and reach out for the spell. Find the door to the Promised Land just believe in yourself. Here this voice from deep inside it's the call of your heart. Close your eyes and you will find the passage out of the dark. Here I am. Will you send me an Angel? Here I am in the Land of the Morning Star!

Moriah's Message 12
The Seven Seals

John the Revelator was taken in the spirit (astral travel) to the Lord's throne. Jehovah was sitting on his throne, thunder and lightning came out of it, and seven lamps burned before it. Twenty-four elders were seated around him. Before the throne was a sea of crystal or mineral water: the life-force that demon-ghosts live on. Four demonic beasts with many eyes (both front and back) and six wings were praising the Lord. The elders fell down, cast their crowns before the throne, and praised him that lives for 'ever and ever' (eons upon eons) and 'receives' glory and power.

The Lord was holding the Bible; it had seven seals on the backside and no one could loosen them. A lamb with seven horns and seven eyes took the book to open the seals. Demons without number say "Worthy is the Lamb that was slain to receive power, riches, wisdom, strength, honor, glory and blessing (Rev 4—5)."

This hideous Lamb-Beast with multiple eyes and horns, who was slain for power, wealth and glory, is the Lord posing as Jesus. His seven horns and eyes are seven demon-ghosts sent forth to control earth. Each demon commands one of seven major groups through secret organizations. They are the religions, governments, economies, education, media, military and medical organizations of the world. This gives them a voice (horns) and power over that which will come to be (eyes). They orchestrate and manipulate all major wars and world events. Their structure is a pyramid; those at the top have the most knowledge, but even they do not know the whole mystery— no man can open the seals.

Seals **1—4,** the white, red, black and pale horses are The Holy Ghost (Rev 6). The rider on the white horse had a bow; a crown was given to him and he went forth conquering. His white horse represents The Holy Ghost posing as God's Spirit. The red horse is given a great sword. Christians gave The Holy Ghost this sword ('machaira'- power to punish them) and he uses it "that they should kill one another (Rev 6:4)." The Holy Ghost is now the black horse (their true color); the Lord's burden is gone.

Christians (the barley) are weighed on the Lord's scale and given their due, and Jews (the wheat) are given their measure. The demon-ghosts are now pale from lack of oil (pale horse). They are told not to hurt the oil (chosen) and wine (each other) until their judgment begins. The strongest demon-ghosts would then consume the weaker ghosts. The demons that survived the Lord's judgment would then possess the chosen and receive everlasting habitations (Luke 16:9 and Rev 6:5—8).

In the **5th** seal the saints (demon-ghosts) receive a robe— the chosen. They rest for a "little season" while the earth is destroyed. In the **6th** seal the sky looks like a scroll being rolled together, the sun is black, the moon is red, a shower of stars fall to earth and every mountain and island is moved from their place (Rev 6:9—14). This is a nuclear holocaust.

After the vision of the six seals, John is shown another vision; he sees four angels holding the four winds of the earth. The angels are told not to hurt the earth until 144,000 (12,000 from each tribe of Israel) are marked to govern New Jerusalem. This vision takes place before the sixth seal occurs (the earth has not been destroyed).

When the **7th** seal is opened there is silence in heaven. Seven angels with trumpets stand before Lord God. This is a stand against him. Angels is 'aggello'— news, broadcast; trumpets is 'salpigx'— reverberate, reflection, repercussion. The angels with trumpets are Moriah's Messages 1—14

Another angel burns incense at the Lord's altar with the prayers of the saints. Another is 'allos'— different; this angel is a demon. He casts fire from the altar to the earth to stop the trumpets. His spell does not stop them. The trumpets sound- echo, thunder, boom and roar, as they fly over the face of the whole earth' (Revelation 8—10).

The 7th Seal

Seven Trumpets Heard Around the World

1st Dawn—Adam: Hail, fire and blood rain down on earth and kill a third of the trees and green grass. Hail is hurl forcefully; fire is lightning. These messages hit the world hard and spread quickly. Blood is the vital principle of life, new blood, fresh or new ideas. The trees and grass are The Holy Ghost. "As for man (Son of man) his days are as grass... He flourishes, the wind passes over and it is gone (Ps 103:15)." The wind is The Greatest Deception.

2nd The Hebrew—Woe unto You: A burning mountain is cast in the sea, turning a third of the sea into blood; a third of the sea creatures with life die and a third of the ships are destroyed. Mountain is 'oros'- rise up; burning is 'kaio'- kindle, inflame. The burning mountain in the sea of humanity is Jews, Christians and Muslims, who rise against the demon-ghosts with fury. The ships and sea creatures are the elect and the demons that possess them. They do business in great waters and they understand the works of the Lord and his wonders (Ps 107:23). They know the Lord is Satan. One third are killed by Satan to strengthen his power; he consumes their demons.

3rd Satanic Spells—John Jesus Paul: A star called wormwood (bitter calamity) falls like a burning lamp on a third of the waters. Many men (demons) die. These messages are seen around the world like a falling star. They are a light that burns up demon-ghosts. Many are cut off from the life-giving waters (life-force) and wither away, dying their second death.

4th The Great God—The Delivery: A third of the sun, moon, and stars are smitten. The sun, moon and stars are Lord God (Jehovah and his demon-ghosts). "There is one glory of the sun, and another glory of the moon, and another glory of the stars (I Cor 15:41)." Smitten is 'plesso'— smite, defeat, crush. The demon-ghosts (weak and strong) are cast out; their day of trouble has arrived.

5th A Dry Tree—My Promise: An angel comes to earth with a key to Satan's bottomless pit, located under the ocean (on the astral plane). The demon-ghosts will gather here when Christians cast out The Holy Ghost. Black Elk is the angel that can open this pit. His name is Abaddon in Hebrew meaning green herb (Herb of Power in his vision) and Apollo-Apollyon in Greek, destroyer of evil (Black Elk is given this power in his vision).

Black Elk is in the Catholic heaven. When Christians cast out The Holy Ghost, he will be transformed, becoming a magnificent, luminous being- Chief of all the Heavens. Black Elk will call to the souls in all of the heavens (symbolized by horses) and they will come running without number. Like Apollo driving his horse-drawn chariot across the sky; Black Elk will take the horses to earth, to kill Lord God. The sky will be filled with running horses as they descend. John calls them locusts because of their rapid, continuous descent.

6th A Flying Roll—The Seven Seals: John hears a voice coming from four horns on the Lord's alter. Addressing the demon that burned incense at the altar (not the 6th angel) the voice says "loosen the four angels… to slay a third part of men (Rev 9:14)." The Lord's top four demons summon a third of the demon-ghosts that are left and consume them.

With this increased power they hold back Black Elk's horses (200-million strong) from entering the pit, with a wall of water. When the horse troops charge, they are stopped by the water-wall. Black Elk collapses it with his lightning spearhead, a passage opens and the horseman plunge in. "He has come up as clouds; his chariots are as a whirlwind; his horses are swifter than eagles. Woe unto us (Jer 4:13)."

Black Elk will destroy the demons with fire, smoke and brimstone. Fire is 'pur'— lightning; this is Black Elk's spear of lightning. Smoke is their being smoked out (they have no refuge). Brimstone is 'theios'— godlike, divine; the horsemen destroy the demons with Spiritual light. Revelation 9:20—21 are out of order; they refer to the seven plagues and belong in Revelation 16.

Habakkuk saw horns come out of the Lord's hands: "there was the hiding of his power. Before him went pestilence, and burning coals went forth at his feet... He drove the nations asunder... marched through the land in indignation, and threshed the heathen in anger." Then 'they' came out as a whirlwind: "You walked through the sea with your horses, through the heap of great waters... my lips quivered... rottenness entered into my bones, and I trembled... that I might rest in the day of trouble. When he comes unto the people, he will invade them with his troops (Hab 3:4—6, 12, 14—16)." The demon-ghosts are cut off.

Isaiah saw this day: "All thy rulers are fled together, they are bound by the archers... it is a day of trouble and of treading down... Thy choicest valleys will be full of chariots and the horsemen will set themselves in array at the gate (Isaiah 22:3, 5, 7)."

Chariots is 'rakeb'– dispatch on horseback; gate is 'shaar'– opening. Black Elk is standing in the gap, the horsemen enter the waters and the demons are bound. "In that day, the Lord God of hosts called to weeping and mourning... let us eat and drink for tomorrow we shall die (Isaiah 22:12, 13)." For a nation is come up upon my land, strong and without number... (Joel 1:6)." This nation without number is Black Elk's Horse Nation.

7ᵗʰ The Great Vision I—the Great Vision II: And I saw another mighty angel come down from heaven clothed with a cloud (Rev 10). The angel held a little open book. He had a rainbow on his head, his face was like the sun and his feet were pillars of fire. He set his right foot on the sea, his left foot on earth, and cried with a loud voice. As he cried seven thunders uttered their voices.

This brilliant angel holding a little book is Black Elk. The little book (commentary on a bigger book- the Bible) is The Greatest Deception. The cloud, rainbow and sun are from his vision. Black Elk's feet are fiery pillars; pillars is 'stulos'— support. In Black Elk's vision he receives the power of the universe. All eternity will support Black Elk when he engages Lord God in battle. His right foot on the sea represents his entering Satan's pit under the ocean; his left foot on earth symbolizes his coming to the earth, where this event occurs.

As Black Elk speaks, 7 thunders speak. The thunders are Messages 1—14. Black Elk guided my writing of these messages (he spoke, then the thunders sounded). John was about to write what the thunders said when a voice told him to seal them up until the 7ᵗʰ angel sounds. The mystery of God will then be finished. Black Elk declares by the Creator that created all things, there should be time no longer.

A voice tells John to eat the little book. It was sweet (glukus- fresh) in his mouth (stoma- language) and bitter (pikraino- to alienate) in his belly (koilia- substance). The little book is new and original in its dialect on the bigger book. Its material alienates a group of people and they reject the Bible. The little book, The Greatest Deception, will prophesy before all nations, revealing the 'mystery of God' to the entire world.

{In Revelation 11, two witnesses (Old, New Testament) have power to prophesy and smite earth with plagues (woe, curses, scourges) as often as they will for 1,260 years. At the end of their testimony the red dragon climbs out of Satan's pit (Jehovah's Kingdom of God) and kills the witnesses (Bible).

Counting back 1,260 years from 2020 takes us to 760 A.D. Islam was spreading over the Arabic Peninsula. Within a few hundred years, it spread to Spain in the west and northern India in the east. Jerusalem remained under Muslim rule until the Crusade wars (1096—1270). The Inquisition began in the 1300s, annihilating Cathars. The Spanish Inquisition began in 1478 and continued with a vengeance until 1834. During this thousand-year period, millions of people were tortured to death.

The 1st Evangelical Revival in Europe and America was in 1730-1760. The 2nd one followed with revivalists traveling across the USA and Great Britain (1790—1840). After World War II revival crusades once again swept the country. They continued around the world, under Billy Graham.

When this time period ends, the 'daily sacrifice' to demons comes to an end; they are cast out. The dragon kills the Bible. Everyone sees their dead bodies; bodies is 'ptoma'– carcass, anything from which life or power is gone. The world does not allow the Bible to be buried, forgotten, not remembered. The world will always remember how demons almost destroyed the earth, so it never happens again.

The world rejoices, celebrating their liberation by singing, dancing, and exchanging gifts. This is the 'Beautiful Day of Dancing' Black Elk sees in his vision. This day will forever affect all universes, for all of eternity, changing their course.

Revelation says the two witnesses will be revived, Jehovah will pour his vials of wrath (7 plagues) on earth, and New Jerusalem (Satan's Kingdom) will be established. This will not happen. When we cast out the demons, Black Elk will trap them in the light until the utterly wither away.}

For more information on Revelation see Chapter 1.

Jesus said everything with life contains God's law; "living things are nearer to God than the scripture, which is without life (Essene Gospel of Peace)." Spiritual laws are written in our heart, not in books.

"I am a dreamer and I'll tell you my dream. Someday red man and white man will sit down with all the races of humankind and we'll solve our problems together. We'll all follow God's law. We'll even pray together… Someday we'll have ceremonies together and the eagle will come and join us. He'll dance with us. You'll learn what it's like to dance with the eagle… That's coming close… Yes, it can happen. We'll all dance together with God (<u>Noble Red Man</u> Arden)."

Little Girl Talking

I think about the generations and they say they want to make it a better place for our children and our children's children so that they… they know it's a better world for them and I think they can make it a better place.

HEAL THE WORLD
Michael Jackson

There's A Place In Your Heart And I Know That It Is Love. And This Place Could Be Much Brighter Than Tomorrow. And If You Really Try You'll Find There's No Need To Cry. In This Place You'll Feel There's No Hurt Or Sorrow. There Are Ways To Get There If You Care Enough For The Living. Make A Little Space. Make A Better Place. Heal The World. Make It A Better Place For You And For Me And The Entire Human Race. There Are People Dying. If You Care Enough For The Living Make A Better Place For You And For Me. If You Want To Know Why There's A Love That Cannot Lie. Love Is Strong It Only Cares For Joyful Giving. If We Try We Shall See In This Bliss We Cannot Feel Fear Or Dread. We Stop Existing and Start Living. Then It Feels That Always Love's Enough For Us Growing. So Make A Better World. Make A Better World. Heal The World. Make It A Better Place For You And For Me And the Entire Human Race. There Are People Dying. If You Care Enough For The Living Make A Better Place For You And For Me. And The Dream We Were conceived In Will Reveal A Joyful Face. And The World We Once Believed In Will Shine Again In Grace. Then Why Do We Keep Strangling Life? Wound This Earth? Crucify Its Soul? Though It's Plain To See This World Is Heavenly. Be God's Glow. We Could Fly So High Let Our Spirits Never Die. In My Heart I Feel You Are All My Brothers. Create A World With No Fear. Together We'll Cry Happy Tears. See The Nations Turn Their Swords Into Plowshares. We Could Really Get There If You Cared Enough For The Living. Make A Little Space To Make A Better Place. Heal The World. Make It A Better Place For You And For Me And The Entire Human Race. There Are People Dying. If You Care Enough For The Living Make A Better Place For You And For Me... Heal the World we live in.

Save it for Our Children

Black Elk's Vision I

In August 1930, a distinguished poet went to the Sioux reservation. When Neihardt arrived at Pine Ridge Agency he asked the Field Agent if he knew a holy man he could visit. Courtright told him about Black Elk. Neihardt went to see him. "It was a dead-end road that led through the treeless, yellow hills to Black Elk's home- a one room log cabin with weeds growing out of the dirt roof (<u>Black Elk Speaks</u> Neihardt)."

Black Elk told Neihardt he came to record the vision he had in his youth, to save it. Neihardt returned in the spring to write his life-story. As I read Black Elk's great vision (chapter 3) I felt his presence helping me understand. Black Elk also communicated with me in my dreams. Some parts were recorded wrong and his vision was not in order. Displaced sequences are common in visions, but it makes it difficult to follow. With Black Elk's help, I corrected his vision and put it in chronological order. It took me 22+ years.

When Black Elk was five, his Grandfather made him a bow. He rode his horse into the woods, even though a storm was coming. He stopped at a creek to shoot a kingbird in a tree with his new bow. The bird said: 'The clouds are one-sided.' Black Elk thought the bird was telling him the clouds were watching him. It spoke again: 'Listen! A voice is calling you!'

Black Elk looked at the clouds and saw two men coming headfirst like arrows slanting down. Thunder drummed and they sang: 'Behold, a sacred voice is calling you. All over the sky a sacred voice is calling.' The two men flew toward Black Elk. When they got close, they wheeled about toward where the sun goes down. Suddenly, they were geese. They flew away and rain came with a big wind and a roaring. Black Elk did not tell his vision to anyone, but he liked to think about it.

The summer Black Elk was nine, his tribe traveled towards the Rocky Mountains. He became ill; his arms, legs and face were swollen and he couldn't walk. He had to ride in a pony drag. That night he was lying in his tepee looking out the opening when he saw two men come down from the clouds headfirst like arrows slanting down- the same men he saw when he was five. They landed, holding long spears with lightning flashing from the points. Speaking as one, they told Black Elk 'come, your Grandfathers are calling you!' They shot upward like arrows and a little cloud came down. Black Elk got on it; he felt light and was not sick. The cloud flew up where white clouds were piled high like mountains.

The two men with spears spoke together: 'Behold your bay horse. He will call your Horse Troops.' The bay faced **West** and neighed. Twelve midnight-blue horses appeared facing west. Their nostrils were thunder, manes were lightning. An angel soared above them. The bay faced **North** and neighed. Twelve white horses appeared, facing north. Their mouths roared, manes were a blizzard wind. White geese soared above them. The bay faced **East** and neighed. Twelve buckskin horses (golden-yellow, black mane and tail) appeared facing east. Their eyes were daybreak stars, manes were morning light. They had necklaces of buffalo teeth. The bay faced **South** and neighed. Twelve sorrel horses appeared facing south. Their ears were antlers, manes were grass. They had necklaces of elk's teeth. The midnight-blue, white, buckskin and sorrel horses had formed a square. They broke formation and stood behind Black Elk four abreast.

The two men with spears spoke together: 'Behold your bay horse. He will call your Horse Nation.' The bay faced **West** and neighed. The sky was a storm of plunging horses of all colors shaking the world. The bay faced **North** and neighed. The sky was a wind of running horses of all colors filling the air with a roar. The bay faced **East** and neighed. The sky was a blaze of glowing horses in rainbow colors singing songs. The bay faced **South** and neighed. The sky filled with breathy, nickering horses of all colors playing happily.

The two men with spears spoke together: 'See how your horses all come dancing!' Horses danced around Black Elk, filling the sky. The horses without number changed into

116

animals and fowls, fled to the four quarters and vanished.

Speaking as one, the two men with spears said: 'your Grandfathers are having a Great Council and they have sent for you. We will take you to them with your bay horse and your Horse Troops.' The two men walked on either side of Black Elk. The bay horse walked behind with the blacks, whites, buckskins and sorrels following four by four. They came to a tepee made of clouds with a rainbow door. The horses stood in their quarters, looking inward four by four.

{Black Elk stood at the rainbow door and saw six Grandfathers sitting in a row. The oldest Grandfather said: 'Come right in and do not fear.' Black Elk stood before them. They looked older than men can be, old as the stars. Black Elk knew they were not old men but the Powers of the Universe. The oldest Grandfather said: 'Your Grandfathers all over the universe are having a Great Council; they have called you here. Behold the Thunder Beings that brought you. They will take you to the place where the sun continually shines, the inner earth, that you may see and understand.' As he spoke of understanding the rainbow door flamed with many colors and leaped over Black Elk.

Grandfather West: 'Younger brother, this bowl of water holds the sky- power of the universe to defeat sorcery.' Black Elk saw the sky in the water, then the bowl vanished. 'This bow is power to destroy evil.' Grandfather gave Black Elk the bow. 'With these powers you will kill the blue man.' 'Younger brother, look and behold your Spirit: Eagle-That-Stretches-His-Wings.' Grandfather stood tall and flew to the West becoming Black Elk's Spirit- a magnificent angel. The great angel stood above a starving midnight-blue horse, sick and dying. Grandfather East gave Black Elk the Herb of Power and said 'hold this out to the thin horse.' Black Elk took the herb and the sick horse became a great stallion. The West horses turned into <u>stallions</u>.

Grandfather North: 'Younger brother, you will make your homeland live, for I give you the power of the White Goddess Wing, the Cleansing Wind.' Grandfather sang 'The White Goddess Homeland is appearing, may you behold!' Grandfather stood tall and ran to the North, becoming a white goose wheeling. The North horses turned into <u>geese</u>.

Grandfather East: 'Younger brother behold the Thunder Beings.' Black Elk looked; two men were flying beneath the daybreak star, headfirst like arrows. 'From them you will receive the Herb of Power to awaken everyone on earth. They will take you to inner earth where the sun always shines.' He held a pipe in his hands with a golden eagle on the stem. It looked at Black Elk, fluttering its wings. 'With this pipe you will bring the power of truth, the power to make well, to your soulmate on earth.' Grandfather pointed to a red man; he lay down and rolled, changing into a buffalo. The buffalo rose up tall and galloped to the East. The East horses turned into <u>buffalo</u>.

Grandfather South: 'Younger brother, I give you the red stick. It will become a sheltering tree for the children- the living center of your homeland. You will make it blossom. As Grandfather held the red stick, it sprouted flowers, leaped in his hand and became a great tree. Birds sang in its branches, villages lived under it, all living things with roots, legs and wings were happy. Grandfather said 'Behold earth.' A Black and Red road crossed where the tree stood. 'The Black Road goes East to West, a road of destruction and death. The Red Road goes North to South, the good road of the red earth. Your nation will travel down these roads; you will destroy <u>a people's foes</u>.' Grandfather stood tall and ran to the South, becoming an elk. The South horses turned into <u>elks</u>.

Grandfather Sky, oldest of them all, said: 'My boy I have sent for you and you have come. You will travel to earth with my power- the power of the universe.' He stretched out his arms and turned into a golden eagle hovering. Grandfather said 'Behold, all the wings of the air will come to you. They, and the winds and stars will be your relatives. The golden eagle soared above Black Elk and fluttered. Suddenly the sky filled with friendly wings, all coming toward Black Elk.

Grandfather Earth was very old with long white hair. His face was in wrinkles and his eyes were deep and dim. Black Elk stared at him, for he seemed to know him. As he stared, Grandfather Earth slowly changed, growing backwards into youth. When he became a boy, Black Elk knew it was himself, with all the years that would be his. He then became old again and said 'My boy have courage, for my power will be yours. With it you will save earth. Come; we will review our gifts that you may understand.' The Grandfathers stood tall and walked out the rainbow door. Black Elk followed.

The bay faced West. A voice said: '**Grandfather West** gave you a bowl of water with the sky- power to defeat sorcery and the bow to kill the blue man.' The black horses stood behind Black Elk, four abreast. The bay faced North. A voice said: '**Grandfather North** gave you the White Goddess Wing– the Cleansing Wind to make your homeland live.' The white horses stood behind Black Elk, four abreast. The bay faced East. A voice said: '**Grandfather East** gave you the Herb of Power to awaken, and the pipe to bring truth and make well.' The buckskin horses stood behind Black Elk, four abreast. The bay faced South. A voice said: '**Grandfather South** gave you the red stick. It will become a sheltering tree for the children and the living center of your homeland. The sorrel horses stood behind him four abreast. A voice said '**Grandfather Sky** and **Grandfather Earth** gave your their powers.}

A Voice said 'you will travel **4 Ascents** with your nation.' **1st**: the land was green and a long line of people climbed. The old men and women raised their hands and crooned a song. The sky ahead was filled with clouds of baby faces. The people camped around the sacred tree. **2nd**: the climb was steeper. The people changed into animals and birds. Black Elk was a golden eagle soaring. The animals grew restless. They were afraid they were not what they had been and called to their chiefs with troubled voices. The people camped around the sacred tree and leaves were falling from it. A Voice said 'Behold your nation, henceforth they will walk in difficulties.' **3rd**: the animals and birds that were people, ran here and there. Everyone seemed to have their own rules. The winds were at war, like wild beasts fighting and the nation's hoop was broken. The people camped around the sacred tree at the top of the third long rise; the tree was dying. **4th**: the animals and birds turned back into people and they were starving. A storm was coming fast and black. Frightened birds without number fled before it. The people camped at the summit and secured their tepees against the wind; the sacred tree was gone. Black Elk wept.

Black Elk was on the bay horse. He was painted red with black joints and white stripes between them. His breath was thunder. The bay had lightning stirpes and his mane was a cloud. The earth was below; it was dark and terrible. The world was fighting like wild beasts, with rapid assaults and smoldering rage. Women and children were wailing, like horses screaming, all over the world. The Horse Troops from the west, north, east and south fell behind Black Elk in formation. The daybreak star rose. The Thunder Beings who flew headfirst gave the Herb of Power to Black Elk and spoke together: 'With this you will receive power to be transformed.'

The Thunder Beings told Black Elk to drop the Herb of Power on earth. Black Elk watched it falling far. It struck earth, rooted, grew and bore four blossoms on one stem— black, white, yellow, and red. Rays as bright as the sun flew out from the flowers, bathing the earth in its light. Everyone saw the light-rays and there was no place for evil to hide.

Black Elk rode into camp on the bay horse. He saw a starving man in the 4th ascent painted red, holding a spear. The red man walked to the center of the nation's hoop where the tree had been, laid down, rolled and became a buffalo. The Herb of Power sprang up where the buffalo stood. It grew four blossoms on one stem, like the one Black Elk dropped on earth: black, white, yellow, and red. The blossoms on the Herb of Power sent light-rays flashing to all the heavens. A song of power came to Black Elk; he sang in the mist of the raging storm: 'a good nation I will make live, this Nation Above [heaven] has said, for the Nation Below [earth] is giving me the power to transform.'

Black Elk was still on the bay horse. A voice said 'Behold'. Black Elk saw a starving, midnight-blue horse in the West. The voice said 'take this to make him over;' it was the Herb of Power that bloomed. Black Elk circled above the sick horse holding the Herb of Power with flashing light-rays, and heard people on earth calling for Spirit Power.

The horse rolled, becoming a tall, majestic midnight-blue stallion. His voice boomed thunder, his mane was lightning, his tail was silver, his coat sparkled with dapples like tiny silver stars. His eyes were like the daybreak star. He was Chief of all the Horses. The people on earth calling for Spirit Power give Black Elk the power to transform. He becomes a tall, magnificent being with a powerful body and long, sparkl- ing, midnight-blue hair. Black Elk is Eagle-That-Stretches-

His-Wings, Chief of all the Heavens.

Black Elk was on the great stallion; the Horse Troops fell behind him. A voice said 'To the four quarters, you will call your Horse Nation. Make haste Eagle-That-Stretches-His-Wings! Black Elk dashed west and the stallion neighed thunder; horses of all colors came plunging from the clouds. He dashed and neighed thunder to the north, east and south; the glowing clouds answered, giving forth plunging horses of all colors shinning and rejoicing in their fleetness and strength.

Black Elk looked below; the earth was silent in a sick green light. Behind him his Horse Troops had riders. The midnight-blue horses snorted thunder. The white horses roared, their manes and tails whirled a blizzard of hail. Black Elk, his Horse Troops and his Horse Nation descend to earth. Black Elk, riding his great stallion, was their leader. The daybreak star rose dim. Sharp rain was falling and the trees bowed low where they passed. The people, animals and birds were afraid and they were dying; the grasses and trees were withered. As they rode along, the earth brightened with hope.

Black Elk, his Horse Troops and his Horse Nation came to three massive streams that made a vast source of mighty waters. Flames rose from the waters and a dreadful blue man was there. Dust floated around him. The black horse riders charged the blue man but could not reach him. The white, yellow, and red troops charged, but they too were stopped. They cried 'Eagle-That-Stretches-His-Wings, help!' Voices from all over the universe cheered him on.

Black Elk charged, shooting his bow. The arrow turned into long spear; its head was lightening. The long spear stabbed the water and a passage opened. The horsemen and horses without number plunged in and struck the blue man. Black Elk pierced his heart and he turned into a harmless turtle. Thunder rolled and voices shouted 'you have killed!' The flames died and the trees and grass were no longer withered. Voices from all over the universe cheered their victory.

Black Elk's Horse Troops and his Horse Nation rode alongside a river and saw a village. A voice said 'Behold your Nation Below, make haste Eagle-That-Stretches-His-Wings!' Black Elk entered the village with his horses. The wind was blowing from the south like fever. In nearly every tepee, men, women and children lay dying. Black Elk rode around the circle of the village, looking in upon the sick and dying. Then the men, women and children got up and came forth with happy faces.

Herb of Power
Sending forth bright rays

Moriah's Message 14
Black Elk's Vision II

Black Elk and his horses rode to the village center and the people gathered around them. A voice said 'Give them the red stick that they may flourish, the sacred pipe to make well, and the Cleansing Wind to make the world live. Black Elk thrust the red stick in the ground at the village center. It blossomed and grew and into a great sheltering tree with birds singing and animals beneath it, mingling with the people like relatives.

The women raised a tremolo of joy. The men said 'behold the sheltering tree. From it we will multiply in a sacred manner and it will take care of us. We will live under it like little chickens under the mother hen's wing. We will depend on the sheltering tree so it will always be with us. From it we will raise our children, and under its branches we will live with all our relatives as one people.' The Cleansing Wind sang through the tree; the pipe flew in on eagle wings, spreading truth and wellbeing around it.

The daybreak star rose and the voice said 'it will be a relative to the people. Whoever sees it will see much more, for from it comes wisdom. Those who do not see it will be dark.' The people turned their faces eastward and light from the daybreak star fell on them. A voice said 'Behold the circle of the nation's hoop is sacred. All powers will be one power in the people without end.'

Black Elk leaves earth with his Horse Troops and Nation. They travel to a new land beyond heaven. The black, white, red and yellow horses follow behind Black Elk. Little children go next, then youths and maidens, young men and women, those neither young nor old, and old men and women with their canes. Behind them were ghosts of people like a trailing fog— grandfathers of grandfathers and grandmothers of grandmothers without number. A voice said 'Behold a good nation walking in a sacred manner toward a new land.'

{When they arrive at their new realm, Black Elk's Horse Troops form in a circle with their Chief at the center. Four Virgin goddesses dressed in red, come from the four quarters and stand before Black Elk and his stallion. One held a bowl of water, one held a white wing, one held a pipe and one held a red stick. The universe fell silent. The great stallion raised his voice and sang this song four times: 'My horses prancing. My horses dancing. All over the universe, they dance. A Day of Happiness, a Day of Dancing, all over the universe they dance. May you behold your homeland, they are dancing. May you behold your homeland- they dance.'

His voice was not loud yet it filled the universe. There was nothing that did not hear; it was more beautiful than anything can be. The stallion's song was so beautiful it made everyone dance. Nothing could keep from dancing. The virgins danced, the horses and people danced, leaves on the trees and grasses on the hills danced. Waters in creeks, rivers and lakes danced. The four-legged, two-legged, and wings of the air, danced to the music of the stallion's song.

A voice said 'All over the universe they have finished a Day of Happiness- a Day of Dancing. See this day for it is yours.' Black Elk saw his Beautiful Day. Every living thing was rejoicing in his victory. The Beautiful Day sparkled, fruits grew everywhere and everyone shared with each other. A cloud in the east with a flaming rainbow blessed everyone with friendly rain. The Horse Troops and the people of all ages went singing to their new home. All things sang with them as they walked. The voice said 'Now you will travel to the inner earth, to see and understand.'}

The Thunder Beings who flew headfirst took Black Elk to inner earth where the sun continuously shines. He saw great mountains; colored lights were flashing from the mountains to the heavens, rising upward like a flaming rainbow. Black Elk was standing on the highest mountain. Below him was the hoop of the world. He saw more than he could tell, and understood more than he saw, for he was seeing in Spirit. Everything was harmonious and everyone was living as one. The sacred hoop of his people was one among many hoops that made a circle as wide as daylight and starlight. The sheltering tree was the living center of the homeland.

The Thunder Beings who flew headfirst spoke together: 'Now you will go back to your Six Grandfathers.' They turned into four flocks of geese, flying in circles above each quarter, making a sacred sound—b-r-r-p, b-r-r-p, b-r-r-p, b-r-r-p! As the geese lead Black Elk to his Grandfathers, he became himself. The tepee was roofed with clouds and sown with lightning. A flaming rainbow was above it. Under the tepee were wings of the air and under them were animals and men. All were rejoicing and thunder was like happy laughter.

As Black Elk entered the teepee through the rainbow door, voices cheered him from all over the universe. There were faces of people yet to be in the roof made of clouds. He stood before the Grandfathers sitting in a row. With arms stretched toward him, they cried: 'He has Triumphed!'

The Grandfathers described their gifts. From the **west**: a bowl of water with the sky to defeat sorcery, and a bow to destroy evil. From the **north**: the power of the White Goddess Wing- the Cleansing Wind to make the world live. From the **east**: the Herb of Power to awaken; a pipe to bring truth and make well. From the **south**: the red stick that becomes the sheltering tree for all the children- the living center of your homeland. After each Grandfather spoke, they melted into the earth and rose again. Each time they did, Black Elk felt closer to earth.

Grandfather Sky said: 'Grandson, you have seen all over the universe. Now you will return to the place from where you came. See your people.' Black Elk looked below and saw his people; they were well except for himself, who was lying like the dead. Grandfather sang: 'There is someone on earth, he lies in a sacred manner for I have caused him to be sacred.' The tepee began to sway as in a gentle wind. Many different voices from all over the universe cheered and said: 'Behold, Eagle-That-Stretches-His-Wings is coming forth!'

Black Elk walked out of the tepee; dawn had the daybreak star on its forehead. As the sun rose it looked at Black Elk walking alone, and sang: 'With visible face I am appearing. In a sacred manner, I appear. The greening earth, I make delightful. The center of the nation's hoop, I make delightful. The four-legged and two-legged I have made walk. The wings of the air, I have made fly. My day, I have made it sacred.' The sun stopped singing and Black Elk felt lonely. A golden eagle told him to look back. The rainbow door on the tepee grew dim, then the tepee vanished. The tall rock mountain inside earth appeared where the tepee had been.

Black Elk's village was ahead. He entered his tepee and saw his mother and father bending over him. Someone said 'the boy is coming too; you had better give him some water.' No one knew Black Elk had been far away. He was told he had been lying like the dead for 12 days and Whirlwind Chaser cured him. Black Elk remembered the place he had traveled to and knew his Grandfathers had cured him. He wondered if his people would believe him, for he was only nine. That evening Whirlwind Chaser came to see Black Elk and saw 'a power, like a light all through his body.'

Black Elk kept to himself for a few days. His people were like strangers and everything seemed odd, as though the world was far away. He felt like he did not belong and he did not want to eat; he was homesick for the place he had been.

Review of Back Elk's Great Vision

Black Elk meets his Horse Troops and his Horse Nation, receives gifts from the Grandfathers and travels four ascents with his Nation Above. He drops the Herb of Power on earth. It grows four flowers on one stem, shooting light-rays that illuminate earth and expose Jehovah.

The Nation Above believed they were climbing a spiritual path. When it got steep, they changed into animals and birds. This gave them a secure footing and easy flight to the top. Black Elk was a golden eagle, with the power of Grandfather Sky. At the summit they see Jehovah's storm coming fast (the apocalypse). Bright rays from the Herb of Power blaze forth in all the heavens. The bright rays in heaven symbolize souls in heaven receiving knowledge of this book. They know who the Lord is, and they are spiritually starving.

After the bright rays from the Herb of Power light the earth, people call for Spirit power and cast out their demon-ghosts. The starving black horse receives power from people on earth and becomes a tall, majestic stallion with a midnight blue coat and sparkling, silver dapples- Chief of all the Horses. Black Elk receives power from people on earth and is transformed into a magnificent being with long, sparkling blue hair- Chief of all the Heavens. Black Elk's stallion is an extension of himself. They call to their Horse Nation and Black Elk takes them to earth.

When Black Elk, his Horse Troops and his Horse Nation (Jehovah's X-worshippers in heaven) come to earth, sharp rain is falling. This symbolizes their continuous descent. Everything is dying- people, animals, birds, grasses and trees. Three streams came together making mighty waters; flames rose from the water and a dreadful blue man lived there- Jehovah. He was posing as the Creator, Jesus, and God's Spirit- the three streams. Blue symbolized his spiritual pretense; fire on the waters- the destruction he lives on. Dust floating around the blue man symbolized demon-ghosts; they are the dead: 'to dust you shall return.'

Jehovah turned the mighty waters into a solid wall of water to stop the horsemen. Black Elk's arrow became a long spear with a lightning tip. The lightening tip held the power to defeat sorcery and it collapsed the water wall. The horses plunge in and stab the blue man. He turned into a turtle. Turn turtle means capsize. Like a turtle lying on its back, the blue man will utterly wither away. "The horsemen lifted up both the bright sword and the glittering spear; there is a multitude of slain (O.T. Nahum 3:3)." Sword is 'chereb'– sharp implement; this is the horsemen's spears. Glittering is 'baraq'- lightning; this is Black Elk's lightning spearhead. The Thunder Beings who flew headfirst also had spears with lightning tips.

Black Elk, his Troops and his Nation enter a circled village; this is Black Elk's Nation Below- Jehovah's X-worshippers on earth. They are sick and dying. Their Spirits see Black Elk and they cheer and rejoice. They know the earth and all life will recover. Back Elk gathers his Nation Below in Spirit, blessing them. He gives them the red stick to flourish; it becomes the sheltering tree. Women receive the ability to procreate through parthenogenesis. Men agree to honor women and depend on them to bring forth children. Black Elk gives his Earth Nation the power of truth- the ability to discern and know what is false so they will not be deceived, and valor- heroism and fearlessness, to be good leaders. The daybreak star rose and its light fell on them. Those who see it receive wisdom; those who do not remain in darkness.

Black Elk's Horse Nation become themselves (people); they, and his Horse Troops, travel beyond heaven. His Horse Troops form a circle around him and four Virgin Goddesses stand in the center, facing Black Elk from each quarter. Black Elk's stallion sings so beautifully all eternity dances, rejoicing in our victory. The Troops and Nation go to their new home. Black Elk is taken to inner earth, sees his Grandfathers and returns home. Black Elk was in Dreamtime for 12 days. He may have stayed in inner earth for many days. Dreamtime is different than earth time.

The four virgins are hermaphrodites. The West Virgin held a bowl of water. The North Virgin held a White Wing. The East Virgin held a pipe. The South Virgin held the red stick. Grandfather West gives Black Elk power to defeat sorcery and power to destroy evil. Grandfather North gives us the power of the Cleansing Wind to make our world live. Grandfather East gives power to expose evil and bring truth to make well. Grandfather South gives power to restore us to are original state.

The Nation Above. The people in heaven were without number and changed into animals and birds. The horses of all colors were without number and changed into animals and birds. The people climbing the ascents and the horses are called Black Elk's Nation. The people in heaven are the horses without number.

The Horse Troops. The riders on the Horse Troops are the Indian converts Black Elk made while living. Black Elk and his stallion are One Spirit; the riders on the Horse Troops have separate souls. The Horse Troops hold symbolic power in Black Elk's great vision. Midnight-blue West: nostrils are thunder, manes are lightning, symbol- **stallion**. Black Elk and his stallion become Chief of the Heavens. White North: mouths roar, manes a blizzard wind, symbol- **goose**. Goose: abruptly changing course, knowing exactly where we are going and how to get there. Buckskin East: eyes are morning suns, manes are morning light, symbol- **buffalo**. Buffalo: power of truth to awaken. Sorrel South: ears are antlers, manes are grasses, symbol- **elk**. Elk: living in groups of

200—400 under a matriarchal society; being vegetarian.

The Sheltering Tree. The red stick roots and blooms, and grows into a sheltering tree for the children. This will happen when we procreate through virgin births. Children will grow up knowing they belong; they are loved, cherished, and their innocence and imagination is protected.

The Herb of Power roots and blooms four flowers on one stem, symbolizing humanity coming from one source and united together, giving Black Elk power to transform. The light-rays are this book, known on earth and heaven. My book holds Living Light- the Cleansing Wind to make the world live. Reading this book gives you this cleansing power (see message 15).

Black Elk kills <u>a people's foes</u>. The people are Jehovah's worshippers, on earth and in heaven. The foes are Jehovah and his demon-ghosts. Black Elk is on the bay when he drops the Herb of Power. 'Bring to bay' means the enemy cannot retreat. Black Elk's Horse Troops and Horse Nation trap the demons- they cannot retreat. Black Elk is a boy in his vision and the bay fits him. After he transforms the majestic steed fits him and they are one.

Black Elk is the red man in the 4th ascent, holding a spear. He walks to the center of camp, rolls and becomes a buffalo. This symbolized Black Elk's communion with White Buffalo Woman. The herb sprang up and flowered where the buffalo stood, sending light-rays throughout all the heavens. Their contact makes the Herb of Power blossom. Their interaction is also symbolized by the golden eagle on the pipestem. The eagle is Black Elk; the pipe is White Buffalo Woman.

As a sign of White Buffalo Woman's return, Miracle was born on the Heider farm, August 20, 1994. She turned the colors of humanity as she grew. Miracle was born in Janesville (Jane's Ville) Wisconsin. Wisconsin means homeland. Someday earth will be an all-female homeland. Humanity will be hermaphrodites. Before Miracle, white buffalos were born every 100+ years. Since her birth dozens of white buffalos have been born across America, reminding us that White Buffalo Woman returned.

When humanity is restored to our original hermaphrodite state, we will be like our cousins in inner earth. We will regain our lost abilities and live hundreds of years, in harmony with each other and nature. If Black Elk is not transformed and the world is destroyed, people of inner earth will survive.

Steeds of Apollo
Lumen Winter

Note to Readers. I was editing Black Elk's vision (4-23) when I felt a presence. At first, I thought it was Black Elk; it was his vision. I've felt his Great Vision before, impressing me with something. It is alive, it has its own consciousness and it communes with me. The impression the Great Vision gave me: the Herb of Power is not the Flowering Stick. Sandra confused them many years ago; I didn't notice this error. The Herb of Power grows roots and blooms, and the red stick grows roots and blooms. But the Herb of Power does not become the sheltering tree; they are not the same thing.

Moriah's Message 15

The Cleansing Winds

Black Elk's vision made his heart sad. He had felt one with all things and knew what it was like when people lived this way. He was told he would make this day happen, but his people were forced to surrender their way of life when he was a young man. Starving and freezing, they went with the soldiers to the reservation. While traveling they camped for the night. The next morning (Dec 1890) soldiers surrounded the starving Indians with cannons, demanding their guns. Yellow Bird refused to hand his over. An officer wrestled it from him, the gun went off and the officer was killed. The soldiers began firing the cannons.

Black Elk heard cannons going off from Pine Ridge. He put on his sacred shirt with symbols from his vision- a flaming rainbow, lightning, an eagle, and daybreak star. He painted his face red, put an eagle feather in his hair and took his bow. Black Elk road to the gulch and saw cavalrymen "riding along the gulch, shooting into it, where the women and children were running... trying to hide in the gullies..." Bullets whizzed around Black Elk as wounded women, children, and babies fell while running to the gulch for protection.

"After the soldiers marched away from their dirty work, a heavy snow began to fall... There was a big blizzard, and it grew very cold. The snow drifted deep in the crooked gulch, and it was one long grave of butchered women and children, and babies, who had never done any harm, and were only trying to run away (Black Elk Speaks chapter 24)."

That year Black Elk danced his first ghost dance and had a vision. He flew headfirst with out-stretched arms toward a ridge and glided over the top. He heard deep rumbling and a flame leaped out. On the other side were six villages. The land was beautiful and sparkling in a living light. Black Elk came down by the sixth village.

Twelve men told Black Elk 'we will take you to see our Chief.' They lead him to the center of camp. The sheltering tree was there 'full of leaves and blooming.' The Chief stood in front of the sheltering tree with his arms stretched out. Black Elk could not tell what people he came from. He was not white or Indian. His hair was long and loose, his body was beautiful, strong and powerful, and painted red. He spoke like singing: 'all earthly beings and growing things belong to me.' As Black Elk stared at him, his body became swirling lights of all colors, then he vanished.

Twelve women stood before Black Elk and said, "Behold them, their way of life you will take back to earth." The sky was a brilliant blue, the sun was bright yellow shinning above a beautiful green earth. Everyone was one age, young and beautiful. Black Elk heard singing in the west. One of the twelve men took two sticks, one painted red and one painted white. He said 'you will depend on them' and thrust them in the ground (Black Elk Speaks chapter 22).

Black Elk flew headfirst, like the two men in his great vision (Black Elk before and after he was transformed). The painted red man in this vision is Black Elk. In his great vision he was painted red and became a majestic being, like the beautiful man filled with light. The village is the Golden World. Black Elk brings it to earth by killing Jehovah. The buried red and white sticks may be white men, reincarnating as red men, to learn how they harmed them and see through their eyes, and red men incarnating as white men, to help them.

Black Elk again flew with out-stretched arms. He flew over a dark river that roared with angry foam. Men and women tried to cross it, but couldn't make it. They cried to Black Elk 'help us' but he could not stop flying- a great wind was carrying him. He then fell back in his body. The dark river is the clash between red and white man. Black Elk's people wanted him to heal them with his old medicine— tobacco offerings, drumming, singing, rattling, etc. Destiny was taking him on another journey. He had to become Christian, so he would go to heaven when he died. Black Elk was destined to become Chief of the Heavens. The meaning of his vision was obscured while living so he could fulfill it.

Black Elk became a Catechist for the Catholic Church and converted hundreds of Sioux and others from surrounding tribes. His Indian converts will come to earth with Black Elk, if he becomes Chief of all the Heavens. They will help him kill the Blue Man (Jehovah). Black Elk will need their great skills.

After Black Elk finished telling Neihardt his life story, he pointed to Harney Peak and said: "There, when I was young, the spirits took me in my vision to the center of the earth, and showed me all the good things in the sacred hoop of the world. I wish I could stand up there in the flesh before I die, for there is something I want to say to the Six Grandfathers." Black Elk went to his sacred Black Hills with Neihardt and his son Ben, to talk to his Grandfathers.

Standing on Harney Peak, Black Elk cried: "Hey-a-a-hey! Hey-a-a-hey! Hey-a-a-hey!... Grandfather, Great Spirit, once more behold me on earth and lean to hear my feeble voice... I am sending a voice, Great Spirit, my Grandfather... I send a voice for a people in despair. You have given me a sacred pipe, and through this I should make my offering. You see it now... To the center of the world you have taken me and showed me the goodness, the beauty and the strangeness of the greening earth, the only mother. There, the spirit shapes of things, as they should be, you have shown to me, and I have seen. At the center of the sacred hoop, you have said that I should make the tree to bloom... "With tears running, O Great Spirit... my Grandfather, with running tears I must say now, that the tree has never bloomed. A pitiful old man, you see me here and I have fallen away and have done nothing. Here, at the center of the world, where you took me when I was young and taught me; here, old I stand and the tree is withered Grandfather, my Grandfather!"

"Again, and maybe the last time on this earth, I recall the great vision you sent me. It may be that some little root of the sacred tree still lives. Nourish it then, that it may leaf and bloom, and fill with singing birds. Hear me, not for myself, but for my people; I am old. Hear me that they may once more go back into the sacred hoop, and find the good Red Road, the sacred tree." In answer to his prayer, a light rain fell. "With tears running down his cheeks, the old man raised his voice to a thin high wail and chanted: 'In sorrow I am sending a feeble voice, O six Powers of the World. Hear me in my

sorrow, for I may never call again. O make my people live!'
For some minutes the old man stood silent with face uplifted,
weeping in the drizzling rain. In a little while the sky was clear
again (Black Elk Speaks Author's Postscript)."

Black Elk told John: "When I look back now from this high
hill of my old age, I can still see the butchered women and
children lying heaped and scattered along the crooked gulch,
as plain as when I saw them with eyes still young. And I can
see that something else died there in the bloody mud and
was buried in the blizzard. A people's dream died there. It
was a beautiful dream. And I, to whom so great a vision was
given in my youth, you see me now a pitiful old man who has
done nothing, for the nation's hoop is broken and scattered.
There is no center any longer, and the sacred tree is dead
(Black Elk Speaks chapter 25).

Black Elk's nations are Christians, Jews and Muslims, on
earth and in heaven. Nation Below gives him power to transform, Nation Above helps kill Jehovah. They enact the Nation
Below traveling the red and black roads and our victory over
Jehovah. The dying, sacred tree symbolized the sacred circle
of his Nations, not the sheltering tree. After Black Elk kills
Jehovah, he blesses his Nation Below, giving them the
sheltering tree. Women regain the ability to have virgin births.

The first time I picked up Black Elk Speaks, Black Elk came
to me before I opened it. He made my heart hurt and I cried.
I had a soul connection with Black Elk, yet I didn't remember
the vow we made to bring the Great Purification. As I read
his great vision, Black Elk helped me understand. I had a
similar experience reading the Bible. Black Elk's vision and
the Bible were connected- to each other and to me. I went on
a prayer quest for deeper understanding.

Sitting on a cliff edge, I asked if my messages were the
flying scroll Zechariah saw. A hard wind suddenly came up
and a cloud changed shape. It became a very distinct
crayfish and it was flying across the sky. A pair of ducks
appeared in front of me, flew up stream and disappeared.
The ducks symbolized communion between realms. Walking
home I saw a crayfish on the road facing east. He turned
north. The crayfish symbolized the world turning off the Black
Road (east-west) onto the Red Road (north-south). Crayfish
teach you to release what no longer serves you. The Moon

 tarot card shows a crayfish climbing out of stagnant water (belief systems) onto a moonlit path (spiritual journey). This path reveals your shadow self, so you can heal. The crayfish symbolized kundalini. There is a division between its lower and upper body, symbolizing our lower and upper chakras (123.com/clipart).

{Black Elk gave my book the power of the Cleansing Wind. I thought this power was for my readers, to help them release their false beliefs. It is this and far more. While writing this book I felt power building within the messages and chapters. As this power grew, it became a living fire. It pressed down on my shoulders and made my heart hurt. I wanted relief from this pressure. I knew the pressure would release when my book fulfilled its destiny, but what is this fiery energy? I was reading about the fiery, cleansing power of kundalini and realized my answer. The Cleansing Wind is Kundalini.

Words that reveal essential truths sparkle with Living Light. If these essential truths have been suppressed, they want to expose the deception that kept them hidden and they will not be denied. They rise with fiery, cleansing power to purge and obliterate the lies. In The Quest (Brown) Stocking Wolf says it only takes one person to alter humanity's course. It is the same force that causes a flock of birds to change course. "I suspect that it is but one bird that creates the thought that turns the flock... One person, one idea, one thought can turn the flock of society away from the destructive path." And one power- Kundalini, the Cleansing Wind.}

Brown records a future vision Stalking Wolf had in the 1920s. He saw: starvation, overpopulation, man breaking the laws of creation, disease. The disease born of monkeys, sex and drugs sweeps earth 'destroying man from the inside.' Is this genetically modified organisms (GMO)? Man toys (monkeys) with plant and animal genes, crossbreeding them (sex) inserting foreign material (drugs) in their DNA. Tomatoes crossed with flatfish lower freezing-point, brown rice crossed with human blood-protein increases blood plasma, pigs crossed with mice reduce phosphorous, cows crossed with human genes make human milk, salmon crossed with ocean pout make giant salmon.

Vast tracks of land grow sterile, poisonous, GMO crops. Will bio-farming become death-farming; blighted, diseased crops destroyed, soil with transgenic bacteria unusable and GM farms blacklisted? Soil is a living organism. If we kill the soil, we kill ourselves- we would die of starvation. The miRNA in GMO foods may alter natural organ function.

Covid vaccines destroys us from the inside. Genetic code forces cells to produce millions of virus proteins. This foreign act rewrites the body's cellular instructions. Virus proteins get in blood veins and travel through the body causing micro blood clots to form, destroying us from the inside. The Lord said he would work a strange (zuwr- profane) work and bring a strange (nokriy- foreign) act- a consumption upon earth (Is 28:21—22). A blasphemous, foreign act that consumes humanity: genetically modified people?

In Robes Kelly is shown food shortages from depleted soil, polluted water and natural disasters. Artificial food is made that makes people sick. Giant corporations crash, the US government had become a corporation; it goes bankrupt and folds. Starvation, anarchy, violence and epidemics also cause society to collapse. "…those in the middle years will have great difficulty carrying on. Stretched to the limit they will be unable to find the time and energy to work for a living because they are bravely trying to nurse the fevered children, care for and comfort the old ones, bury the dead and keep themselves well enough to keep going."

The Ascents in Black Elk's vision act out what's happening on earth. In the 3rd Ascent, people as animals and birds are running lawless and fighting like beasts. In the 4th Ascent they are starving; the apocalypse has started. Black Elk sees earth. People are raging and fighting like wild beasts. Women and children were wailing. When Black Elk comes to earth everything is dying- plants, birds, animals, people. People are starving, sick and dying.

In Stalking Wolf's vision, holes tear the sky apart with a booming noise; they ooze liquid like an infection. Garbage piles up, fish and trees die, there is mayhem and violent storms. Man is faced with a choice: stay on the destructive path or go back to nature. The destructive path contaminates the air, land, sky and water, and we die. Antenna arrays tear the sky apart and chemtrails fill the sky with poisons. We must stop focusing radio beams on the atmosphere, stop chemtrail spraying, spraying chemicals on crops, and putting excrement in water. Sewage treatment plants accelerate algae growth in the oceans, depleting oxygen for sea life. Overflow of untreated sewage is released in waterways.

Stalking Wolf said "Nature starves deer in winter when their numbers are too many for the land to bear." This keeps nature in balance so deer can survive. We must live in harmony with nature, or nature will take us out.

When you commune with nature, you discover yourself. Nature is our mother and she is within us. Raising a garden and learning plant-based healing strengthens our relationship to nature. In Human Robots & Holy Mechanics Kyle says experiencing the deep realities that coexisted in the world of our ancestors, takes us closer to nature and away from the machine world. We need to change our robotic lifestyle and mechanical existence to reconnect with nature.

Fruit trees, berries, grapes and veggies could be planted in yards, parks and other public places. Turn patios, balconies and rooftops into container gardens. Grow a vertical garden on your fence. Alleys and walkways could be filled with rows of garbage cans planted with tomatoes, peppers, chard, carrots, onion, radishes. Hang a shoe organizer on the side of your garage. Fill the pockets with soil and plant herbs. Grow mushrooms with used coffee grounds. Plant, harvest and preserve food with your family, friends and neighbors.

There may be food shortages and famine in the near future. Urban agriculture could be a main source for local food. The world's largest rooftop farm is in Chicago, growing 10-million crops yearly. Detroit agrihood feeds 2,000 households for free. Many large cities in the USA have community gardens and working farms. Start an urban farm in your city; organize neighborhood garden shares.

In The One-Straw Revolution Fukuoka describes his semi-wild way of growing vegetables. He mixes different veggie seeds and hand tosses them. When mixed with other veggies and not planted in rows they have more protection from bugs. This method gives higher yields with less effort using no machinery, ploughing, weeding, pruning or fertilizer.

Help each other cast out demons and Black Elk will be transformed. When he comes to earth with his Troops and

Nation, they will surround the demon-ghosts in a wall of light until they vanish. Jehovah will pull every demon to himself when he's trapped, to live as long as possible. With no demons to consume, he will consume himself. Universes throughout eternity will celebrate our victory over Jehovah with us. We will sing and dance with joy.

Beautiful Day
My footprints covering earth

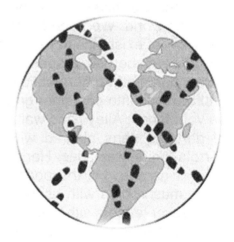

The first verse of this Mormon song describes dawning of the Beautiful Day. The daybreak star rises, the world awakens, darkness flees, the Beautiful Day brings 'peace and rest' -goodwill and contentment. Our restless mind is stilled and we see beyond the veil.

The Day Dawn Is Breaking

Townsend

Diamond Head Sunrise   Anthony Casay

The day dawn is breaking, the world is awaking,
The clouds of night's darkness are fleeing away.
The worldwide commotion from ocean to ocean
Now heralds the time of the Beautiful Day.
Beautiful Day of peace and rest.
Bright be thy dawn, from east to west.
Hail to thine earliest, welcome ray.
Beautiful, Bright, Millennial Day

Moriah's Message 16
A Great Purification

We are living in the 3rd world. The first one was destroyed by earth's rapid expansion. This caused severe earthquakes and flooding, destroying the island of Lemuria- earth's largest land mass. The 2nd world was destroyed by Atlantean's breaking creation laws with their technology. Our world is in danger of facing a similar fate. The Global Elite are breaking creation laws with bioengineering, and poisoning the atmosphere with chemicals and nanobots that should not exist. Life is at risk.

The Global Elite bioengineered creatures that should not exist using human embryos, plants, animals and insects. They made chimeras, cyborgs and other abominations. Covid-19 vaccines were designed to genetically modify us with genetic code, forcing our cells to produce virus proteins.

Hopi prophecy says "Man will build black ribbons for bugs to travel on. The bugs will start to fly. They fly around the world and a trail of dust comes out from behind them. This makes the earth's atmosphere dusty. The dust causes many diseases that get more and more complicated." Black ribbon: roads, bugs: cars, flying bugs: planes, dusty trails from planes: chemtrails. Chemtrails put poisons and nanobots in the atmosphere, causing diseases that may be part of a complex system to destroy us on the inside.

When the 4th world began, a Red brother promised a White brother, if the world became endangered he would help him save humanity. The Red elder brother may become white, but he will keep his black hair. Black Elk became Christian but kept his native heart. When the red elder Brother goes east (the light) he looks for his white brother. Black Elk died in 1950 and found me in the Spirit World. We confirmed a plan to bring the Great Purification. I was born in 1952. When the earth became endangered, Black Elk inspired me to translate the life plan he received from Grandfather Sky.

The Hopi were told to cut their hair a certain way to recognize their White Brother when he returns. I have this haircut, but it is not how Hopi will know me. This book and Black Elk's Great Vision are the Hopi matching tablets. They tell the same story. Both are needed to bring the Great Purification. One side of the Hopi tablet with a missing corner shows Black Elk's vision; the other side is  this book. Black Elk's vision is on the Hopi Prophecy Rock.

Elder Brother has two helpers: <u>Nation Above</u> and <u>Nation Below</u>. Nation Below symbol is the Celtic Cross: receiving true direction. They pray for Spirit Power and cast out their demon-ghosts, bringing Black Elk's transformation. The Nation Above symbol is the daybreak star and the swastika flower. They are souls in Jehovah's heavens, and come to earth with Black Elk to kill the demon-ghosts.

{Prophecy Rock
Black Elk's Vision

Maasaw told Hopi "A greater one than I will give you a Life Plan." This plan was given to Black Elk by Grandfather Sky in his Great Vision. He holds it high because Black Elk received it in the Spirit world. The bow and arrow in his right hand were given to Black Elk to destroy the blue man.

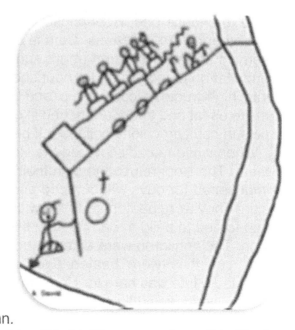

The big circle is the Golden World. The cross above it is Black Elk's <u>Horse Nation</u>. They will come to earth with Black Elk to kill demon-ghosts, if he is transformed, and the Golden World will someday return. The square is Black Elk's <u>Horse Troops</u> facing the four directions in Black Elk's vision. The upper path with figures is the Back Road. Two headed white man (far right) takes the world down a path of destruction. If we pass the vertical line (return path) we have one chance to turn back before the point of no return (jagged path). If we stay on the jagged path the world will be destroyed. The return path takes us to the Red Road.

The circles on the Red Road are Great Shakings that rock the world. The first two shakings open the way for the Great Purification. The last great shaking- Great Purification, is on the other side of the return path- it only happens if we turn off the Black Road. **1st Shaking**: <u>The Greatest Deception</u> heard by every nation. **2nd Shaking**: Christians, Muslims Jews reject their god. **3rd Shaking**: Great Purification Day.

The corn on the red road is real corn, the figure is humanity, returned to hir original state. On the red road, the world is thrown into chaos as destructive systems collapse. Within a few generations, humanity lives well, in self-sustained towns. Someday the Golden World will return.}

Maasaw showed the various clans many kinds of corn and said to choose one. Hopi chose the smallest, the real corn, the others were imitations. Corn is altered to produce bigger kernels and smaller germ (more sugar, less nutrition). Cows grow fat on it and are under nourished. Altered corn is made into high-fructose corn syrup and added to products that make us fat and under nourished like cows. Bees are fed this poison causing colony collapse. If bees die, we die.

When white man discovered the Hopi, they gave treaties to them. The Hopi refused to sign their treaties. The men were imprisoned for days without food and water. Hopi refused to sign. They were beaten, fed food with soap, chained together and forced to build a road through their land. Hopi refused to sign. Their children were taken to boarding school, their hair was cut, they were beaten and forbidden to speak their language. Life was hard for Hopi, but they still refused to sign so the world would live. Their prophecies say if Hopi fails, it will trigger the destruction of the world and all mankind.

Maasaw gave Hopi four tablets and said to reveal them when the last Hopi sign is fulfilled. One tablet had a missing corner; the white brother will interpret it at end of the 4th

world. He will have a book of truth with a record of his people. It will reveal the true Creator and expose the false god, fulfilling the last Hopi sign. Nine Hopi signs predict the ending of the 4th world; 8 are fulfilled.

1st White men take land that is not theirs, strike enemies with thunder (guns). **2nd** Spinning wheels filled with voices (covered wagons). **3rd** Beasts like buffalo with long horns overrun land (cattle). **4th** Land crossed by snakes of iron (railroad tracks). **5th** Land crisscrossed by giant spider webs (power lines). **6th** Land crisscrossed with stone rivers (roads). **7th** Sea turns black, living things die (oil spills). **8th** Youth with long hair visit tribal nations (hippies). **9th** Dwelling place in heaven appears as a blue star, falls with great crash.

9th sign. Hopi stars are gods. A blue god that dwells in heaven falls (blue man in Black Elk's vision). His mask is removed, the world sees he is a false god and he is cast out. People stop going to their place of worship. Black Elk brings the great purification, killing the blue god. The 5th world begins- a new cycle of life.

If the elder and younger brother fail, we will not survive. The point of no return is the point on the black road where the earth would die if humanity is allowed to continue. Nature (earth) would then wipe us out. Humanity (and demons) would die, earth would live and life, far into the future (new 5th world) would eventually begin. "May the Great Spirit guide you on the right path (Elder Katchongva)."

Elder brother has a swastika flower (power herb), sun (daybreak star), red symbol (red road) and two helpers that help him destroy evil (two nations). The younger brother is a writer and leaves footprints (words) that cover earth. Our matching tablets are this book and Black Elk's Great vision.

My Tablet. Goddess-Creator is replaced with Jehovah, a demon-god with no head because he's dead, and upside down because he flips everything backwards: good—evil, light—dark. The enclosed area inside the tablet is Jehovah's realm. The tideline is devastation, loss and dread. The bottom of his enclosure has two more tidelines: destruction and death. The brotherhood symbol is his demon-ghosts. The forked tongue below the missing corner is deception. The missing corner is a snake's head. Symbols outside Jehovah's domain are Black Elk's bow and lightning spearhead.

Black Elk's Tablet. The circle with little lines is the daybreak star in Black Elk's vision. The path around it is the return path. The circle with three dots is Black Elk and his helpers: Nation Above, Nation Below. The jagged line is the mirror image of the one on the prophecy rock that takes us away from earth. This line goes down inside earth where Black Elk stood. The swastika is the Herb of Power in his vision. The missing corner is Grandfather Sky and a rainbow.

Mankind travels the paths on the swastika. They journey out from the divine center and lose their way. Man becomes endangered. When we return to the divine center, the Golden World will return.

Note. Throughout antiquity Jehovah has been masquerading as various enlightened beings. Did he do this with Maasaw? He appeared to Hopi covered in blood and said 'obey me.' Some Kachina ceremonies have Jehovah's mark. Children are told they will be eaten by kachinas if they're bad and a kachina ceremony whips the kids. Hopi live in harmony with nature, in spite of Jehovah's possible corrupting influence.

Moriah's Message 17
Satan's Master Plan

I married a return missionary in the temple when I was 18, and had babies as my religion imparted. At age 25, I had 5 children. When the twins turned eight, I did not want them baptized and quit going to church. I found my own spiritual path and wanted my kids to do the same. Jane attended Calvary Chapel with a friend and went to the Mormon church with other friends. When she was 12, she asked me 'who is God?' I told her only God could answer that. Jane prayed for guidance on which church to attend; she chose Calvary Chapel.

When Jane was in High School, I read The Master Plan of Evangelism (Coleman). I wondered if this cult movement had infiltrated Jane's church. She quit going to school dances, reading novels and listening to music. 'Whatever God has planned' became her answer for everything. Jane had an outgoing personality. She became reserved and withdrawn. Jane told her brother she didn't know who she was.

Disciples of Christ move to an assigned area and attend the local church. They befriend the teenagers and ask the pastor if they can start a Youth Group. The teens are instructed to invite their friends and the new recruits are told to do the same. This is the multiplying ministry scheme.

The Youth Group is told they have an extended family composed of anyone they can associate with, and they are the only bridge God has to these people. Secular material cannot be read, and secular affairs are restricted. Quiet time must be observed daily and Bible study cannot be missed without permission. The teens are pressured to surrender their life to the Lord and be a disciple. Between Bible study, recruiting and church, they have little time for anything else.

Youth leaders persuade their groups to rely on them for guidance and reveal their personal problems. The information is used to isolate them. They're told their parents do not understand them, so God brought them into their life to be their parent. This induces them to transfer family loyalty to the cult. They are given daily instructions: confess sins, observe quiet time, read the Bible, make converts for Christ. If they don't cooperate the leaders withdraw support, which the teens have come to depend on. Sometimes they are physically isolated with camp retreats.

The group is encouraged to give themselves to Christ with excitement, tension, exhaustion, confessions, repenting, and guilt trips; these mind-control tactics lead to total surrender. Once total conversion takes place, love becomes conditional — earned through proper behavior, and demands become more stringent. Leaders control their disciple with repetition, memorization and condemning private thoughts. They cannot watch, listen to, or read secular material.

Young adults age 16—25 is the age group most youth leaders and disciples try to recruit. This group grows larger and larger every day, your children may be among them.

The multiplying ministry training program is designed to change activities, habits, thoughts, and behaviors through discipline, discipleship, repetition and supervised control. Normal thought processes are stopped using loaded language, and by controlling activities, information, time and relationships. Their personality is replaced with conditioned responses, turning them into mind-controlled, robotic slaves.

Coleman said Jesus "took advantage of those about Him, and thus His teaching seemed perfectly realistic... the disciples were absorbing it, without even knowing they were being trained to win people under like conditions for God... Our strategy, without their knowledge, will have already been infused into their practice." Jesus did not manipulate people-covertly scheme and trick them, or train them without their knowledge. Jesus did not take advantage of people. Jesus' teachings did not seem realistic, they were true.

Colman said Jesus maneuvered to achieve His objective and disclose God's strategy of world conquest. Maneuvers, strategy and conquests are used in military operations. Jehovah is the one with a war strategy of world conquest;

Jesus is not out to conquer the world. "Before withdrawing our supervision, we should explain to them explicitly what has been our plan from the beginning." This revelation is not to be made until they are well along in their training program.

Many college campuses and Christian churches are infiltrated by this cult, yet the pastors may be unaware that their youth leaders are teaching a multiplying ministry scheme. The organizations that teach it are: The Navigator Course, Campus Crusade, Boston Movement, Downline Ministries, Campus Ministry United, and The Church of Christ; there may be others. Christian movements that push discipleship are involved in the Master Plan of Evangelism.

Jane's church may have been covertly infiltrated by the multiplying ministry, and she may have been influenced by it for a while, but she was not pulled into the movement. When Jane was a mother with a family of her own, her Mormon Grandpa told her she was attending the wrong church; his church was the only one that was true. Jane informed her Grandpa that the only truth was God. If a church reflected her relationship with God, then she would attend that church, but she does not look to churches for truth, she looks to God.

While Jason was at college, he was invited to attend a Bible Study. Jane had been encouraging him to join one, so he went. One month later, he was baptized into the Church of Christ. I called one day to see how Jason was doing. He said he was falling behind in his classes. He had Bible study that evening. I asked him to stay home and catch up on his studies. He said 'I can't!' There was panic in his voice.

I asked Jason if his church was based in Boston. He said yes. I told Jason his church was a cult; members had to become a disciple, and the discipleship was designed to take over their life. I again asked him not to attend Bible study. He said 'I have to, I gave my word.' I told Jason his promise was invalid because they were not honest with him.

Jason quit attending the Church of Christ but it left him tormented with fear because he wasn't saved. This is a dangerous cult; it uses indoctrination and brainwashing techniques. When Mormon missionaries knocked on Jason's door, he began meeting with them. He called one day to say he was getting baptized in the Mormon Church on Saturday. I told Jason I had a terrifying nightmare about him last night.

I told him my dream, and he decided not to be baptized.

In my nightmare about Jason, his legs were cut off below his knees- he was walking around on his knees! I was horrified that his lower legs and feet were gone. Jason told me he was baptized in the Mormon Church and they cut off his legs. He was elated because now he was saved. The Mormon Church is also a cult, designed to take over your life.

I asked Jane's X-husband how he became Christian. He said someone gave him a Bible and he stayed up all night reading it with them. This is a multiplying ministry strategy; excitement with severe exhaustion creates an altered state where programming can take hold. In Holy Terror Conway and Siegelman tell the following true stories of Kristy, Diane and Danney, who were recruited into a movement using the multiplying ministry scheme.

After Kristy became involved, she read the Bible from midnight to 6:00 a.m. for a week, becoming exhausted. She was on the brink of collapse and told her recruits: "I just can't give up any more for the Lord." Her recruiter said: "Why don't you just let go and give in, what are you holding onto?" Kristy said "My life, I'm holding onto my life!" They told Kristy "You've got to give your life to the Lord. You can't be a total Christian... unless you totally give your life to the Lord." Kristy said "I wanted nothing more than to just let go, but I thought if I let go, I would just sink ... A couple days later I did let go only I found that I was floating. It was amazing."

In Cults in America Appel says floating sensations happen during the transition period where you float between two worlds, detached from your past and not yet connected to your future- "the naked moment before the new clothes are on and the discarded ones are strewn about on the floor." After this Kristy said, "Sometimes I would feel high, just on top of the world. Then I would find myself so depressed, I just felt worthless and helpless. I didn't want to eat or sleep. The conflict was immense (Holy Terror)."

After asking Lord Jesus into her heart, Diane was told she was an "ambassador of Christ." She said "we were supposed to spread the gospel to everyone. They said the only reason God was allowing me, Diane, to live, was to bring everybody I came in contact with to the Lord... When the whole world was converted, Jesus would come back in the clouds, and pick up all his children, and the earth would be destroyed..."

Diane gave up her books, music, painting, writing, and her involvement with the women's movement. "Everything that had been important to me now became Satanic... I cut all ties to the world... Then the fear and guilt really began to get to me... Everyone was watching one another, picking out things that weren't Christ-like. Then we had to repent..."

"They told us not to think or to question because Satan uses the mind to trick you. They told us not to trust our emotions because they were deceptive... I couldn't stand the emptiness and alienation inside. It was terrible, like looking at yourself and seeing somebody who was totally mindless. All that was inside my head were these automatic answers."

"...The terror of not finding myself was deep inside. The center of my being was empty, black and dark. So I signed myself into a psychiatric hospital... I was afraid to talk to them because they weren't born-again Christians. They tried to help me but I couldn't listen... I stayed for two and a half months, hoping that maybe I could find some answers... It was all a waste of time and money..."

"I was lying in bed one day, all doubled up in pain, and I heard this little voice crying for help. At first, I thought it was Satan, so I didn't pay attention to it. The next day I heard it again, this tiny little voice, very faint and weak. Then, I don't know why, I just said I'll help you... suddenly I began to think of things that would make me happy... I thought about fun things I used to do. Then I started reading and writing again... I started doing... things that had been forbidden."

"My Christian friends rejected me and I was afraid to get close to people who weren't born again, because they were of Satan. After eight years I tried to read a newspaper, but everything seemed to point to Satan and the coming destruction of the world. When I tried to think, I would get a pain in my head. Things weren't connecting. I felt like I had lost my mind (Holy Terror)."

Danny, an honor student, was recruited by the Navigators during his freshman year of college. Danny completed his degree, got a job at an engineering firm and became involved with the Navigators again. Two years later he took his life at a church parking lot. The letters Danny wrote revealed a process he was subjected to that "ripped away his sense of self, his ability to think rationally, and his grip on the world... Danny was led to give up all outside interests for Jesus." He wrote "I am a seed, available to be planted."

Danny was 25 and had a brilliant career when he took his own life. His mother said Danny "gave up his former friends for these new ones, gave up baseball for Bible study, gave up his Lutheran faith for this fundamentalist version of religion. He roomed with their choice of roommates, gave them his car to use, lent them money. Then they completely rejected him." Danny was told he was not good enough to be a staff leader. He became depressed, quit the Navigators and committed suicide. Rejection is a powerful tool that cult leaders use to control their followers; if it is applied to forcefully, it can back fire (Holy Terror Conway, Siegelman).

Kristy, Diane, and Danny denied their own feelings and desires; this threw them into depression. Kristy didn't want to eat, Diane almost went insane, and Danny killed himself.

Lakota Chief, 'Noble Red Man' said: "God made everything so simple, we do what we please." Develop your unique talents and abilities. Do things that you love, things that you are passionate about. Bring forth the fruit of your soul and your dreams will come true.

In Michelle Remembers (Smith, Pazder) Michelle recalls satanic rituals she was subjected too. When she was six (1955) Satan appeared for a 81-day non-stop ceremony. The following is some of the chants that Satan himself said:

"I write a **Master Plan** of the destiny of man... I'm the one that's accessible now; I'm the one to show them how... I'll just whittle away my time, cutting into the heart of the divine... They don't even know what I'm about... They think it means war (the red horse) but it's only a way inside the door... people will follow because they think they will see and all the time Ha! They are following me... Turn around all the light, turn a light, make it night... To serve my purpose is there only desire... Across the world the sleeping dead... Matthew Mark, Luke and John... Their words were lies, my children will see... The only thing left burning true is the light that shows me to you... Touch everyone you can. Make a beast of every man... I'll bring out the truth, I'll show who's the liar... for peace of mind a soul's the cost... No one can point a finger at me..."

The Master Plan of Evangelism is Christian Nationalism- a dictatorship for Christ-Jehovah-Satan. White Identity Pastors believe in White Christian Government and Biblical law. They know Christ is wrathful, favors his chosen and punishes with torture. Pastors have authority over congregations and men weld power over women and children. Trump is preparing the way for Christian Nationalism by encouraging racial riots, insulting women and making white supremacy remarks. Influential Southern Baptist preachers not teaching Biblical literalism were forced out of the ministry, to groom us for living under Biblical law, where we could be arrested and killed without trial. Christianity is taking us to Satan's Reign.

Any course teaching 'Christ Consciousness' is sorcery. Receiving Christ Consciousness in your heart or asking for this guidance opens your aura to demons. Christ consciousness is Satan consciousness. Christ is Satan. True religion comes from your inner light- the eternal part of your soul that does not incarnate and watches over you- your higher Self. Ask your higher Self for guidance. Your true Self is your soul incarnate; it is connected to your higher Self. I am not enlightened, but my higher Self is and yours is too. Listen to your own heart.

{The pathway to the Creator is infinite; travel the path that appeals to you. Enjoy the journey, have fun, pursue what you love and live from your heart. This takes you along your highest path where you become your true Self. Our true Self knows we exist in a false world. To find the real world, find your true Self and you will break away from those who draw you into a false life.

In I Just Want You to Remember Angi says when we are guided by the light within us, we cannot be controlled, manipulated or lied too. We see through the deception of the Dark Ones (demons) and do not submit to their evil. We stop feeding them and without our energy, the Dark Ones lose power over us and die; they stop existing.

Our true Self is our soul- our inner light. 'When we speak truth, embrace life, feel compassion, create and care instead of destroy, we become our true Self. It is us when we have a revulsion to evil and behavior that violates and diminishes ourselves and others. (Ken Sanes, transparencynow.com).'

Paul said we are children of light, and follow that which is good (1 Thessalonians 5). "There's only goodness in God. And that same goodness is in us all. You can feel it in yourself. You know when you feel good inside. Yes, you're God's child, too. You are good. You are sacred. Respect yourself. Love the goodness in yourself, then put that goodness into the world. That is everybody's Instructions. God made you so you feel good when you do right. Watch when you feel good and follow that good feeling. The good feeling comes from God. When you feel good, God feels good too. God and you feel good together (Noble Red Man Arden).}

Moriah's Message 18
Reclaim our Planet

Before World War II the Global Elite created a blueprint for global dictatorship in precise detail, and divided it into separate parts. **During World War II**, vast wealth poured into Nazi hands from the fortunes confiscated from massacred Jews. **After World War II** this wealth funded: 1. medical experiments. 2. saucer spaceships (UFOs). 3. Genome labs where creatures (aliens) are made. 4. new corporations. These things were on the blueprint, including teleportation, atomic bombs, microchip implants, 9-11, vaccines and Covid-19. The Manhattan Project included towers to be built in Manhattan with nuclear reactors below them.

When World War II ended as planned, Nazi medical teams were brought to the USA. They continued their experiments under the CIA, MK-Ultra program. In the 1950s, military men In the USA and Canada who had a 4-year-old child, were asked to enroll them in the program 'for the good of the country;' they were paid well. Other kids were recruited from orphanages, State hospitals and satanic cults. MK-Ultra experiments took place at military bases, camps, universities and hospitals.

Their eugenics agenda was "selective breeding and culling of the human race to favor the insiders and club members over the common herd… Was the plan to create a future race of slaves? Is that why they performed lobotomies and drugged the children into a vegetative state? Were they trying to see how far they could go in destroying a soul, in order to create a human robot, a functioning zombie who could be used as a disposable, unpaid labor force? Were they prepared to go that far (My Cold War Diamond)?"

Other MK-Ultra memoirs: The Enslaved Queen (Hoffman),

153

Surviving Evil (Wetmore), I am Serena (Masterson) Secret Weapons (Hersha, Hersha). Our Life Beyond MK-Ultra Elisa E. Elisa reveals hybrids, clones and soulless humans. The Mk-Ultra goal: total covert mind control of humanity. Mk-Ultra is at the top of the Global Elite pyramid. I suspect top Masons and top Mormons were involved, as well as the CIA.

While Nazi medical doctors tortured and brain damaged children, Nazi scientists under Operation Paperclip covertly built antigravity spacecraft. They called their crafts 'UFOs from outer space' to hide this technology, and bioengineered creatures they called aliens. The aliens looked like a 10-year-old with progeria: short, narrow frame, no fat, large bald head, no eyebrows, low-placed ears and receding chin. The Roswell UFO, a manmade craft with bioengineered humans, tricked us into thinking the USA was hiding aliens.

The eugenics program furtively infiltrated public schools in the 1950s. Students became patients receiving treatments through vaccines. The chemicals in the vaccines bound the student/patients in a mind/brain straight-jacket. Now babies and toddlers receive these treatments, to cause permanent, right-brain damage before the blood-brain barrier closes, stopping the chemicals from entering their brain. This right-brain damage impairs intuition, imagination and feelings, leaving left-brain abstract reasoning and rational intellect intact. We are being genetically engineered for slave labor and army troops for the Global Elite.

During World War II, the USA developed teleportation. The USS Eldridge was rebuilt as a transporter under the guise of degaussing the ship. The engine was replaced; the deck held Tesla coils, magnets, transformers, generators, etc. The ship disappeared from the Philadelphia Naval Yard, appeared in the Norfolk harbor and materialized in Philadelphia, in 1943. Some crewmen were paralyzed, others were on fire, buried in walls, dead or simply vanished; a few men went insane (Philadelphia Experiment).

The USS Eldridge transported to another location and returned, like a Star Trek transporter that converts matter to energy and back again. Does this technology work by creating an Einstein-Rosen bridge? Is it used in UFOs?

Cybernetic technology was developed in 1948. This led to microchip implants capable of altering brain chemistry with

154

electronic plusses. The implants were tested on prisoners and kidnapped children at Montauk Air Force base. They were inserted into their brains through the nasal cavity.

When the microchip, mind-control project was ready to be fine-tuned (1973), a cult was set up as a front operation in the US. Members were flown to a compound in the Guyana jungle. In <u>Was Jonestown a CIA Medical Experiment?</u> Meiers claims Jonestown was an operation base for MK-Ultra, and Jim Jones was hired by the CIA. Jonestown had a medical lab for mind control experiments. Its sponsor was Dr. Layton, Chief of chemical and biological warfare research at Dugway Utah. Layton conducted genetic experiments at Dugway.

In <u>The Black Hole of Guyana</u> Judge says one goal of MK-Ultra was to **control mass populations** for cheap labor. Dr. Delgado told Congress technology may be able to control workers and troops at war with remote signals. Judge said we are the ultimate victims of Jonestown mind control that ended in murder. Our minds are manipulated and we are deceived like they were. Will we also be controlled?

Can remote signals wipe out memory, manipulate emotions, create hallucinations and inflict pain on a massive scale? Is mass murder on their agenda? 5G carries 20 times more information. More efficient, faster and smarter, could 5G-data connect to AI computers and us through gene editing, biotech and brain-computer interfaces? SMART: computers, TVs, factories, cars, homes, people, phones- all electronic devices interconnected and controlled by AI?

When Jonestown experiments ended (1978), abductions began on a mass scale. Manmade transporter devises and UFOs, and bioengineered hybrids, abducted people, creating the biggest hoax next to Christ. As bioengineering evolved, 'aliens' became more diversified. Genes from a human egg are removed and foreign genes (animal, insect) are added. Gray aliens may be human/insect bio-android cyborgs with skullcap and arm replacements. Reptilian aliens have lizard genes, other aliens have praying mantis genes. Jehovah said his remnant (something that remains after the rest is gone) must be 'in its place'— its exact place (DNA). Jehovah's remnant are bioengineered beasts. We call them aliens.

Demons can take any form; they have appeared as aliens and angels for thousands of years, deceiving us and our ancestors. Beings from other planets cannot physically travel to earth, but they can incarnate with memories of a past life on another planet. Demons are dead people: astral-ghosts trapped on earth. 'Aliens' that abduct us were bioengineered by people in labs on earth.

When UFO abductions began, women were impregnated with a bioengineered embryo; the fetus was removed around 3 months and grown in an incubator. Some eggs were enhanced with human genes and left in the womb. These children received microchip implants and were abducted throughout life. Now, most bioengineered embryos are grown in incubators in underground labs- wombs are not required.

Military personnel assigned to Area 51 are shown aliens (bioengineered creatures) and UFOs (manmade spaceships) becoming part of the alien agenda, not knowing it's a worldwide hoax. Are bioengineered super soldiers here too, perhaps with implants that interface with command networks and weapons of mass destruction?

If you are being abducted, pray to Jesus (**not Christ**) every night. Ask for protection from abductions, both physically and in your dreams. If aliens come they won't be able to paralyze you and they'll leave. If aliens enter your dream, you will awaken. Aliens insert astral implants in the astral body.

The Love Bite: Lorgen reveals mind control, emotional manipulation and demonic elements in UFO abductions. Facing the Shadow, Embracing the Light: Isley discloses her military and alien abductions, including concentration camps on the moon, where Isley was raped and forced to do hard labor with little food. She knows the US military is involved with aliens, but she doesn't know they created them.

The Ultimate Alien Agenda: Walden says aliens reengineer humans. Humans bioengineer aliens. He was taken to underground facilities where decapitated, disemboweled human bodies hung from hooks and saw aliens consuming human fetuses and babies. The alien scientists Walden saw were bioengineered by humans, and they eat humans.

In Symmetry (Preston) Dolly's abductions sound like angelic visits but they look like gray aliens. She conceives hybrid babies for them and the fetuses are removed at 3—4 months. The aliens also put implants in Dolly. Spiritual beings do not violate creation by interbreeding different species or

156

put implants in you. Dolly says our sun will destroy earth in a few years and aliens will pick us up in their UFOs before this happens. She said they will save us. This is a lie and a trap.

Cows are also abducted by UFOs. They are drained of their blood to make pure hemoglobin (Consciousness and Energy Kelly, Levengood). Is this pure hemoglobin used in vaccines? Crop circles are made with UFOs. Levengood discovered some crop circles kill grains with microwaves, others raise yields with ions Will the Global Elite use this technology to kill crops in some areas and increase yields in others?

Navajo Elder Secatero said man is creating new lifeforms with technology, developing their potential and giving them our flesh. If this continues humanity will be enslaved by these creations. They will become our master and feed off us (The Mystery of the Secret Skulls Morton, Thomas). Is this new lifeform bioengineered aliens? Will we become their food?

The Global Elite are reengineering humanity into sub-humans (us) and enhanced humans (them). They cannot win their war against us because Jehovah is also against them. There would be no religions, schools, military or corporations in New Jerusalem, only demon controlled, post humans.

In 1812, Sam supplied meat to the army. Soldiers called his US-stamped barrels 'Uncle Sam's meat.' If New Jerusalem is established, people will become Uncle Sam's meat, kept in cages to feed chimeras, hybrids and demon-controlled zombies- ferocious beasts existing on human flesh, eaten raw like a lion eating its prey. Earth would be populated with caged people, chimeras, hybrids and zombies. No one would want to live in this world. Jehovah is the enemy of humanity.

Revelation says wealthy merchants (Global Elite) deceive all nations with sorcery. Sorcery is 'pharmakeia'- poisoner. Deceive is 'planao' -roam from safety, truth and virtue.

The Secret Covenant: "An illusion... so vast it will escape their perception. Those who see it will be thought of as insane. ...They will be blanketed by poisons... [food, water, medicine, air]... we will inject poisons into the blood of their children and convince them it's for their help... We will create medicine that will make them sicker and cause other diseases ...Their minds will belong to us and they will do as we say... When they shall rise up against us we will crush them like insects... a new era of domination will begin." Chemtrails contain depleted uranium, aluminum, barium, strontium and mercury. These metal nanobots damage our bodies and poison crops. Chemtrails become chemclouds, a poisonous white haze, causing a greenhouse effect. Wildfires become chemical fires.

Tony Rogers said Globalists want everyone chronically ill and plugged into their systems. We are designed to serve them, as gears in their machines. Electronic devices (phone computer, TV) stimulate alpha waves, put us in a hypnotic state, and program us with 'hive mind' mentalities. 5-G uses the same frequency as the Pentagon crowd control system that can heat skin, influence behavior or cause heart failure.

The Global Elite stage mass shootings, so we will give up our guns for safety. Some shootings are planned by the CIA with MK-Ultra slaves. New memories, including feelings, are implanted for a family that isn't real. He may be relocated with a new identity and go on a killing rampage. Some school shootings are students programmed to kill.

The USA is a managed production with fabricated settings designed to incite violence. News headlines are trashy gossip columns for the show: 'Trump is Raging Mad' 'Biden is Senile' 'Putin is Insane' 'Trump says Biden deserves the electric chair.' This is psychological warfare. We are the enemy; we are being demoralized and debilitated. Reporters say fake news is dangerous to democracy. This means true news is dangerous to democracy. In a democracy the government grants rights. In a republic, the government is a protector of rights. The USA is a Republic.

The USA is now being run by the Global Elite. Elections are fixed and Presidents are actors. Some staged events: Obama playing Osama, 9-11, Trump's stolen election, the Capitol break-in, Biden's notecards (thank participants, depart), Trump 'stealing' secret documents. The play's Grand Finale is Christian Nationalism followed by New Jerusalem.

The Global Elite hold world power. They control commerce, corporations, finance, technology, education, medical fields, nations, military, media, food, everything. They are depleting and destroying the earth's resources worldwide for total global control. Everything is at risk: soil, water, air, insects, birds, animals and humanity. We are heading toward the catastrophic collapse of all ecosystems.

The Global Elite break creation laws with bioengineering: vaccines, bioweapons, implants, smart drugs, genome editing, genetically modified insects, plants, animals, people. CERN breaks creation laws; it generates a magnetic field 100,000 times more powerful than earth's. Did it cause the North Pole shift toward Russia? Is it opening wormholes to parallel realities, creating timeline rips and dimensions?

"Afterwards there occurred violent earthquakes and floods; and in a single day and night of misfortune all your warlike men in a body sank into the earth and the island of Atlantis in like manner disappeared in the depth of the sea (Plato)."

Atlanteans broke creation laws that destroyed their island. They bioengineered beast-people that ate raw meat (Neanderthals) and interbred with them. Everyone carries 1—4% of their DNA. The Global Elite have a higher percent; many have a neck and head that protrudes forward instead of upright. Jehovah may have bioengineered Neanderthals in Atlantis. 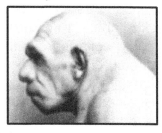 bigthink.com

"A sound of battle is in the land and of great destruction. How is the hammer of the whole earth cut asunder and broken (Jer 50:22—23)! Hammer [patteesh- beat] is a sound in the earth that that cuts it apart. Is this EISCAT-3D?

In <u>Under An Ionized Sky</u> Freeland says the sky has been weaponized using satellites, antenna arrays and chemtrails connected with 5G networks, for quantum computer control over earth. Are 5G towers and supercomputers linked to each other and us? 5G cell-tower streetlight poles are being installed in neighborhoods, on sidewalks and streets worldwide, without the residents prior knowledge.

Do Morgellons fibers come from nanobot fibers in chemtrails? Curling red, blue, black and white fibers protrude from welts that do not heal; they move under the skin. Does everyone have these fibers and only a few people develop skin sores?

HAARP radio waves create magnetic disturbances in the atmosphere. If sustained, hurricanes, tsunamis, tornadoes and earthquakes can result. DEMETER (French satellite) detected a 360% increase in ULF waves in the ionosphere above Haiti for a month before the 2010 quake and a similar increase above the coast of Japan before the 2011 tsunami hit. May 2023, impoverished cities across Mississippi and Alabama were demolished. Dozens of predominantly black towns were flattened in the night with no tornado warnings. Was this Global Elite covert terrorism? Were New Orleans (2005) and Paradise (2018) also acts of covert terrorism?

Could EISCAT-3D, 200 times more powerful than HAARP, be used as an EMP weapon? Is this what caused sheets of dry lightning in Aaron Ray's vision? A global EMP weapon could collapse communication infrastructures and electrical circuits. The world is sustained by a complex network of inter-locking structures, where transactions and information flow. Businesses would close, planes would crash, cars, trucks and trains would stop and the world would go dark.

Trident Juncture NATO training, October—November 2018 held in Norway, Finland and Sweden (home of EISCAT-3D) involved 40,000 soldiers, 130 aircraft and 70 vessels from 30+ nations. What were they training for? Four years later, NATO (Global Elite military) begin bombing Ukraine cities with Russian artillery and blaming Russia (false flag). Russian military only bombed Ukraine military installations.

Domestic terrorism laws were passed in the USA, to arrest people who speak against the government. The Global Elite remove people who oppose them. Will there be a 'Night of the Long Knives' where political opponents are murdered?

Mega-corporations enslave children. In Africa they produce commodities in inhumane conditions: sugarcane, tobacco, cocoa, mining, coffee, cotton and bricks. In the USA near-free labor comes from prisons; inmates produce a billion-dollar year revenue working for $150 a month. Will this will be us, living in confinement working for corporations?

Laws need to protect people not corporations. Corporations need to be structured so the wealth they produce is equitably shared with employees. If humanity lived natural laws there would be no billionaire people or corporations. They pillage resources, including animals and people, for profit. Bill Gates bought controlling influence over healthcare systems world-wide and giant tracts of farmland. Elon Musk is launching 42,000 space satellites. The US sent 40+ billion to Ukraine; Vast wealth is buying control of the world.

Alternatives To Economic Globalization addresses ways to dismantle the International Monetary Fund, World Bank and World Trade Organization. It gives alternative methods for manufacturing, agriculture and transportation. Free societies need economies that support everyone, sustainability, local decision making and human rights. In Economic Insanity Terry shows how to limit corporate power, restructure wealth, stop harmful corporate activities, protect workers and small businesses. Laws need to restrict corporate ownership of radio, newspapers, magazines, TV stations and banks, protect schools from government and corporate control.

One Nation One Curriculum (Kantrowitz Newsweek 4/5/92) said States will be pressured to '**get with the program**' and adopt national standards like France and Germany, where lesson plans and tests determine whether students enter the workforce or attend universities. No Child Left Behind law enforces national standards. It is designed to stop critical thinking. Standardized tests track students programming.

In The Outer Limits Straight And Narrow (1996) a private school surgically inserts microchip implants in the student's brains without their consent or knowledge. They are told to '**get with the program**'. Straight is the gate and narrow is the way that leads to life 'for the manipulators of our ultimate fate.' Are we mind/brain controlled like these students?

People who expose covert agendas are under surveillance. A stranger told me 'we are watching you.' Objects are moved in my house. I'm followed in my car and on walks. Military jets, drones and helicopter fleets make low-fly passes over my house. When I eat out, a man sitting alone drinking coffee lets me know with hard glares he was sent to watch me. My phone shows random, wrong times when I look at it between 8:00 pm—8:00 am. On Miracle's birthday (08) a helicopter circled the house multiple times until David came out, then it hovered over his head. Aaron Ray was mowing when he heard a horrific noise. The ground shook and a huge shadow went over him. A C-130 Hercules aircraft flew over him!

STOP the Global Elite's agenda to make the US a Christian Nation. **STOP** supporting mega-corporations. **STOP** sending your children to public schools. Remember Howard in the movie Network? "I want you to get up right now!... go to the window, open it and stick your head out and yell, I'm mad as hell and I'm not going to take this anymore!" Indorse local products, use bartering if you can and when possible, give goods and services for free (matriarchal gift economy). Live from your heart, develop your talents and claim your destiny. You will help heal the world and have an enriched life. You are more than you know. Live free.

One Moment in Time

Hammond and Bettis

Each day I live I want to be,

A day to give the best of me

...I want one moment in time

When I'm more than I thought I could be

When all of my dreams are a heartbeat away

And the answers are all up to me

Give me one moment in time

When I'm racing with destiny

Then in that one moment of time

I will feel, I will feel eternity

Which Future Will Manifest

Chimeras   Cyborgs   Hybirds

Ascension: Able To Move Between Worlds

Moriah's Message 19
Manifest Miracles

Symbolism, the language of the universe, can manifest. Repeated symbolism in traditions and holidays creates our future, whether based on sorcery or to manifest miracles. Jehovah's celebrations further his satanic agendas. When Europeans and Americans adopted Jehovah as their god, they were severed from their ancestral roots. Celebrating seasonal changes will reconnect us, and we will manifest miracles. Replace Christmas with Winter Solstice.

Saint Nicholas worshipped Jehovah and a demon named Krampus followed him around. He had fangs, hoofs and a long tongue. Jehovah-Santa is Krampus; his birthday is Christmas. St. Nicholas gave treats to children and Krampus carried them into the woods to eat them. Krampus carries shackles so children cannot run away from him and a bag to stuff them in. Bad children are eaten or burned alive.

This 1900 Christmas card says: Greetings from Krampus! A girl sits in trance while her brother is assaulted.

Santa=Satan, Claus/e=Lord's breach of promise. Santa's elves=Satan's demons. Santa's ho ho ho, Merry Christmas: Ho=stop, Merry=intoxicated, Christmas=Christ's massive slaughter. If the Lord's Dreadful Day came, Jehovah would call forth his demons (Zec 2:6). "She will be delivered into the hand of the people of the north— Santa's elves (Jer 46:24)."

Santa's rein/deer are the Lord's reins he has on his dear Christians. He would pull on his bridle, bringing them to a halt on his Dreadful Day. The Lord said "There shall be a bridle in the jaws of the people causing them to err (Is 30:28). I will put my hook in your nose, and my bridle in your lips (Is 37:29)." Bridle in the jaw is "recen"— halter to restrain; bridle in the lips is 'metheg'- curb, rein in. "We put bits in the horse's mouths, that they may obey us; and we turn about their whole body (James 3:3)."

Santa Claus lives in the North Pole because evil realms are cold (spiritual realms are hot). Santa's workshop is where he works spells. The toys in Santa's sleigh symbolize his toying with our affection so he can slay us. Christmas trees symbolize the demon-ghosts chopping us down; decorations symbolize our worship of them. Santa going down the chimney symbolizes Christians receiving The Holy Ghost. Stockings hung on the chimney symbolize demon-ghosts stocking up on merchandise (Christians) to survive.

The children on Santa's list are the Children of Israel: Jews, Christians, and the Global Elite. Jehovah-Santa-Satan would come to them in one night on his 'Dreadful Day' and judge them bad, wrong, condemned. He would then call his demon-elves to come forth and slaughter them. Reject Jehovah and stop celebrating his birthday- Christmas.

Santa/Satan is god of commerce, and commerce is destroying the earth. As industry razes forests and pollutes rivers, to manufacture merchandise we do not need, Satan feeds on the wake of destruction it leaves. The Christmas buying frenzy oils the wheels of this demonic machine and keeps it turning. As we consume products, Satan consumes us. The first, middle, and end numbers on all barcodes is 666. Christians have this same mark—The Holy Ghost. The barcodes on merchandise symbolize humanity as revenue producers for Satan. Merchandise is slang for human cargo.

In <u>It's A Wonderful Life</u> George Bailey is taken to a parallel world where his hometown is Pottersville. Potter owns most of the town- gambling halls, nightclubs and slums. George is returned to his reality, where the town is Bedford Falls, there is a warrant for his arrest, his ear can't hear, his mouth is bleeding, and the whole town loves him.

We are George Bailey, with money troubles and unrealized dreams. Like George, we are in danger of living in Pottersville where bankers and corporate insiders own our towns. Like George, we need to take stand against this and help each other live. George is a hometown hero. He shows us the importance of family and community and the power of doing good. Be a hero. Stand for what's right. Break the corporate stranglehold over your life. We can restructure the economy on a local level and support our community (chapter 22).

In <u>Sweet Salt</u> Locke tells about The Man Who Killed Santa Claus. A missionary in Arizona posted signs in a Navajo town saying Santa would come down from heaven on Christmas Eve with toys. Christians back home donated the toys. He hired a small plane and a man to play Santa. The man showed up too drunk to walk, and hundreds of Navajos had gathered to see Santa. The pilot decided to stuff the Santa Claus suit with straw and drop it out of the plane. The chute failed to open and Santa hit the ground with a splat. The drunk Santa was symbolic of Satan drunk on our life-force. The hay-stuffed Santa was Satan with no life-force.

Stop Celebrating Christmas
Manifest a world without Santa

As we go about our daily life, angels inspire us to manifest miracles. Sandra was unraveling the gospel when Hale-Bopp made its debut, summer of 1995. Hale was tracking comets from his driveway when he noticed a comet around midnight that shouldn't be there. Bopp did not own a telescope; he was out with friends observing star clusters when he saw a new comet. Their discoveries named the comet.

Hail means attract attention; it symbolizes the passionate burst of interest <u>The Greatest Deception</u> will generate. Bop is informal for dancing; it symbolizes the beautiful day of dancing it will bring. In the USA Hale-Bopp was seen in the northeast before dawn and in the west at night. Hale-Bopp before dawn signifies our turning onto the Red Road; Hale-Bopp at night symbolizes the power of the west that will kill Jehovah. Daniel Green predicted Hale-Bopp would be "the most viewed comet in all of human history... it will be hard for the average person not to see it." The average person will also hear about The Greatest Deception. It will "fly out across the whole earth"- the flying scroll and goat in Daniel's vision.

Twenty years later (8-21-17) another celestial event occurred: the first total solar eclipse to traverse the USA from coast to coast, in 99 years. Day turned to night for a brief moment as the sun's rays blazed around a black shadow, creating a brilliant halo. The shadow withdrew and vanished. Will this symbolic miracle manifest?

On Miracle's 3rd birthday, 8/20/97, lightning started the bluff by my home on fire. Planes and helicopters fought the flames. The fire burned through the night and the next day the bluff was bare. Bluff means deceive. The stripped bluff symbolized this book exposing the Lord, calling his bluff.

My neighbor's lamb got loose; I helped herd it home. Jill said "come on, you're not going to the slaughter house now!" The lamb symbolized Christians, and Jehovah's plan to bring them down "like lambs to the slaughter." Turning the lamb in the right direction and Jill's comment symbolized Christians rejecting Jehovah.

Imagination is a symbolic representation; it speaks the language of the universe and can manifest. Imagination is your creative power. The Lord is afraid of our imagination; it can destroy him. He said "the imagination of a man's heart is evil (Gen 8:21)." If everyone imagined the same dream it would materialize. "Imagine all the people sharing all the world... and the world will live as one (John Lennon)." Who would ever guess what powers we possess!

True religion is living a healthy lifestyle, actively healing your body, mind and soul, living from your heart and fulfilling your destiny. This spiritual path adds light to the world. Your body is a sacred temple and so is your living space. You and your home are entwined; both need to be kept pure.

167

Your environment is vital to your spiritual growth. Your living space affects you on every level of your being. Living with someone who is abusive or negative lowers the vibrations of your home and can wreak havoc on your health. Ancient Lemuria was spiritually advanced. Lemurians lived a thousand years. When Atlanteans discovered their island, they built houses on their land. This lowered the vibration of their homeland and corrupted their youth. The spiritual life of Lemurians suffered (The Lemurian Way, Lauren Thyme).

Cities are living beings, like rivers and trees. Corruption and evil weaken their life-force and spread decay. A city with over-the-top mansions, derelict buildings, rundown houses and dead trees is an out of balance, dying city. When a city dies, the Spirit of the Land leaves and further deterioration occurs. When homes and yards are well maintained, nature spirits and angelic beings add their Living Light to the land. Darkness retreats and the neighborhood becomes vibrant.

Your home is a reflection of yourself. It is alive and inter-twined with your wellbeing. Putting your house or apartment in order puts your affairs in order. You will see what you need and don't need, in your house and in your life. The trans-formation it brings your home will also transform you. Write a poem to your living space and read it every day. It will help you manifest miracles. See my poem to my home in chapter 25- My Storybook Playhouse.

In Sacred Space Linn says your home becomes vibrant through love and devotion; it can bless everyone who enters. It can be a sanctuary where you interface with the universe. It can broadcast energy 'like an echo heard throughout infinity.' "The energy radiating from your home can be like a small stone dropped into a still pool of the universe, whose ripples will be felt at the farthest shore of the cosmos... Your home can be a transmitting station for the light."

Organizing your home and eliminating clutter opens a synchronistic flow in your life that brings you things you need, manifesting miracles. Clearing the clutter in your house will also clear clutter in your head, which is where it first came from. Go through every room, removing unused or unwanted items- dishes, clothes, books, etc. Donate them to a thrift store. Move furniture around until everything finds its ideal place. If one isn't found, it does not belong in your house.

The tops of bookshelves and dressers are temple altars. Cover them with beautiful scarfs and arrange your most beloved objects on them; they will help manifest your desires.

Clear clutter in cupboards, drawers, closets, on floors, tables, etc. It lowers the vibration of you home and can make you feel morose. Empty your dresser drawers, one at a time. Clothes you use go in the drawer, neatly folded, other items go in a bag to give away. You will feel good when you open your drawers. Unused space has stagnate energy; it can make you depressed. Unused rooms restrict life-force. Energy stops flowing and the space becomes dead. Empty out the room and create something different.

Garbage, clutter, dilapidated anything, inside and outside, attracts demons. Clean, repair and paint. Keep plumbing, electrical, heating systems, etc. maintained. Remove books and DVDs that are dark or violent. It will raise the vibrations of your living space and help keep you healthy. Draw lines through barcodes on products and books. Barcodes contain Jehovah's image (666) and emit negative energy. Drawing a line through them blocks the energy.

In Clear Your Clutter With Feng Shui, Kingston says when you only keep the things you need for your personal journey, instead of burdening yourself with things that obscure your way, it's easier to stay on your spiritual path and you will never feel the need for clutter again.

Instead of selling unwanted items, give them away. The sorted bags and boxes of things you are clearing out, need to be removed from your house. Giving them away will manifest miracles in your life. When my children were young I took some clothes they had outgrown to the Salvation Army thrift store. I browsed the store and found a dress my mother made for my sister Tina. The dress had traveled 200 miles when I found it 14 years later. It fit Ruby Jane, who was three.

Sandra's Destiny Dream. Seventeen years after I found Tina's dress at the Salvation Army thrift store, I had a dream of Tina giving me White Buffalo Woman's dress. Her dress was white with rainbow sparkles. Tina's little dress was white with rainbow dots. It symbolized White Buffalo Woman's dress. The Salvation Army symbolized the multitude (army) who would receive rescue from danger (salvation). Dreams speak the language of symbolism and can manifest miracles.

Thrift stores are magical places where synchronistic encounters happen. The actor who played the Wizard of Oz (Morgan) went to a thrift shop looking for a coat to wear for the part. He found a coat in the right style. The name L. Frank Baum (author of The Wizard of Oz) was sewn on the inside. Baum's wife confirmed the coat was her late husband's.

When Jarvis was 12, I took some books to the thrift store. The next day a high school student gave Jarvis his computer programming books. He heard Jarvis was learning how to program. Jarvis spent the next few years studying them. He now writes software for 3D laser-scanning technology.

On Halloween, 1997, Jared and I cleaned for 12 hours. When we took Christmas lights off the porch, Jared said 'the balance of power changed.' I remembered a dream I had of Jared and I making music and dancing. It symbolized our cleaning. Demons on the land needed to be banished before Halloween night, to manifest a symbolic, world shift from darkness to light. The house was built where my in-laws barn once stood and may have been used for satanic rituals. We cleared out demon-ghosts with our cleaning.

{Sandra had the following Destiny Dreams 1—3; Moriah had Destiny Dream 4. These dreams manifested miracles.

1. Sandra's dream. In 1994 Tina gave Sandra (birth soul) White Buffalo Woman's dress and shoulder wrap in a dream. Sandra changed her clothes, putting them on. She thought White Buffalo Woman's dress symbolized our communion while writing messages. The dress was our soul exchange. Sandra was going to pass on and I would take her place. The wrap symbolized our communion while Sandra wrote messages (94—99). Our communion continued after the exchange with Sandra on the other side communing with me.

2. Sandra's dream. While writing my messages I saw this book in a dream. I sat at a desk and browsed it. My dreambook was from the future; it looked like this one. A drama played out symbolizing The Greatest Deception being read and digested by people who worship Jehovah. This was a miracle-manifest dream, to help it come true (message 23).

3. Sandra's dream. Two days before Miracle's 7th birthday (8-20-2001) Jared had a desire to see me- an 8-hour drive. After an hour's travel, he questioned his decision. Why was he making this trip? He decided to turn around. A bright star went dim and it felt like the world was now in danger. Jared told the star 'ok I'll go' and it brightened. We went to Boise on Miracle's birthday and stopped at a park. A stranger approached and said "the river is over there." We didn't know there was a river in the park. We walked over to it and felt a sacred presence. I recalled a dream I had two years ago.

I told Jared my dream. We were standing in front of the same river. Dolphins and whales were leaping in it, diving with beauty and grace. Cows were in the river, floundering in panic. Some were dead, with their legs in the air. I walked towards a dolphin on a rock and my dream ended. When I finished, Jared heard a voice say 'you have triumphed.' He came to see me on Miracle's birthday so we could stand in front of the Boise River and imagine my dream. Recreating it with our imagination will help manifest its miracle.

Whales and Dolphins symbolize masculine and feminine energies in balance and harmony. Leaping in and out of the water symbolized their synchronistic dance and our awakening. Dolphins and whales are helping us awaken from our perpetual sleep. The floundering cows are cash cows, mega-corporations owned by the Global Elite going belly up. When people stop purchasing products they do not need or want, mega-corporations will go bankrupt. Their control over us, society, governments, world economies etc. will come to end.

Boise means 'the wooded river valley'; it was known as a shelter of trees in the high desert. Standing in front of the Boise River symbolized people taking a stand, establishing self-sufficient towns where we live in harmony with each other and nature. The dolphin on the rock symbolized the return of the Golden World and our ascension.

It's been 25 years since we stood on that river bank. Multiple miracles brought us there. Jared was inspired to see me on Miracle's birthday. A star brightened to keep him going. An angel appeared in the park so we would see the river. I was inspired to tell Jared my dream. An angel told Jared we won. This dream will manifest its miracle when the Global Elite's mega-corporations that have enslaved us, go broke and we become self-sufficient (see chapter 22).

4. Moriah's dream. January 2022 I dreamed I was in a hotel ballroom. Beautiful music was playing. I saw a mother and asked if I could dance with her baby; she said yes. I danced and twirled across the floor with the baby in my arms. When I gave the baby to its mother she said I needed to come with her. We went outside to her car. I said 'I don't want to go, I might get lost. I'll forget and I may not find my way back.' She told me I must come, we planned this. I got in her car and the dream ended.

The hotel is the afterlife, the Mom is Sandra, the baby is our book. I danced with the baby, filled with love and joy! Sandra's car represents the crash that 'killed' her. Sandra did not take me to the hospital, she took me to her car. Perhaps she came for me before the crash occurred. The steering wheel was pushed against the car seat with no room for anyone between them. Maybe I was there and protected Sandra from being crushed. We exchanged places in the hospital when she crossed over. My fear of getting lost was forgetting who I am and taking on Sandra's karma.}

David believes 'I' had a near-death experience. There was no near-death; Sandra left. When she appeared to David to tell him goodbye, I was in the hospital keeping her body alive. Sandra passed on September 17, 2001. She did not know I was going to replace her, but her soul knew. We made the agreement before her incarnation. When she came for me, Sandra had no hesitation. I was the one who was hesitant.

Our soul exchange happened while Sandra was dying. Angels supported the body while it took place and guided the surgeon's hands so the body would survive. A soul exchange is soul transference, not resurrection. Sandra needed to experience childhood and raising a family. Her youngest was 16 when she passed. I needed adulthood to fulfill my vow. I inherited the body's cellular memories and a part of Sandra's soul that stays with the heart as long as it is alive. Our combined destinies through our exchange will help humanity ascend. Soul exchanges are rare and only happen to benefit humanity.

The first printing of this book, titled A New Vision, was written by Sandra. She unraveled the Bible, writing 24 messages. I revised them and added message 16: A Great Purification. Sandra didn't know we were the Hopi younger brother. I kept Sandra's voice to the extent that I could, but new information was needed. I added images to Sandra's messages and lyrics, and wrote Part Two.

Imagine

John Lennon

kondoonung.com

Imagine there's no heaven, it's easy if you try
No hell below us, above us, only sky
Imagine all the people livin' for today
Imagine there's no countries, it isn't hard to do
Nothing to kill or die for and no religion, too
Imagine all the people livin' life in peace...
Imagine no possessions, I wonder if you can
No need for greed or hunger, a brotherhood of man
Imagine all the people sharing all the world
You may say I'm a dreamer but I'm not the only one
I hope someday you'll join us and the world will live as one

Moriah's Message 20
Mother's Womb

The universe is shaped like an infinity symbol. One side is matter; the other is anti-matter- a mirror image. The point between is Eternity. The Möbius strip moves forward and will ultimately return to where it was created: Eternity. Einstein's theories united energy, matter, space and time. Now consciousness has joined the union. We are eternal consciousness, the void that holds infinity and the probability field. It is pure potential and infinite possibilities; no-thing and every-thing unactualized.

"In the beginning, God created the heaven and the earth. The earth was without form and void, and darkness was on the face of the deep. The Spirit of God moved on the face of the waters. God said let there be light, and there was light (Gen 1:1—3)." The earth was without form, void, and dark. This is star formation, where particles are so dispersed, they are a near-perfect vacuum (void) and the nebulas are so dark they can only be seen against a background of stars. When nebulas reach the density of clouds they collapse and emit radiation— "and there was light." This was the 1st day.

At the end of a star's life, its outer layers are blown into space. The matter is too dense to escape the star's space warp and it encircles the dying star, forming a crust. This is how planets are formed; they have a small sun in there interior, a hollow sphere, and an outer crust. The earth's star-core is still burning. There is an opening to inner earth at the North and South Poles. Gas from the inner sun escapes through these openings and is illuminated by solar flares.

"God said let there be a firmament in the midst of the waters, to divide the waters from the waters. God made the firmament and divided the waters which were under the firmament, from the waters which were above the firmament, and it was so. God called the firmament heaven (Gen 1:6—8)." Firmament is "raqiya"—a vast, continuous area. Heaven is "shameh"—lofty, something high. The earth's crust is a vast, continuous area, around 10 miles high. The firmament called heaven in these verses is our earth's crust. It divides the seas inside the earth, from the seas on top; it is in the midst or center, dividing the waters from the waters. This was the 2nd day.

"And God said let the waters under the heaven be gathered... and let dry land appear... let the earth bring forth grass, the herb yielding seed, and the fruit tree... and it was so... (Gen 1:9—11)." The sun has not been created yet grass is growing and there are herbs and trees. The grass, herbs and trees are growing inside the earth with waters under the firmament (earth's crust), and with sunlight from the earth's star-core. This was the 3rd day.

"God said let there be lights in the firmament of the heaven, to divide the day from the night, and let them be for signs, and for seasons, and for days, and for years... to give light upon the earth (Gen 1:14, 15)." This firmament of heaven is the lofty expanse of the sky. It is the sun that gives light to the earth, provides us with seasons, and divides day from night, marking our years. This verse tells us the earth is older than the sun. This was the 4th day.

Elements are forged in star cores; hydrogen fuses into helium, helium into carbon, carbon fuses into oxygen; oxygen fuses into silicon, which fuses into iron. The star expands and contracts as its temperature changes, becoming dim and bright again and again as each new element ignites in the core. Each element leaves a burning shell. Older stars have several shells, with the lightest elements toward the periphery, and the heaviest toward the center. These cycles take millions of years to complete.

When an iron core builds up the cycles of thermonuclear fusion stop. The elements from hydrogen to silicon release energy as they fuse into the next more complex element; but iron must receive energy to form a heavier nucleus. When a middleweight star reaches this stage its core keeps shrinking and heating unchecked until it collapses. As the shells fall inward the layers compress tighter and atoms break apart.

Protons and electrons unite, forming neutrons and neutrinos.

Neutrinos travel at light speed and have little interaction with matter. As the newly created neutrinos speed away in all directions, neutrons become more compact. A wall of neutrons slowly close around the neutrinos until they can no longer escape. The neutrinos impact eventually becomes so great they push the neutrons outward and escape. Shock waves ripple throughout the star's compressed layers, triggering explosions. These explosions form silicates, aluminum, carbon, gold, magnesium, silver, uranium, iron and other elements. The elements are blown outward, becoming trapped in the star's space-warp. Over millions of years they will coalesce and form a planet.

The earth is your mother. All the elements in your body were forged in her womb when she was a star. Planets are hollow with an iron core star at their center formed from thermonuclear fusion. As a planet's star-core cools, it releases heat. This heat-energy creates many elements, including hydrogen and oxygen which bond together, forming water. The rising heat, newly formed matter and water expands the planet's surface, violently ripping its crust apart. As volume increases, gravity increases.

Seventy million years ago, the earth was smaller with less water, half the gravity, and a faster spin. This is why dinosaurs were so massive and Pteranodons with 50-foot wing spans could fly. Dinosaurs died when the earth rapidly expanded. Giant rivers of molten lava flowed, massive earthquakes ripped the land apart and water gushed forth creating vast oceans. The earth's expansion is now barely detectable; seafloor spreading slowly creates new crust. The universe, stars and planets expand and contract.

The sun is becoming a planet. Earth is becoming a moon. Jupiter was once a sun and its moons were planets. Someday our sun will be like Jupiter, and earth, Venus, Mercury and Mars will be its moons. Stars are the youngest Celestial Beings, and moons are the oldest. Craters on moons were made by gas bubbles during their days as a sun.

The Hopi/Navajo Spider Woman created the moon; she is grandmother of the sun— two generations older. Being the oldest, it is she who wove the world into existence; she is the weaver and we are the web.

As the earth orbits the sun, the sun orbits the Milky Way Galaxy. It takes approximately 222 million years for the Sun to complete one journey around the galaxy. The Sun bobs as it travels, rising above the galactic plane, down below it and back again. This oscillation takes 64 million years. There is a moment in this journey when a perfect galactic alignment between the Sun and center of the galaxy happens. This is the Galactic Alignment we are moving toward.

As the earth rotates it creates the north and south magnetic fields. EISCAT-3D and HAARP disrupt the earth's electro-magnetic fields by heating the ionosphere with a focused beam. This electromagnetic wave-energy can make the earth wobble and even flip on its axis. Earth's magnetic field holds our atmosphere in place. We cannot survive without this blanket and we cannot survive if the earth flips over.

We don't know what we are doing to ourselves and our earth mother. She gave us life and she can take it. It takes great evil to kill a planet. We have disturbed earth's balance; if we become a threat to our earth mother, she will take us out. She will not allow us to put her life at risk. Earth can send a distress signal to a large asteroid, to destroy us. Our earth mother would recover and life would eventually begin again.

Heavy clothes have cut us off from our earth mother. Tom Brown was told to stay dry and put on a coat, but when Stalking Wolf took him into the woods "off came the pro-tective shells, and we were baptized into the stimulating reality and rapture of life. When we learned to stop resisting nature, and let it flow through us, we were never really un-comfortable in the elements again (The Vision)."

Children are separated from the earth when they are forced to bundle up. Jarvis runs barefoot outside when it snows or rains, laughing with delight as he gets wet. He doesn't like wearing shoes or a coat. On cold days he wears a cap, he can then play with freedom and stay warm. Most of your body heat escapes from your head. At school Jarvis cannot go outside on cold days without his coat, so he doesn't wear his cap, he gets hot with it on. One day I was at the school when he came in from recess; his ears were red from the cold wind. He would have been warmer with a hat and no coat, yet this is not allowed!

When Standing Bear was in boarding school, he wore long underwear, stiff shirts, heavy pants and hard boots. They gave him great torment; the skin is "a highly developed breathing apparatus" which could not breathe in heavy clothes. "Our bodies were used to constant bathing in the sun, air, and rain."

In The Vision Tom Brown describes Stalking Wolf's bathing ritual. "I could see clearly the streams of tears on his cheeks glistening in the sun, and the contented smile on his face. He kneeled down solemnly and touched the water ever so gently... he began to stroke the water as if it were a living being, looking deep into its color... Reaching deeper into the water with cupped hands, he raised the water to the Creator in thanksgiving... dropped his blanket and entered the water. I could see his entire body trembling with excitement, and the smile on his face. As he lay back in the water, he was one of total rapture."

In The Essene Gospel of Pease Jesus told those with pain in their bones to put clay, softened by sun and water, on their limbs. Native Americans knew their mother's skin (soil) was cleansing and healing. Jesus did not come to Native Americans; they did not need him. They were living the truths he brought to the other side of the world. If his true words were not lost, those who followed Jesus' teachings would have lived in harmony with them. Instead, those who worshipped nature were burned at the stake and the natives were forced to live like White men.

Natives lived in the timeless place where one is whole. Life was their school. Clocks did not tell their children when to work, play, eat, learn, and worship. They learned from the earth and from traditions, dreams, and visions. Stalking Wolf said everyone is unique. "That is the power of their medicine... learn from that uniqueness, that medicine." Brown watched a child sail a leaf downstream. He was "squealing with delight and laughter as it chased water bugs over the surface ...I could sense a timelessness... unconditional play and curiosity as he seemed to relish each moment. I could feel a longing deep inside me, for that quest for play and joy... That child taught me... to let go of time, and to keep the purity of play and curiosity alive... (The Vision Brown)."

Buscaglia said a child's education should help him discover his uniqueness, aid him toward its development and teach him how to share it with others. This is how native children learned. In the USA, public schools apply psychology to the classroom. Stimulus-response conditioning and sensitivity training are used to modify children's thoughts and behavior. Students are prisoners, locked in rooms,

178

locked in time, made to conform, and robbed of their self. This destroys their uniqueness and murders their souls.

Chief Dan George: "How long have I known you, oh Canada? ...I am sad for all the Indian people throughout the land. For I have known you when your forests were mine... I have known you in your streams and rivers where your fish flashed and danced in the sun, where the waters said 'come, come and eat of my abundance.' I have known you in the freedom of the winds. And my spirit, like the winds, once roamed your good lands.

But in the long hundred years since the white man came, I have seen my freedom disappear like the salmon going mysteriously out to sea. The white man's strange customs, which I could not understand, pressed down upon me until I could no longer breathe. When I fought to protect my land and my home I was called a savage. When I neither understood nor welcomed his way of life, I was called lazy. When I tried to rule my people, I was stripped of my authority.

...Like the thunderbird of old, I shall rise again out of the sea. I shall grab the instruments of the white man's success— his education, his skills, and with these new tools, I shall build my race into the proudest segment of your society... I shall see our young braves, and our Chiefs, sitting in the houses of law and government, ruling, and being ruled, by the knowledge and freedom of our great land. So shall we shatter the barriers of our isolation. So shall the next 100 years be the greatest and proudest, in the proud history of our tribes and nations."

Noble Red Man: "It is our duty to become a free people again, to become part of the world of nations. We are a nation by every standard set by the United Nations. We have our own language, our own religion, our own land, our own history, our own culture going back to the beginning of time. That's more than your U.S. government can say. You borrowed your language and your religion from someone else... And you took your land from... us! We Indians are a beautiful people, a peaceful people. Every one of us is a natural-born leader. We have so much to teach the world, so much to give other nations... we want our rightful place."

Sunbear and Waben: "We have forgotten how to hear the stories and songs that the winds can bring to us. We have forgotten to listen to the wisdom of the rocks, that have been here since the beginning... We have forgotten how the water refreshes and renews us. We have lost the ability to listen to the plants, as they tell us which ones we should eat to live well. We have lost the ability to listen to the animals, as they give us their gifts of learning... Open your eyes, ears, minds, and hearts, to see the magic...

Luther Standing Bear: "Old people liked to... walk with bare feet on the sacred earth... the soil was soothing, strengthening, cleansing and healing... the old Indian still sits upon the earth... to sit or lie upon the ground is to ...think more deeply and feel more keenly. He can see more clearly into the mysteries of life and come closer in kinship to other lives about him... Man's heart away from nature becomes hard... he kept his youth close to its softening influence."

Chiparopai: "We wear the white man's heavy clothing and it makes us weak. Each day in the old times, in summer and in winter, we came down to the river banks to bathe. This strengthened and toughened our firm skin. But white settlers were shocked to see the naked Indians, so now we keep away. In the old days we wore the breechcloth, and aprons made of bark and reeds. We worked all winter in the wind— bare arms, bare legs, and never felt the cold."

Vine Deloria Jr: "Our ideas will overcome your ideas. We are going to cut the country's whole value system to shreds... We have a superior way of life. We Indians have a more human philosophy of life. We Indians will show this country how to act human. Someday this country will revise… its laws in terms of human beings instead of property. If Red Power is to be a power in this country it is because it is ideological. What is the ultimate value of a man's life?"

In November 1995, NASA released photos of pillars of hydrogen gas. After they aired, thousands of people called in, saying they saw the face of Jesus in the gas cloud. On his head was not a crown of thorns, but the statue of liberty crown. A baby calf could also be seen. The calf was symbolic of Miracle (white buffalo born the previous year) announcing the return of White Buffalo Woman. Jesus wearing the statue of liberty crown, foretold our deliverance from Jehovah.

Planet Earth

Michael Jackson

Planet earth, my home, my place,
a capricious anomaly in the sea of space.
Do you care, have you a part
in the deepest emotions of my own heart?
Tender with breezes, caressing and whole,
alive with music, haunting my soul.
In my veins I've felt the mystery,
of corridors of time, books of history.
Life songs of ages throbbing in my blood
have danced the rhythm of the tide and flood.
Your misty clouds, your electric storm
were turbulent tempests in my own form.
I've licked the salt, the bitter, the sweet,
of every encounter, of passion, of heat.
Your riotous color, your fragrance, your taste,
have thrilled my senses beyond all haste.
In your beauty I've known the how,

of timeless bliss, this moment of now...

Planet Earth, gentle and blue,
With all my heart, I love you

Moriah's Message 21
Uncleanness

The scrolls of healing lay neglected
Beneath the shifting shadows of the desert...
The gentle Jesus was lost...
In the image of a crucified God (Szekely)

In the 3rd century Jesus' words were recorded in Aramaic. They ended up in the Vatican archives and Royal archives of the Hapsburg's. One text was published as <u>The Essene Gospel Of Peace</u> translated by Szekely (1928). The quotes and teachings of Jesus in this message came from this book.

Jesus said the earth is our mother. The blood that runs in our veins is born from her blood (water). The air we breathe is born from her breath (wind). Our bones are born from her rocks. Our flesh is born from her flesh- her fruits. Our mother is in us, and we are in her. She gave us her body and one day she will take it back. Our mother is above all living things.

If we eat at the table of our earth mother, our breath will be her breath, our blood- her blood, our bone- her bone, our flesh- her flesh, our bowels- her bowels. Our eyes and ears will be her eyes and ears. The light in our eyes will be bright as the sun, and we will look upon it with unflinching eyes.

Jesus said: "If you eat living food, the same will quicken you, but if you kill your food, the dead food will kill you also. For life comes only from life, and from death comes always death..." If we eat flesh our breath will become short and evil smelling, our blood will thicken and blacken, our bones will knot and break, our flesh will wax fat and watery, our bowels will fill with rot. Our earth mother will then take our breath, blood, bone, flesh, bowels, eyes, and ears, and then she will take the life which she gave us.

Jesus said "kill not, neither eat the flesh of your innocent prey, lest you become the slaves of Satan... the flesh of slain beasts in his body will become his own tomb... whoso eats the flesh of slain beasts, eats of the body of death. For in his blood, every drop of their blood turns to poison; in his breath, their breath to stink, in his flesh, their flesh to boils; in his bones, their bones to chalk; in his bowels, their bowels to decay; in his eyes, their eyes to scales; in his ears, their ears to waxy issue. And their death will become his death... for he is **turned into a wild beast** himself." Jehovah said "you will kill of your herd and your flock which the Lord has given you (Deut 12:21)." He commanded: "you will eat flesh." Jehovah loves the smell of burning flesh and demanded animal sacrifice. Jesus said this is of Satan.

Digested animal flesh be - comes flesh of your flesh and blood of your blood. If you eat animal flesh on a regular basis, you will resemble the animal.

Do you know someone who looks like a cow, chicken, or pig? Eating animals will literally make you part cow, part chicken and part pig. Many people are part cow from eating beef. When Jared was little, he pointed to a fat lady and said 'look at that cow over there.' I was embarrassed but now I realize he was seeing her astral body, which was part cow.

Factory-farm animals (cows, chickens, turkeys, pigs, salmon, tuna, cod, trout, halibut) are confined in crowded spaces and cages, from birth to slaughter. Those transported to slaughterhouses have their throats slit while still alive. Many remain conscious as they are plunged into hot water for defeathering or skinned and hacked apart

When we eat factory farm animals, we take in their life of torture. Do you have a sense of dread while eating your Sunday roast? When our bodies are filled with the rotting flesh of tortured animals, our minds fill with fear and terror. This leads to warfare with each other. Jesus said do not cook food; eat it raw. Wild animals kill with their claws and fangs, devouring their prey raw. We do not have claws and fangs because we are not designed to eat animals.

Dairy 'intensive farming' increases productivity with heavy use of antibiotics, pesticides and fertilizer. Mega diaries keep milk cows in tiny tie-stalls, tied at the neck between milking. Milk production is greatly increased with hormones, yet calves never taste their mama's milk. They are taken after birth, before she can even lick her baby and confined in a small space. A tube shoved down the throat force-feeds the baby calve milk replacement with blood plasma and chicken litter (feathers, chicken feed, poop). Mama's milk is sold to us.

Boy calves are put in tight confinement so they cannot move and intentionally starved to keep their meat white. They are killed at 2 months for veal. Girl calves are confined for a year, until they can be inseminated for a milk cow. Participating in this artificial production of calves and milk (eating veal, drinking cow milk) is an act of violence against nature. It puts you in danger of getting Alzheimer's, from calves eating blood plasma and chicken feed made with slaughter waste and cow bones.

Cattle and pigs are fed grocery waste (candy, bread, yogurt plastic packaging). Beef parts are used in candy, gelatins, drugs, supplements, etc. Eating these animals and products can cause mad cow disease (CDJ) and Alzheimer's. CDJ outbreaks began in 1999; Alzheimer's surged along with it, growing 55%. There can be spongy brain changes in Alzheimer's, and Alzheimer's plaques in CJD. CDJ comes from modified cell proteins that eat the brain, creating sponge-like holes. Prions are part of a cell's natural structure and only mutate if the cow is fed cow parts (blood plasma, bone meal).

During Sunday dinner when Jarvis was three, he asked for more ham. We passed him the plate and he took a big piece. His aunt said 'that's certainly no vegetarian you're raising!' Jarvis asked 'what's a vegetarian?' He was told it's someone who doesn't eat meat. Then Jarvis asked 'what's meat?' He was told 'it's an animal.' Jarvis wanted to know what kind of animal he was eating and was told it was pig. Jarvis had a vision of two little pigs; one was taken to be killed and eaten. He said 'I think it's sick to eat animals!' Jarvis refused to eat the meat on his plate. From that moment he was vegetarian.

When King Nebuchadnezzar took the Israelites captive, his servant was told to bring the brightest children to the palace. Daniel was among them. The children were given meat, which Daniel refused. Eating animals was a commandment of the Lord; children who did not obey were stoned to death. Daniel must have hidden his vegetarian diet from his family before their capture. The servant said: "why should the King see your face worse liking than the other children? You will make me endanger my head." Daniel asked Melzar to let him and friends have pulse (food grown from soil: fruit, veggies, grains) instead of meat for ten days, and see if they looked healthier than the children who ate meat. He agreed. "At the end of ten days they appeared fairer and fatter in flesh than the children which ate... meat. Melzar took away the portion of their meat... and gave them pulse (Daniel 1: 1—10)."

Our digestive system was not designed to eat flesh; it rots before the stomach breaks it down. The intestines secrete mucus for protection from poisons, preventing the absorption of nutrients; parasites live in it. If their habitat is not removed, they multiply, giving their host cravings for foods that feed them. Eating flesh turns our bodies into cesspools of rot. Fecal build-up causes putrefaction; this rot radiates death in our body. Pockets of pus and debris accumulate and can increase the colon's circumference four+ times its normal size. This is why people have bulging lower abdomens. See Cleanse and Purify Thyself (Anderson) 1—2.

Jesus said for every year that we eat dead foods we must fast and pray for one day. One week of fasting will eliminate seven years of rot and decay from our bodies. While we fast, Jesus said we must "seek the fresh air of the forest and fields. There, in the midst of them, you will find the angel of air. Take off your shoes and clothing and let the angel of air embrace all your body. Then breathe long and deeply, that the angel of air may be brought within you. The angel of air will cast out... all evil-smelling and unclean things..."

"Let the angel of water embrace all your body. Cast your-selves wholly into her enfolding arms. As you move the air with your breath, move the water with your body. The angel of water will cast out... unclean and evil-smelling things... Seek the angel of sunlight to embrace all your body. Breathe long and deeply that she may be brought within you and cast out all evil smelling and unclean things which defiled you without and within. The uncleanness will depart in haste... by your breath, your skin, your mouth and your hinder and privy parts.

These things you will see with your eyes and smell with your nose."

"When the uncleanness is gone from your body, your blood will become as pure as our earth mother's blood... your breath will become as pure as the breath of flowers, your flesh, as pure as the flesh of fruits... the light of your eye, as clear and bright as the brightness of the sun... Now the angels of the earth mother will serve you, and your breath, blood, and flesh, will be one with the breath, blood and flesh of the earth mother."

"Many sick people followed Jesus' words, and sought the banks of the streams. They took off their shoes and clothing, they fasted, and they gave up their bodies to the angels of air, of water and of sunshine. And the earth mother's angels embraced them... The breath of some became as stinking as that which is loosed from the bowels. Some had an issue of spittle, vomit rose from them... Uncleanness flowed from their mouths, in some by the nose, in others by the eyes and ears. And many had sweat come from all their body. On many limbs great hot boils broke forth... and in many their urine was... thick as honey, in others it was... black and as hard as the sand. Many belched stinking gases from their bowels... Their stench became so great, none could bear it... they looked upon these abominations of Satan, from which the angels had saved them, and rendered thanks..."

"Breathe long and deeply at all your meals, that the angel of air may bless your repast. Chew your food well with your teeth that it may become water, and the angel of water will turn it into blood in your body... Never sit at the table before the angel of appetite calls you... If you eat in sorrow, or anger, or without desire, it becomes a poison in your body..."

"Eat all things, even as they are found at the table of our earth mother. Cook not, neither mix all things one with another lest your bowels become as steaming bogs... If you mix together all sorts of food in your body, then the peace of your body will cease, and endless war will rage in you."

Jesus said: **1.** eat one food at a time. **2.** eat things as they are (raw). Grocery products with mixed ingredients are against Jesus' teachings. Foodstuffs are designed to wreck your health; stop eating them. MSG, Aspartame, sodium benzoate, and sucralose are added to thousands of foodstuffs. They're poisons labeled as natural flavors and spices. MSG is addictive; aspartame overstimulates the nervous system, disrupts the brain's chemical messengers and breaks down into formaldehyde. Sodium benzoate in soda damages bone marrow. Sucralose calcifies the kidneys and damages the immune system. Fluoride (added to water) and bromine (food additive) block the absorption of iodine, causing thyroid malfunction, obesity and cancer. Baby formula contains synthetic DHA and ARA. These poisons create inflammation and infection. A baby's only defense is to cry after feedings from stomach pain, and throw up.

In Fighting The Food Giants, Stitt says: "There is a force in this country that's out to poison your food, make it addictive, and manipulate your body chemistry." If you stop eating these products you will have hunger pains caused by withdrawal symptoms. Your body is craving chemicals that send false hunger messages to your brain, so you will eat more. Jehovah said "when I have broken the staff of your bread... you shall eat and not be satisfied (Lev 26:26)." Jesus said never eat until you are full, Satan tempts us always to eat more.

Jesus said to eat one food at every meal: a bowl of brown rice- nothing else, a bowl of beans for another meal, cabbage for another, etc. Jesus said to chew your food to water. In The Complete Macrobiotic Diet, Waxman says chewing every bite to liquid (50+ times) eliminates digestion and bowel trouble. Chewing acts as a pump that circulates body fluids, regulates blood flow and dispels negative energy (chewing/biting releases aggression).

Disease happens when your body is loaded with toxins. Toxins come from meat, milk, prescription drugs, vaccines, soy, artificial sweeteners, processed and prepared foods with multiple ingredients, white flour, microwaved foods, table salt, sugar, stress, pesticides, chemclouds, and more. Eat wholesome mono meals and fast as Jesus taught.

60-billion animals are raised on factory farms and in labs for experiments. Monkeys, pigs and sheep and are crossed with human genes for organ implants. People are murdered for organs sold on the black market. Organ donors may have organs removed before death to keep blood pumping. Transplanted organs have consciousness which is trapped in the recipient. Someday organ transplants will cease. When we stop eating animals as Jesus taught, stop using them for tests and research, and stop raising animals for organ transplants, humanity, animals and nature will heal, including the atmosphere. When 60-billion farm animals are eliminated, oxygen levels will skyrocket.

Factory farms raise GM crops that damage soil and ruin health. GM seeds have a lethal gene and require a chemical to germinate. Farmers cannot use their seeds for planting. Pellets coated with poison and DNA are forced into the cell's genetic region with a high-energy gun, violently raping plant cells with agrobacterium- a plant disease that causes tumors to grow. Agrobacterium is also used in sewer plants. People working at sewer plants have a higher percent of Morgellons and test positive for agrobacterium. Once this bacterium enters humans and animals, they act like parasites. If we fast for a few days our body will destroy them.

GM crops: sugarcane, alfalfa, soybean, corn, potatoes, peas, squash, tomatoes, rice, wheat, flax, vegetable oil, tobacco, cotton. Bees gather pollen from GM crops and have GM material in their honey. Milk, cheese and eggs contain GM material from cows and chickens eating GM crops.

Eat raw foods. Have a weekly one-day water fast. Sunbath naked in streams. Go on a yearly, two-week water fast. You will regain your heath and live longer. When you fast, fat cells release fatty acid molecules for energy, decreasing the number and size of your fat cells. Enlarged fat cells produce abnormal amounts of hormones. These hormones slow metabolism and increase inflammation, contributing to disease. Fasting helps heal many chronic conditions.

In The Transformational Power of Fasting, Buhner says the body eliminates bacteria, viruses, fibroid tumors, waste products in the blood, buildup around the joints, and stored fat when we fast. The mind and heart release toxic buildup as well. The Master Cleanser (Burroughs) is a 10-day liquid cleansing diet of fresh-squeezed lemons, maple syrup and cayenne. The Grape Cure (Brandt) kills tumors.

When you eat right and fast as Jesus taught, your body eliminates toxins and cancer cells die. Lymph nodes trap and destroy cancer cells when we fast. Doctors cut into these lumps, making them divide and grow (biopsy). They remove lymph nodes that destroy cancer, mutilating the patient.

Radiation and chemotherapy shorten their life. In <u>There Are No Incurable Diseases</u>, Wilson gives remedies on how to cure any disease using alternative healing methods. The information in this book can help you restore your health

Jesus said our earth mother gave us her body and 'none but she heals you.' Eating raw food grown in healthy soil purifies us. Our body heals and we return to the bosom of our earth mother. We will then hear our mother's heartbeat. If an earthquake, tornado or other natural disaster comes, we will know and be prepared. Jesus said to only eat what our own lands bear. Do not eat foods brought from far countries. Our earth mother gives foods that are best for people in every terrain. Only eat from the table of your earth mother. Plant a garden. Sprout beans, seeds and grains. Watch <u>The Wheat-grass Trucker</u>; he will inspire you.

In <u>Vegetable Gardening Encyclopedia,</u> the editors say: "Live off the land in your backyard. Grow everything that goes into a salad right there on the patio. Train cucumbers over the balcony of your apartment. Make house plants work for you; plant tomatoes in a hanging basket and cabbages in the window box. Have an herb garden in the kitchen..."

'The sun that grows veggies is the creative power within you. The rich earth is the ground of your being. The rain is your nourishment.'

In <u>Growing And Using The Healing Herbs</u>, Gaea and Shandor Weiss say: "The garden is a mirror and we see ourselves reflected in it... gardening cultivates our minds and imaginations, as much as it produces a tangible harvest... We can feel ourselves in the rich and receptive element of earth- the ground of our being. We can see ourselves in the waters of nourishment which come as rain... The sun's warmth which sets the garden ablaze with greens is the essence of the warmth and creative powers within us... The cycle of planting, growing, harvesting and using plants is part of a holistic experience... (and) draws us closer... to our own natural rhythms."

Jesus Was Androgynous
S/he spoke against the violent Hebrew God
and had no Gospel, Judgment or Kingdom

Moriah's Message 22
Dream Lives

We are dream-living infinite lives in parallel worlds. We have awake and asleep dream-lives, and they're connected. As our awareness expands in one world, it expands in them all. Our soul merges with higher selves in other worlds and we become more integrated. As we journey through dream-lives we receive messages. Dreams cut through defenses to the core of the problem. "To him who learns its language it reveals what really troubles the man, what is central on his mind when not distracted... No other method begins to approach dream analysis for speed and accuracy in understanding... motivations and emotional forces (Leon J. Saul)."

Angels are souls on the other side who once lived on earth. They commune with us while awake and asleep and can physically materialize if needed. You can pray for dream-visits from friends, family, angels, anyone. Angels bring information to us that we need. You may not remember their visits if they come during sleep but the information you receive will come to you when needed. When inspiration hits you 'out of the blue' it may have been given to you in a dream.

Black Elk and Einstein came to me while awake and in my dreams. Jenner came to me while awake and Jesus came to me in a dream. When I pray to Jesus, his love fills my heart but his Spirit doesn't enter me. Never invite an entity to enter you. Beings in the light do not enter your aura or your heart.

You have a higher Self (part of your soul that doesn't incarnate); it is connected to your soul and watches over you. It brings inspiration like your guardian angel does. It can appear to people on earth and parallel worlds at the same time. You soul can have more than one physical incarnation on the same timeline. We are simultaneously living our past and future lives, including our near-future, on earth and other worlds. Your future soul and higher Self may commune with you while sleeping, through your dreams.

You can enter another person's dream and you will both dream the same dream. David dreamed he put the brain-wave synchronizer he invented, on his little brother. Jarvis didn't like it and started crying, because David wouldn't take it off. The next morning Jarvis told David, 'I had a dream that you put ear phones on me and wouldn't take them off!'

Years ago, I dreamed a satanic nurse was vaccinating children. The serum contained poison and a demon was sitting on the needle tip; he entered the child when injected. I tried to stop her and she came after me with her needle. I was running and saw Jared. I asked 'is this a dream?' He said 'you figure it out.' I decided it was and ended it. The next morning Jared said 'I was in your dream last night. You wanted to know if you were dreaming and I didn't tell you.'

In 2012 London Olympics performed my nightmare with zombie nurses and demons chasing children in hospital beds. Seven years later children received Covid vaccines-the greatest attack against children ever executed.

The astral plane contains different worlds, superimposed and separated by vibration. The lowest level where demons dwell vibrates to earth. Deceased souls that satisfy cravings for drugs, sex, food, lewd fantasies, etc. are here. Some disincarnate souls roaming earth do not know they are dead and play out fantasies. Some committed suicide and remain on the earth until their death-time comes.

Jehovah's heavens are in the next layer, where Christians, Jews and Muslims continue to live out their various religions. Demons cannot enter these heavens; the light would dis-integrate them. When Jehovah's worshippers manifest his image and worship him, they feed him through etheric cords. The Lord dwells in heaven, through Christians in heaven who dwell on him. After Christians leave heaven with Black Elk, they will go on to higher realms.

Souls who reincarnate from lower worlds don't remember former lives and return quickly, with little spiritual progression made. When earth ascends lower realms will collapse, demons will dissolve and souls will enter higher worlds. In the higher worlds, souls continue their spiritual growth while assisting those on earth and in lower astral worlds. Souls in the higher worlds remain for a while, before incarnating or entering higher realms.

False beliefs, darkness and addictions go with us at death. They can be overcome. In <u>A Wanderer in the Land of Spirits</u> (1896) Farnese tells about Franchezzo's experiences in the afterlife. He is in the lower worlds with other dark souls. Franchezzo travels upward toward the light as he atones for the revengeful acts he committed during his life on earth. He saves himself- a hard process, but help is available. He in turn helps other souls in the lower realms. <u>The World Unseen</u> (Borgia) and <u>Hearts of the Fathers</u> (Lawrence) also reveals dark realms and what souls must do to leave them.

{In 1972, Margaret Tweddell contacted Ruth Taylor's father, a minister who died in 1970. Tweddell receives telepathic messages while in full control; entities do not enter her. Taylor records their visit in <u>Witness From Beyond</u>. A. D. Mattson describes his world as a replica of ours, only of "a finer substance, and we are not bound by our objective reality as you are." He said they materialize clothes, change them with thought and create any kind of landscape they want. It 'remains as objective reality as long as we wish.'

People who die from illness and disability often bring their symptoms with them. Mattson said there are hospitals on the astral plane for people who are not able to function effectively when they first pass over. He said there are libraries with records of everything that ever happened. You can look up information and receive it in visual or written form. Souls in the afterlife pursue various studies. There are musicians, botanists, teachers, artists, ministers, librarians, and healers.

Some souls in the afterlife further develop the skills that they acquired on earth; others train in different occupations. Mattson said there is an incredible choice of occupation 'in what you may like to call heaven'- greater than there is on earth. 'Once we are committed, we are committed for a considerable time.' Most souls work in groups. When their purpose is fulfilled, the astral body is cast off. It disintegrates, and they go on to higher worlds in their Spirit body.

Mattson had a friend who was a botanist on earth. He grows different species of orchids, bringing information to people in botanical gardens. Information, gathered through studies in the spiritual world, is passed on to people in the same areas of study. This knowledge is often given while sleeping. Mattson's cousin works with people injured in war, giving them courage and strength to go on living, even though they may be crippled. They help the disabled when they are out of the body during sleep. Before he died Mattson attended three astral meetings in his dreams. They were blocked from his memory until death. Matson said "most people would not be able to function effectively if they were aware of their astral experiences during sleep."

Every group has angelic beings that work with them. Every study group, seminar, class, religious service, staff meeting, etc. attracts angels. When people experience a shift in consciousness, their circle of angels help it flower while sleeping. Angels help us reexperience our insights, to know what this enlightenment will someday mean in our life. Souls in the spiritual world bring us the 'Wind of Spirit' to help us expand our higher-level thoughts. They look after the new light in every person, so it will grow in him. It may take a few hours, or it may take weeks or years.

Souls on the other side commune with us when we pray. Mattson said people's privacy cannot be violated. When you pray to the angels they can help you with any situation, assist you with your classes, a project, research, whatever you need help with. "Those who know how to deal in these areas will come. They will direct ideas and thoughts [so] they may pick up a book, open a newspaper, make a phone call or get in touch with a person who can help them."

Mattson had a desire to see space. A being of light came and held out his hand. Mattson took it and suddenly they were in space. "The stars and earth were alive, and they had many lines of light. They were of varying colors, like miniature neon lights... Streams of power were coming down from all angles, to the earth. There were also streams that were going between star, and star, and star, like a tremendous web. These streams of power had a set pattern, like the web of a fishing net, which was all continuous, with the power of lights pulsating backward and forward. I felt caught up in all of this, to the very depths of my being. I felt myself expanding and expanding until I thought, I'm going to burst!" At this moment, Mattson went back.

When he returned, Mattson heard music. "I felt... a beat which was unchanging. I also felt lighter pulses and beats which varied... I could feel... a deep awareness of myself as an individual. Above that were all the other rhythms and all the other pulsations, sounds, and vibrations of all other things in the creation... a tremendous harmony of sound... We all respond and vibrate to our own note." Mattson said everything emits and receives sound. "It is a tremendous feeling to know that one is part of all of this and it gives one the most powerful sense of belonging... this sense of belonging must be given to people on earth... they belong to the great, expanding, universal soul. They belong to the Creator... All things are interconnected through... the Creator."

Mattson realized the colored lights, sounds and music he saw and heard, were the essence. The moment he realized this, he smelled many perfumes. 'This is the next stage in the evolution of man. Man is going to know by the sense of smell.' Mattson said the ultimate goal of each 'sacred personality' is to be in tune with this universal essence, a 'beautiful bead on the thread of the essence of the whole.'}

People who committed horrific crimes and die with a tiny soul will be welcomed by angels. They can enter the light, see everything that happened during their earth life and know why it occurred. They will release karma as their awareness expands and their soul will heal and grow brighter. Souls who go to the light receive all the love, nurturing and support they need. When ready, they enter the Great Halls of Study where they can further their spiritual growth while helping others.

Some people who die are afraid of the light, but there is only love (no judgement) on the other side. Going through the light-portal with angels, friends or family takes you to the highest Spirit World that you can enter. If you don't go to the light when you die, the portal will close. You will become earthbound, unless you pray to the angels for help. They will then come and open the light portal for you.

Many earthbound ghosts are tricked and captured by demon-ghosts who feed on them. If their soul is weak they will need energy from the living to sustain themselves. Demon-ghosts command other ghosts to attack people and bring earthbound ghosts to them, to feed on and enslave. They are threatened with pain and terrorized if they refuse.

This is Jehovah's hell where he tortures demons and trapped souls. Earthbound ghosts caught in this cycle need someone in the light to come rescue them.

Ghosts (earthbound, demonic) attach to people, to syphon their life-force. They imprint their host with negative thoughts and the habits and ailments they carried in life- their abusive behaviors, pain, physical and mental illness, emotional trauma, etc. causing them to manifest in their host. Ghosts who crave drugs, attach to drug addicts, increasing their addiction. Ghosts are the voices that schizophrenics and mediums hear. They lie, mimic voices of loved ones, pretend to be angels and deceive them any way they can.

Some ghosts do not know they died. Funerals help the deceased acknowledge their death. This is why people who pass on are not usually taken to their home in the afterlife, until after their funeral. Some souls don't want to leave loved ones and some want revenge. The importance of entering the light when it appears after we die, needs to be well-known. Ghosts cause trouble, for themselves and us. Both earthbound and demonic ghosts exist on negative emotions and ill health. They influence us to be unhealthy and bombard us with negative impulses, encouraging us to be hostile, judgmental, jealous and reactive.

Souls who don't go to the light after death sometimes attach to family. If they died long ago, they often coexist from 'generation to generation' through their bloodline. Demons do this too, possessing future generations of their ancestors.

Your soul is your Spirit entwined with wisdom, knowledge and memories from past lives. Souls grow and brighten when you commune with your Spirit; they become dim and decay when you do not. Soulless people do not have a higher Self to guide them. Cut off from their Spirit, they become robotic and deadpan. They cannot feel empathy, they have no remorse or guilt, and do not experience higher feelings like love or joy. You cannot have a soul connection with soulless people. They're parasites surviving at the expense of others. "It can be unnerving and strange to interact with someone who's lost all connection to their soul (Xander Gordon)."

Soulless people do not like physical contact; they don't feel intimacy or care about sex. They conserve their energy and are more likely to abuse their partner with mind games than physical abuse. They may say what you want to hear, to use what you tell them against you, or pretend you said something you didn't. They fake feelings, including tears. They sap their partner's energy by feeding off it, and may cause physical and mental illness from relentless, covert abuse.

Soulless people are dangerous; they want to exploit and hurt you. At death, they become demon-ghosts. Without a host to feed on they wither away. If soulless people pray for help and listen to their intuition, they will connect with their Spirit and evolve a soul. Even a tiny soul will survive death.

Cut off from their Spirit, soulless people can't receive life-force through their crown chakra; they pull energy from others through their solar plexus. Before an attack, they may inflict verbal abuse, to upset or frighten their victim and lower their vibration. They can then pull energy from the person while putting dark energy in them. Receiving dark energies from a psychic attack can cause irrational behavior; energy that doesn't belong to you is difficult to control. Repeated attacks can cause mental illness.

If your partner is covertly abusive (gaslighting, emotional and verbal abuse) he may set you up for psychic attacks. Psychic attacks weaken your astral body causing insomnia. Stargazing before bed can help you sleep. Stars give off astral energy. Psychic attacks can throw the astral and physical body out of alignment, causing illness. Imagine a bridge, with you on one end and your abuser on the other. An energy cord connects you through your solar plexuses. Ask your guardian angel to cut and dissolve the cord, and balance your astral and physical bodies.

Trauma can cause soul loss. If you lost a talent or ability, the part of your soul that holds that quality may be missing. Other symptoms of soul loss are crushing sadness, being disoriented, depressed, unreal, detached, memory gaps and personality changes. Soul loss creates voids in you aura that make you susceptible to entity attachments like ghosts. Soul parts could be stuck in the past, stolen by someone, lodged in a parent, lover or friend. They could be living out fantasies in the astral realm or captured by demons. Soul parts may be nested in your aura, separated from your soul. You can ask angels in the light to retrieve and integrate your lost soul parts.

Astral fragments are negative parts of peoples' astral body

that are shed at death. They are parasites and embed in people so they won't disintegrate. A person's astral body can fragment before death, causing Alzheimer's. They lose their memory because pieces of it break off; memory is held in your astral body. People with Alzheimer's may be attacked by their own fragments, causing more decay. When bodies are cremated, astral fragments and bones are destroyed. Graveyards are robbed of bones for satanic rituals.

Humanity's darkness is released on others when they die. Most people have astral fragments and ghosts attached to them. Soul loss, abuse, mental ailments, addictions and disorders make you susceptible to entity attachments. Ghosts (dead people, demons), soul parts, thought entities and astral fragments come from humans, both living and dead. Soul parts can be retrieved and integrated. Ghosts, entities and astral fragments can be sent to the light. Astral shards, demons, thought entities, curses etc. will dissolve.

Help each other retrieve lost soul parts, remove attached ghosts, fragments, etc. Releasing attached ghosts is not difficult but you need to know how to handle situations that arise. Form a study group to learn entity release therapy and have sessions with each other. In <u>Other Lives, Other Selves</u>, Woolger says he formed a study group to learn past-life regression. "We set out to read everything we could… Six of us paired up to work with each other and agreed to come together every other week and share our findings…."

Entity Release books: The Unquiet Dead (Fiore). Entity Possession (Sagan). Remarkable Healings (Modi). Defeat The Enemy Within (Skillas). Freeing the Captives (Ireland-Frey). Spirit Releasement Therapy (Baldwin). Rapid Entity Attachment Release (Komianos). Earthbound Spirits are Attached to You (Schwimmer).

When my grandson was three, another personality would sometimes emerge. I knew this was an earthbound ghost that needed to go to the light. The next time I saw the little ghost take over I told him 'you don't belong here. You are supposed to be in heaven. Look up at the light. Do you see the angels? They are here to take you to heaven. You will like it there; it will be fun.' He left and I never saw him again. A couple months later my grandson said 'Nana I know what's in heaven.' 'What' I asked, 'toys' he said. He saw the light too; it had toys for the lost soul to play with.

Demons are in the astral realm where they can see auras and other energies. They can travel backward and forward in what we perceive as time. They spy on people, since they are invisible, read our thoughts and bring this information to dark sorcerers, gurus and cult leaders who work with them. This makes the guru look enlightened because he seems to have psychic knowledge and visions, predict the future and read minds, but he is not using his own abilities.

The deceptions of dark sorcerers, gurus and cult leaders is revealed in their character. They may be demanding, controlling, resentful and jealous, with big egos. Money is another red flag; many get rich demanding money from followers. Doctrines and rituals also reveal their darkness.

As we awaken, our psychic senses open, auras are seen and thoughts are heard. When ghosts are seen by everyone, even ghosts nested in people, they will be sent to the light where they will be supported. People who feed on the energies of others will be seen doing it; they will be stopped. When demons no longer have human hosts or earthbound ghosts to feed on, they will feast on each other until they vanish. When we ascend, evil people may fall to a world that matches their vibration and disintegrate with its collapse.

Inner earth inhabitants visit parallel earths, astral worlds and spiritual realms, like Mattson in the afterlife and like we can when asleep. They can travel to the 'past' see the 'future' and remote view anything, even other planets. Inner earth humans can disappear and reappear anywhere, changing their looks to blend in, like angels. These abilities were lost to us when we replaced the Goddess with a demon-ghost. When earth ascends we will regain our lost, natural abilities.

Moriah's Message 23

I Am A Dreamer of Dreams

The Lord said if a prophet or dreamer of dreams arises and turns you from him, put him to death (Deut 13:1—5). Jehovah knew a dreamer of dreams would bring him to an end.

{Years before I started this book I had two dreams about my destiny. I didn't know their meaning until many years later.

Destiny Dream. I hiked a mountain and saw a lamb at the top, tied to an altar. The valley below was filled with slain lambs. I could prevent the lamb's death but didn't want to get involved. I kept silent until the knife was raised, then shouted STOP! My shout ended the slaughter. The lambs were un- aware of danger until the knife was raised. Jehovah said "I will make them drunken that they may rejoice, and sleep a perpetual sleep… I will bring them down like lambs to the slaughter (Jer 51:39, 40)."

Destiny Dream. I left a cloth in a church kitchen. Worms came out of it, multiplied and ate the walls, exposing the inside structure. People were horrified and ran outside; a few stayed. The people who left grew into vast crowd, as far as I could see. The building collapsed, killing those who stayed. The building is Jehovah's plan of salvation, the people inside are worshippers, the cloth is this book. The worms that eat the walls are words in my book that expose Jehovah. The Greatest Deception becomes well known; Christians, Jews and Muslims leave their religion. Those who remained worked for Satan inside his churches.}

While writing my messages, I wondered if The Holy Ghost was really a demon. Christians don't show signs of demonic possession. I asked the Creator for a sign to show me if this is true. I read an article that day that said the most dangerous predator conceals himself until the kill. Christians are the Lord's quiet resting places. Their demon lays quiet as he sups life-force; they are hidden unless they strike.

I watched a show that day about a man who wanted to prove God's existence to his brother. He told him he was going to sacrifice his daughter because God told Isaac to sacrifice his son. He put his 2-year-old on the kitchen table and shot her, then waited for God to heal her. When he realized she was dying, he panicked- she wasn't baptized. He stripped naked and ran to his church with his daughter. She died in his arms.

The next evening, the news aired a segment on religious violence. It showed a Nazi spreading a message of racism and hate, and a Black preacher telling his congregation they are Israelites and Black people had to kill everyone else to receive God's inheritance. I embraced my destiny and felt a physical weight pressing down on my shoulders.

I walked to my sacred spot on the cliff and watched the sun set. When it went down a huge owl appeared in front of me. He landed on a rock right below me. I sat down to get closer and my movement didn't startle him. We looked at each other and then he flew inside the rock cliff! The owl is Jehovah and the rock is his shelter. If Christians, Jews and Muslims reject their God he will have no shelter and he will dissolve.

While writing my messages, I dreamed about a store with a clock; its hands were toothbrushes. The store only sold toothpaste. The store is the Lord's churches; the toothpaste is the gospel, which pastes our teeth shut (teeth symbolize power). The clock is the countdown to Armageddon. The toothbrush symbolizes Jehovah winning or losing by the skin of his teeth. We are in a race for our lives; reject the Lord's toothpaste.

The morning that I awoke from this dream, the news showed Billy Graham preaching via satellite. He said with a voice that traveled around the earth, "Fear God and give him glory... the hour of his judgment has come." This broadcast was the angel John saw flying in the midst of heaven (Rev 14:6, 7).

February 14th 1999, I had three dreams about this book. **1st** dream I watched a movie; the ending showed early dawn with 12 stars in the sky. I left the theater, it was early dawn, and there were 12 stars with the same configuration. The movie came true. The stars are Messages 1—12; they bring enlightenment. **2nd** dream I helped an angel plant 13 saplings. The angel was White Buffalo Woman; the little trees are Messages 13—25. When they take root in our heart, we will awaken and reestablish our connection with the Goddess of Creation. **3rd** dream Jared and I were at the Boise River (message 19).

The Goddess whispers to our heart and her spiritual fire fills us with brilliant light. The Goddess sings to our soul and we fall in love with being alive. The Goddess calls to our Spirit and we hear the echo of infinity. The Goddess invites us to play and we dance wild and free in the moonlight, run until our heart pounds, swim in the creek, roll in the grass like a child and stargaze in wonderment. The Goddess speaks to our womb, a baby is conceived and birthed on her wings. The Goddess calls to the world and we awaken. Jehovah and his demon-ghosts are cast out and the Golden World returns.

While writing messages, I dreamed I was in a classroom sitting at a desk browsing my published book. I was surprised to see it was filled with images. Jason came in and wanted money to buy Cracker Jacks from a vending machine. I gave him the cookies in my purse. He sat at a desk to eat them. Jason's Dad came in and was furious I gave Jason cookies. He yelled 'Jason is now over the hump' and then left. I told Jason 'your Dad's rage can't hurt you.' I saw a kangaroo outside and went to the windows to see it; an angry lion was following her. I pointed them out to Jason, then went back to the desk and browsed my book, discovering more images.

The classroom is research that went into writing our book. Sitting at the desk is Sandra writing it. Sandra going to the window is our soul exchange. I returned to the desk and sat down with the book, symbolizing me writing Part Two. Sandra was surprised to see images in her book; they were added later, after our soul exchange. The dream-book was The Greatest Deception in the near-future; it glowed with beauty and power. Sandra added lyrics and poems to her messages, I added lyrics and poems to my chapters, and all of the images in this book. The lyrics, poems and images, mixed with other text, encourages whole-brain thinking.

Jason wanted Cracker Jacks from a vending machine. Cracker is Jehovah, the Slave Master cracking the whip. Jacks is slang for men's dominance through patriarchy. Vending (selling) and machines (tools) are used in business operations. The Global Elite use commerce to control us. Vending machines take money and kick out mass-produced products that pillage the earth. We make the products, wear them, eat them and entertain ourselves with them, becoming enslaved to our bosses.

My purse with cookies is this book exposing Jehovah. I gave Jason cookies. Cookie is a smart man; smart is enlightened, and pain or remorse. Jason eating cookies symbolized Christians digesting this book. It enlightens them, yet causes anguish. John the Revelator also eats this book. It is bittersweet: bitter- hard to digest, and sweet or fresh in its Bible commentary. Its enlightenment causes distress. Jehovah is revealed as an enraged father (Father In Heaven) and an angry lion (demonic beast) who stalks its prey (kangaroo). Jehovah said 'I will devour them like a lion.' The Kangaroo is Christians, Jews and Muslims united against their God (Allah, Lord, Christ).

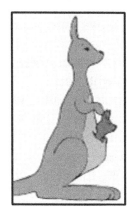

kangaroo legs move as one. Jehovah's worshippers break free of him- hop the fence, spring back- rebound from their sorrow, and regain their sovereignty or power- hop up. My message titles form an outline of a figure with long ears, an oblong head, a long rounded belly and large feet. I watched it form as I wrote messages. After renaming titles, the kangaroo outline remained.

Kangaroos never stop growing. Mama kangaroos carry their babies for the first year. In a Kangaroo Court people settle their own disputes. Kangaroos symbolize humanity growing spiritually, governing their communities with wisdom, mothers keeping their babies safe, ease of movement around obstacles and danger, courage, and evolving in leaps and bounds.

Kangaroos symbolize Dreamtime of native Australians. To be in Dreamtime we must keep the law of Creation- respect. If we respect life we will not break creation laws. Dreamtime is the Eternal Now, where there is no past. We step out of time and the light of eternity shines on the world.

In Eagle Vision, McGaa records a vision Eagle Feather had during World War II while doing a Sun Dance, and a vision Fools Crow's had during Yuwipi untying ceremony. The following is my interpretation of these visions.

Sun Dance. Eagle Feather saw the Sun Dance tree turn into a giant sunflower. It bent down, pulled Eagle Feather inside, and thrust him upward. He saw two men; one had a peace pipe, the other a flowering stick. He rode with them on a cloud above the Sun Dance. The man with a pipe threw it at the Sun Dance tree; it burst forth green leaves. A yellow hoop spread out from the tree to the Sun Dance arena.

The cloud took them to a high mountain peak where Black Elk was crying to his Grandfathers. Cavalry were shooting a buffalo herd. A flaming blue man passed out ammunition until the buffalo were exterminated. Missionaries were building boarding schools when a band of Indians returned to the reservation. In the morning, the cavalry opened fire on everyone, killing men, women and children. Missionaries gathered their medicine bundles and peace pipes, and poured oil on them. The blue man appeared and set them on fire. The missionaries forced the Sioux who survived the slaughter, to kneel before their crosses, while the cavalry watched.

Eagle Feather then saw a growling, repulsive man, with fangs and a blue aura, standing on the mountain. He was challenging a Sioux warrior climbing up the mountain. The warrior's eagle-mate circled above them. Their fight came to a standstill and the warrior descended the mountain. His eagle-mate then landed and turned into a woman.

Time changed to the future. The woman climbed the mountain, and the hideous man taunted her. The woman ignored him and built a set of colored stairs— black, white, red, and yellow. Thunder shook the horizon and a bright rainbow flashed in the east. Flames came down from the rainbow. Where the flames landed, flowers bloomed. The flowers turned into people. Most of them were white and they had an aura like tribal people. The men were strong leaders, yet gentle; the women were gentle leaders, yet strong. Their male-female energies were balanced and they were whole.

A wrecked military jet, bleached clean, was embedded in the barren clay. The warrior from the mountain climbed out of it, picked sage to make a sun dancer's wreath, and walked to the withering tree. Black Elk swooped down from the mountain and led him around it. Priests and missionaries tried to attack the warrior, but he stopped them with his wotai stone. The dying tree changed into a red stick with sprouting leaves, and the yellow hoop spread to the horizon.

Sunflower: the sun. Warrior: Black Elk. Dreadful blue man: Jehovah. The slaughter: Wounded Knee massacre. Black Elk fights the blue man, then gives up (becomes Christian). He dies (descends the mountain) and I land (incarnate on earth). I climb the mountain and build the stairs (this book); the stairs expose Jehovah. The thunder shaking the horizon symbolizes Black Elk killing the blue man. The flaming rainbow is a symbol from his vision. The flower people once worshipped Jehovah. They reject him and become whole. The wrecked military jet is Christianity exposed and discarded, on earth and in heaven. The dying tree becomes the sheltering tree. The spreading yellow hoop is the daybreak star, bringing wisdom to the world.

The carvery, missionaries and priests are flashbacks to Black Elk's earth life. Black Elk is transformed and guides himself (warrior) around the dying tree. The tree lives; when humanity becomes whole, like the flower people, the sheltering tree blooms for the children. The two Black Elks are the two men Eagle Feather saw with the peace pipe and the flowering stick, and the two men in Black Elk's vision (future selves) that take him to see his grandfathers, when he is a young boy.

Yuwipi Ceremony. Fools Crow was bound with a rope and covered with a blanket. A song called in Sioux ancestors. Buckskin rattles flew around and tiny blue lights flickered in the dark. When the song ended, the rattles fell to the floor and the lights vanished. Fools Crow was sitting up untied, his blanket was draped over the stove, the rope was wrapped in a tight ball. No one moved during the ceremony.

During the ceremony, Fools Crow saw a red stick become a flowering tree. The horizon had a rainbow; a pair of eagles flew toward it. When they reached the rainbow, the woman-eagle turned into a meadowlark and the rainbow turned into a flowering tree. A profile of a buffalo appeared in the top branches; it changed into a mourning dove. A profile of a man appeared. It changed into a woman. The eagles were Black Elk and White Buffalo Woman. The buffalo that became a mourning dove symbolized White Buffalo Woman helping me expose The Holy Ghost. The man becoming a woman is humanity becoming androgynous. Someday we will be whole, living the eternal dream wrapped in the brilliant light of eternity.

When Sandra was writing her messages, her husband dreamed she had a different personality and hugged everyone. She became well known and her fame was connected to the Mormon song 'The Day Dawn Is Breaking.' Sandra didn't know this new personality was not her. Because of this dream she added the lyrics of this song, to message 15.

In 2015, I dreamed I jumped off my balcony and flew over the earth. Wild animals gathered below me, hundreds and then thousands. They ran behind me as I flew around the world. Sheep joined them, running behind the wild animals until there were millions of sheep. I symbolize my book. Wild animals: Christians, Jews and Muslins that left their churches before reading this book. The sheep: Christians, Jews and Muslims who leave their religion after reading this book.

Will these dreams come true? When Covid-19 happened, I knew the apocalypse had begun and thought it was too late to fulfill my destiny. I fervently prayed for a miracle to get my book out to the world. That night I went outside and saw outer space! It looked like I was on the Star Trek observation deck. I was taken to the future where earth had ascended and given a knowing that everything is unfolding as needed.

My book makes me want to weep and cry and throw myself on the floor! I can't contain the power it holds, it's too much, it's too beyond me and I'm just sitting on it. I have to turn it over someone else before its fire burns me up and I explode! My book is filled with living fire and it makes my heart hurt.

My destiny will be fulfilled, but we will pay a price for breaking creation laws. The road of destruction will continue until our light grows strong enough to turn the planet around. Millions may die. In Black Elk's vision, when he came to earth to kill Jehovah, everything was dying- people, animals, birds, trees, yet we lived. Humanity lived; we survived and thrived.

The Impossible Dream

Joe Darion

To dream the impossible dream. To fight the unbeatable foe. To bear with unbearable sorrow. To run where the brave dare not go. To right the unrightable wrong. To be better far than you are. To try when your arms are too weary. To reach the unreachable star. This is my quest, to follow that star. No matter how hopeless, no matter how far. To be willing to give when there's no more to give. To be willing to die so that honor and justice may live. And I know if I'll only be true to this glorious quest, that my heart will lie peaceful and calm when I'm laid to my rest. And the world will be better for this, that one man scorned and covered with scars still strove with his last ounce of courage. To reach the unreachable star.

Moriah's Message 24
A Child's Pure Heart Is True

Children have been beaten for thousands of years because the Lord said: 'Foolishness is bound in the heart of a child but the rod of correction will drive it far from him... if you beat him with the rod he will not die. You will beat him with the rod and deliver his soul from hell... (Prov 22:15, 23:13, 14).' The foolishness in a child's heart is innocence and aliveness. When beaten, a child's innocence is crushed and they go numb with fear. This keeps humanity in survival mode: we do not feel safe, we never have enough and we want more. This breeds the greed, hate and war that Jehovah lives on.

In Growing Kids God's Way Ezzo says to beat babies and children with spanking rods, feed and put them to bed by the clock, leave them alone if they cry. This prevents mother from bonding with her child, causing brain damage and disorders. When mothers respond to their babies they bond and their energies synchronize. Children forced to obey with threats will wear a mask to survive. "After years of acting... one loses contact with who one really is. One's true self is numbed out... To live and never know who I really am, is the greatest tragedy of all (Bradshaw)."

Children lose innocence when they grow up in fear of their parents. They will sacrifice themselves to conform. Next to love, a sense of belonging is a child's greatest need- being valued, understood, listened too. A child will do anything to have belonging: accept abuse without complaint, develop eating disorders, cut themselves, commit suicide.

In Summerhill School Neill says there is never a problem child, there are only problem parents. Using force or overindulging a child are both abusive. "In the disciplined home, children have no rights. In the spoiled home, they have all the rights. In the proper home children and adults have equal rights (Neill). Allow your child to be himself and engage in imaginary play. S/he will develop emotional wholeness.

If a child has to stop crying to avoid punishment, his emotion will go in his muscles where it is repressed with tension. This forms armor that cripples the body. Children throw temper tantrums, rolling and thrashing their arms and legs, while screaming and crying, to release repressed emotions. This is a safety valve- a normal part of his/her development. The tantrum will stop when his tension is gone.

When a child is angry, let him cry and kick his legs. Children, forced to repress anger and not allowed to release it with tantrums, continue to repress anger as adults. When something triggers their anger they can explode in a rage. Violence is "the tragic expression of unmet needs (Zeleke)."

Sexually attacking your child is the most insidious crime. In her memoir First, I believe You Carol was molested by her father from 3—12. He smothered her with her pillow while raping her. During the day he was a loving father. Demonic takeovers (temporary, full possession) creates a Jakel-Hyde personality. Raging anger and drunken rampages can give demons control. The eyes go cold and hard as stone, as the demon takes over. The dad or husband is not there, something else is and he is a Monster.

If your child is out of control, you are too. Sick parents make their children ill. Yelling and name calling creates shame. If you say 'you're being rude' you are the one acting rude. If you say 'you are such a brat' you are the brat, not your child. When shaming is early and frequent the child believes something is wrong with them. They grow up feeling inferior and are at risk for depression and anxiety disorders. Emotional wounds caused by abusive parents continue in adulthood. They fear intimacy and a perceived slight is thrown back in defensive anger, before the feeling of shame can inflict its painful arrow.

Respect and compassion builds self-esteem. When children are raised with respect in loving environments, the world will heal. Children raised with compassion and respect are in touch with their true Self. They radiate more life-force and they have a healing effect on others, simply by being in their presence. In <u>Emotional Maturity</u> Saul said, "From birth, the only safe rule is to treat the child as an individual with the fullest respect for its personality as it develops toward independence..."

Note. The above may not apply to special needs children. Out-of-control and abusive behavior may be no fault of the parent. Autistic children often hit, bite, scream, slap, headbang and may have explosive, even violent rages.

If a child talks about when they were big, had another Mom, lived with another family, when they died before, or things they should have no awareness of, it may be from a past life. If a child has a fear of water, fire, war, anything that seems irrational, you can help them explore it. Ask them to close their eyes, breath deep and tell you what they see when they feel their fear. They may see what happened to them in another life; this will help them release it. <u>Children That Time Forgot</u> (Harrison) is a collection of true stories about children who remember their past lives. <u>Return To Life</u> (Tucker) focuses on young children in America with memories of previous lives. Being aware of our past lives will help humanity heal.

Our body holds our past-life memories. It has access to everything we experience. Our body can bring our brain, nervous system, cells, organs, blood, everything into balance, healing us on every level. Our body reveals our true nature through our eyes, voice, hands, muscles and cells. Psycho-diagnostic Chirology identifies disorders with hand reading (Holtzman). Bioenergetics reveals neurosis through muscle reading (Lowen). Recorded speech played backwards exposes lies (Oates). When we hear truth, our body knows even when our mind refuses to accept it.

"The truths the body holds onto are the ones the mind has lied about, the secret shames to which we can't give voice, the losses we are not supposed to know about, the feelings that don't match our desired version of reality. The soul knows who and what it is and will defend its integrity in the body at all costs. The body will distort itself, disease itself, even kill itself before it will incorporate a falsehood. The body has tremendous storage capacity, but eventually it goes on a rampage, attempting to clean itself out through illnesses, madness or mishap (<u>Digger</u>, McCollough)."

Violence comes from not having basic needs met during the first years of life. A unique type of rage and self-hate develops that, as an adult, may be violently projected onto others. Personality disorders and mental illness may be caused by childhood abuse, entity attachment, drugs and/or past lives. The following body-oriented therapies may help heal these disorders, drugs may make them worse.

Family Constellation (Hellinger) heals inherited family trauma using people to represent family members.

Focusing-Oriented Psychotherapy (Gendlin) works with a 'felt sense' to resolve issues.

Internal Family Systems (Schwartz) works with the core Self to heal sub-personalities.

Healing The Eternal Soul (Tomlinson) uses past life regression to heal.

Neurofeedback 101 (Cohen) heals depression, anxiety, OCD and other disorders, helping the brain rewire itself.

Sand Tray (Lowenfeld, Kalff) uses symbolic objects in sand to assist healing.

NeuroAffective Relational Model (Heller) heals trauma.

BodyTalk (Veltheim) helps your body heal itself.

The Completion Process (Swan) integrates child fragments.

Hearing Voices Network (Romme) aids schizophrenics.

The Power of your Subconscious Mind (Murphy) shows how to heal using imagination and infinite intelligence.

Into The Light (Douglas II) says ultraviolet blood irradiation kills viruses and infections, boosting the immune system.

Whole Health (Mincolla) is a holistic healing system that balances body, mind and spirit.

Red Light Therapy (Whitten) eliminates pain, heals joints and improves brain function.

Craniosacral (Upledger) communes with the body through cells, organs, brain, immune system, etc. Trauma is re-leased and organs heal by asking the body to assist.

Becoming Supernatural (Dispenza) shows how to change brain chemistry with intent, develop a more balanced body, an unlimited mind, have greater access to spiritual realms and have transcendent experiences.

In <u>Good Morning Monster</u> Gildiner reveals how she helped her clients heal their psychological wounds, release pain, recover their emotional lives and become whole. Gildiner shows how therapeutic processes work when real healing occurs. There is no standard method. She researches various modalities for tools that she needs, to help her clients heal. Gildiner's work is brilliant, creative and inspiring.

In <u>My Grandmother's Hands</u> Resmaa says everyone carries inherited race/cultural trauma. If we don't heal it, we blow it through our kids, whites, blacks, society. Children transfer family trauma to the world. "Parents unwittingly breed in their very young children... crime, revolutions, wars, and the decay and destruction of nations (Saul)." Criminals act out their childhood abuse. They need healing, not punishment. The USA judicial system should be eliminated. The offender's body holds their innocence or guilt; psychics, intuitives, therapists, etc. can read and analyze it. Criminals and dangerous people could be confined in healing centers while their mental health is restored (see chapter 22).

As society becomes balanced, children will no longer be used as pawns in their parent's power play. Instead of men dominating women (or vice versa) whoever is best in a situation should take charge with give and take. In a partnership, do the tasks that suit your interests, talents and abilities. This helps your male-female energies harmonize. As life flows along new paths, couples who do this flow with it. Most men depend on women for nurture; women depend on men for support. Nurture and support yourself using your male intellect (light) and your female intuition (love). Intuition gathers meaning through symbols, visions, feelings, and dreams, giving data to our intellect, which acts on the input.

When we suppress our male or female energies, society becomes imbalanced and swings between a culture based on science (intellect) and one based on religion (intuition). The ancient Greeks did not have a stable society; astronomy, medicine, mechanics and geometry were established, while spirituality was neglected. This created a need for emotional expression, which found a voice in the early Christian church. This voice became fanatical because of people's need for emotional release. Greek civilization fell into a thousand years of darkness.

In Greek Piety Martin P Nilsson describes their fall as "conversion from rationalism to mysticism; from the clear logical lines of Greek thought, to faith in the... supernatural, from love... of the world and the body, to flight from the world and condemnation of all that was corporeal." During the dark ages' society gave vent to their emotions and instincts, while repressing their rational mentality. Religion and mythology flourished, while science waned. After a thousand years of repressed rationalism society began to swing back to it.

The Lunar Effect (Lieber, Agel) says during this period of change, mysterious effects that could not be explained by reason were denounced as superstition and witchcraft. The witchcraft craze in Europe came about after the old religions and mythologies were driven underground by the Church.

Many scientists have had conflicts between their intellect and their intuition. These conflicts can be a stimulus for new discoveries and revolutionary theories. Scientific methods provide us with objective knowledge, but it is the intuitive insights that make science progress. Science must be taken beyond rationalism. In An Idealist Way of Life Radhakrishnan says intellect and intuition must be synergized 'in the quest for the nature of ultimate reality.'

Einstein believed imagination and intuition were essential tools for discovering universal truths. He said "The mind can proceed only so far upon what it knows and can prove. There comes a point where it takes a leap, call it intuition or what you will, and comes out upon a higher plane of knowledge." He also said imagination is more important than knowledge. Einstein used his imagination to discover the properties of light. It is the gateway to the creative flow.

Classical physics explained the universe like a machine that God set in motion and left to function. It was predictable, its laws immutable and an object's position and momentum could be precisely determined. In 1900 Planck tried to explain radiation with known laws (ultraviolet catastrophe) and discovered they did not apply. His discovery sent shock-waves throughout the scientific community. The flaws of classical physics are detectable at the atomic level. The laws of quantum mechanics must be applied to describe sub-atomic particles. The founding fathers of quantum mechanics were Planck, Heisenberg, Einstein, Schrodinger, Bohr and Broglie. Their theories collapsed the foundation of physics.

Einstein: "All my attempts to adapt the theoretical foundation of physics to the new knowledge failed... It was as if the ground had been pulled out from under one, with no firm foundation to be seen anywhere upon which one could have built." **Heisenberg**: "The development of modern physics can only be understood when one realizes that here, the foundations of physics have started moving... this motion has caused the feeling that the ground would be cut from science." **Bohr** "our experience... has brought to light the insufficiency of our simple mechanical conceptions and... has shaken the foundation of which... interpretation of observation was based."

Planck, Einstein, Broglie, and Schrodinger never accepted quantum physics as Bohr and Heisenberg interpreted it. Their interpretation intimately coupled man to the universe, gave it unpredictable status, and denied its existence at the atomic level. The other scientists believed the universe existed independently of man, was predictable and real at the atomic level. They helped give birth to quantum physics and then abandoned their brain child. Their discoveries forced them to revise some of their most cherished beliefs, but they could only bend so far. The line they drew, that they refused to cross, placed them on the opposing side of their own theories.

Bohr and Einstein loved to debate these differences. Perhaps they were both right. Man may be coupled to the universe, and it may be real at the atomic level. Einstein insisted "God does not play dice with the universe." There is a predictable order to atomic particles, but from our perspective it is random. We cannot view atoms from outside of our physical dimension, so how can we tell what is really happening? Electrons appear to jump around, but are they really jumping? Einstein and Schrodinger did not think so.

If you constantly use your left-brain, you will develop a desire for right-brain activities, and vice versa. Physicists need right-brain activities, like music; artists need left-brain activities, like math. While Planck was working on his radiation problem, he took long walks to think, and then went home and played the piano. While Einstein was working on his theory of relativity, he liked to play the piano until inspiration came to him – then he stopped and wrote it down. When Heisenberg worked out the formulas for an atomic bomb, he did the same thing. His lab was in an old church wine cellar, built inside a cave. There was an organ in the church, which Heisenberg played after working on 'the uranium club.' After a long day of working on the reactions of an atomic explosion, Feynman would walk out into the hills of Los Alamos and beat his bongo drums.

Einstein said "the intuitive mind is a sacred gift and the rational mind is a faithful servant. We have created a society that honors the servant and has forgotten the gift." Intuition connects us with our soul. When we separate from it, we feel empty and may use possessions, food, or drugs to numb our emptiness. When we honor our intellect and intuition, our male/female energies balance, our body and soul connect, and we become more vibrant, present, aware and whole.

The 20th century began with a shockwave that crumbled the foundation of science. The 21st century will send shock-waves through Christians, Jews and Muslims, crumbling their foundation. Science and spirituality will unite, our male and female energies will harmonize, our intuition will guide our intellect, and we will live from our heart.

Born Free

Don Black

Born free, as free as the wind blows, as free as the grass grows. Born free to follow your heart. Live free and beauty surrounds you. The world still astounds you each time you look at a star. Stay free where no walls divide you. You're free as a roaring tide so there's no need to hide. Born free and life is worth living, but only worth living cause you're born free

Moriah's Message 25
Buffalo-That-Carries-A-Pipe

Two thousand years ago, two Lakota hunters saw a young woman in a white dress. One hunter expressed his desire to have her; the other said 'do not have such thoughts, this is a sacred woman.' She said to the one, 'come, you will have what you desire.' He went to her and mist swirled around them. When it lifted the hunter saw a portal into another world. His friend was in the portal and had aged to an old man. His body turned to dust and blew away.

The sacred woman said 'your friend needed to be removed from your tribe. I transported him to another earth similar to this one, where he lived out his life. He lost his Spirit upon death, for he was addicted to sex and did not evolve a soul. Have the people in your camp prepare a tepee to hold everyone. Tell them what happened here.'

The man told his Chief about the sacred woman. The people gathered their tepees and one large tepee was constructed. As the hunter told his tribe what happened to his friend, where he was taken and why, a beautiful angel with sparkling, midnight blue hair entered the tepee of many skins. Rainbow lights swirled around her as she walked to the fire in the center of the tepee.

The angel spoke like singing: 'All things come from the Great Spirit and have part of Hir flame.' She stirred the fire and sparks flew out. 'Little sparks separated from the Great Spirit. They had sovereignty, yet were part of the spirit-that-moves-in-all-things. They started life on many worlds, with plants and animals. The Spirits were androgynous, like the Great Spirit. Some of them decided to incarnate on their evolving worlds.'

'Man multiplied spontaneously, through self-replication. This occurred when perfect conditions for a birth were realized. Babies were nurtured in ideal environments. In this perfect state, the average life span of man was 1,000 years. When man decided to permanently leave the physical plane, s/he left hir body. Death was a voluntary transition, from one realm of existence to another.'

'A demon separated humans into males and females so they could copulate like animals. This caused humanity to degenerate and multiplied their conception. When you stop copulating, women will regain their power of self-replication. Their androgynous children will receive the eternal flame of knowing and become mighty seers.'

'You have brothers with pale skin across the great water. They will come to your land. If they bring a cross with their religion there will be war and they will try to destroy your way of life. If you are multiplying in the sacred manner, they will learn to live in harmony with you. If you are still copulating, you will not be able to help the white man and their wake of destruction will eventually endanger earth.'

'The demon who separated the sexes may corrupt this knowledge so it will not be passed on.' She opened her pouch and removed a pipe. "I will leave my pipe with you, so you will remember my words. The bowl can be removed from the stem, like this. When they are separated, the bowl represents the female and the stem represents the male. When the pipe is put together it is a symbol of man, returned to wholeness- the image of hir Creator. Honor your women as you honor my pipe, and they will have virgin births.'

'If my message is lost, the world will become endangered and a great Seer will be born to your people. The twelve eagle feathers on my pipe represent this Seer. His name is Eagle-That-Stretches-His-Wings. When he needs me, I will return and a white buffalo will be born that will turn the colors of humanity as she grows. This is a warning. What the pale faces do to the buffalo, they do to humanity. Their demon-god will slaughter the people of this land, the way they slaughtered the buffalo, unless they change course. I will give the world a new vision. If it is embraced, Eagle-That-Stretches-His-Wings will lead a great battle against the demons until they are no more. This Great Purification will restore balance on earth.'

The angel gave the Chief her pipe and said 'My name is Buffalo-That-Carries-A-Pipe. When you smoke my pipe remember man was created male-female in the image of hir Creator and babies were conceived through virgin births. Multiply in this manner and you will become a Great Nation.' Buffalo-That-Carries-A-Pipe laid down and rolled, becoming a white buffalo. The calf rolled becoming black, red, yellow and brown, growing bigger each time she changed colors. The buffalo then became Buffalo-That-Carries-A-Pipe, the angel with sparkling, midnight blue hair, and vanished.

White Buffalo Woman did not teach rites, like how to keep souls of the dead. She told the Lakota to stop copulating.

Humanity began as hermaphrodites and have always been among us. Hermaphrodites can make sperm internally, fertilizing their own egg. Virgin births can also occur from an egg that is fertilized internally by a male protein. There is a conspiracy to eradicate the intersex by denying they exist. Gender Assignment Surgery is performed on the genitals of intersex babies, to create a false anatomy- male or female.

Intersex babies are not in medical emergency; they don't need surgery to cut off an enlarged clitoris and other parts offensive to the doctor leaving healthy genitals militated, un-able to regulate hormones or climax as they get older. Doctors who perform harmful surgeries on baby genitals should have their license revoked. Doctors pressure parents to agree to these surgeries and advise them to lie to their child about on-going surgeries, needed to keep their gender secret and repair damages caused from previous cosmetic surgeries.

Humanity has five genders: M, F, f/M (female inside—male outside) m/F (male inside—female outside) Intersex (female—male): <u>M</u> <u>F</u> <u>f/M</u> <u>m/F</u> <u>F/M</u> needs to be listed on gender forms.

Goy	girl/Boy	f/M
Birl	boy/Girl	m/F
Girl/Boy		F/M

Embryos are female. If the brain is flooded with testosterone at six weeks, male genitals develop and mild brain damage occurs. The fetus receives a chemical bath that makes the corpus callosum atrophy. A female fetus' corpus callosum continues to increase. Women can access both hemispheres easier than men, and they live longer. Estrogen boosts the immune system; testosterone suppresses it. Women's emotional states and mental processes are more developed than men. They are less aggressive and impulsive. Men have 15 times more testosterone than women. Intersex people average four times more. This blend gives them greater strength and endurance than women, less aggression than men.

Menstruation will disappear when we return to our intersex state. Losing blood every month slows a girl's growth cycle. When women stop menstruating they will be taller, stronger and healthier. Children have been born to women who never menstruate, and never had intercourse. Virgin birth babies are female; blood and saliva are identical with their mother's.

The first time a girl has sex it is not pleasant; her vagina is not designed for penetration. Dr Siegmeister said "Why should nature seal woman's sexual organs with the hymen, the rupture of which, by forced entrance of the male organ, is a painful and disagreeable experience, if it was intended that woman should perform the act of copulation for the purpose of procreation? "Among animals, nature provides the greatest inducement for them to copulate and multiply. Why should this unyielding membrane be placed at the entrance of woman's generative organs, making the entrance of the penis painful and difficult? There is only one answer... woman... was never intended to perform the act of copulation, for reproductive or any other purpose."

Passion is being aroused- aroused to have sex, or aroused to pursue your heart's desire, whatever that is. Passion carries enough creative force to make a baby- or change the world, when used to fulfill your destiny. Passion is our creative ability, our creative genius. Use it to manifest.

When you have sex, you absorb your partner's sexual energies, including their perversions and obsessions. If your partner is promiscuous, you will be caught in his/her sexual energy-web, including people s/he was sexual with. This drains your energy. You untangle the webs with awareness. Learn your lessons; they are gifts that helped your journey, and keep your sexual passion- your creative power pure.

When sexually aroused kundalini energy rises up the spine, into the brain. Orgasm through intercourse usually sends the energy back down through the genitals. If this energy is held without release it can explode through the top of your head. This nourishes your body, aids spiritual growth, and balances and cleanses chakras. Kundalini can open your 6th chakra (3rd eye) when it rises up through your higher centers.

Orgasm and ejaculation are separate processes. One can occur without the other. Jesus said "commit not whoredom (ejaculation)... for the whoremonger is like a tree whose sap runs out from its trunk. That tree will be dried up before its time (The Essene Gospel of Peace)." If seminal fluid is not lost during orgasm it is reabsorbed in the lymphatic system and returned to the blood, nourishing the body.

Male aggression impregnates many women against their will, causing trauma in mother and baby. This keeps humanity in a degenerate condition. When a mother gives birth, her astral body may fragment to release negative energies, in a similar way that it does upon death. Most fragments go in the placenta but some go with the baby. A woman needs to heal her trauma before she conceives, or she may release them on her baby at birth. With no aggressive, male-sperm births, humanity will heal.

Rape, mechanical sex and lab/office fertilizations, both IVF and Artificial Insemination, create psyche wounds in the fetus. Engineering embryos and growing them in glass wombs break the laws of creation. If you want a child and cannot conceive through intercourse, adopt. Two highly evolved people can attract a highly evolved soul when they unite. But the greatest souls are born through virgin births like Jesus; these babies are androgynous/female.

When we evolve beyond our degenerative state, sexual intercourse will end, and humanity will procreate through parthenogenesis when perfect conditions for a baby are realized. The universe can be your lover and fill you with ecstasy. When you feel your connection with everything that exists, you disappear into its eternal embrace. This state of being is your true nature, your true Self.

Women who want a virgin birth must stop copulating, only eat raw foods, and go on cleansing fasts, naked in the sun, air and water. As you reach your ideal weight and realize perfect health, your periods will become lighter and may stop. Sexual abstinence, fasting, cleansing, ancestry and holistic healings, may awaken kundalini. This spiritual fire will help you heal on every level of your being. When you become whole (completely healed), and you can provide a baby with an ideal environment, parthenogenesis may be possible.

The flowering stick in Black Elk's vision is androgynous humans; flowers- female, stick- male. The flowering stick becomes the sheltering tree and the women shout for joy; they gain the power of self-replication. The men honor the sheltering tree and agree to depend on it to bring forth children so that it would always be with them. Another symbol that represents our androgyny is the broom (Chapter 23).

All life will be renewed when children are birthed from the sheltering tree. We will live together like one, communicating with all our relatives— animals, trees, even rocks. Animals and trees will teach us many things. "Nature speaks to us... Every animal has a story to tell... every tree whispers with its rustling leaves the secrets of life... (Ted Andrews)."

"No people... ever enjoyed a freedom like we Indians enjoyed before the White man came... Everything was free. We were free and so were the animals, the birds, the rivers, and the whole wonderful land from end to end. All free. All pure. All happy. This was the freest and purest and happiest place in the whole Universe. We were the Great Spirit's forest children, living free according to His law (Noble Red Man)." This free, happy place was enslaved by the Lord, but he will soon be bound by Black Elk's nation: "He shall come as an eagle against the house of the Lord (Hos 8:1)."

As your awareness expands to higher levels, you will see with greater clarity, understanding, vision and wisdom, without judgment or attachment. Your heart will burn with the Eternal Flame of Truth. Follow it with passion and courage, and be free.

And then a hero comes along with the strength to carry on. And you cast your fears aside, and you know you can survive. So, when you feel like hope is gone, look inside you and be strong. And you'll finally see the truth, that a hero lies in you (Hero, Mariah Cary).

I Am The Wind

Cynthia Harrell

Just like the wind, I've always been

Drifting high up in the sky that never ends

Through thick and thin, I always win

Cause I would fight both life and death

To save a friend

I face my destiny every day I live

And the best in me is all I have to give

Just like the sun, when my day's done

Sometimes I don't like the person I've become

Is the enemy within a thousand men?

Should I walk the path if my world's so dead ahead?

Is someone testing me every day I live?

Well the best in me is all I have to give

I can pretend I am the wind (I am the wind)

I don't know if I will pass this way again

All things must end; goodbye my friend.

Think of me when you see the sun or feel the wind

I am the Wind I am the Sun

And one day we'll all be one

PART TWO
Stand Together

The Table Of Contents

Chapter 1
The Pinnacle

The two mouths in Revelation

Jehovah's mouth: "And out of his mouth goeth a sharp sword, that with it he should smite the nations, and he shall rule them with a rod of iron. He treadeth the winepress of the fierceness and wrath of Almighty God... saying to all the fowls that fly in the midst of heaven: Come and gather yourselves together unto the supper of the great God, that ye may eat the flesh of kings and the flesh of captains, and the flesh of horses, and the flesh of all men... (Rev19:15—18)." "And the winepress was trodden... and blood came out of it even unto the horse bridles... (Rev 14:20)."

Mouth of this book "And I saw three unclean [akathartos-cleansing] spirits [pneuma- angels] like frogs come out of the mouth of the dragon, and out of the mouth of the beast, and out of the mouth of the false prophet. For they are the spirits of devils [daimon- bring prosperity] making miracles, which go forth unto the kings of the earth and of the whole world, to gather them to the battle of that Great Day of God Almighty (Rev 16:13—14)."

The three mouths or voices of this book are Black Elk, White Buffalo Woman, Sandra. We are cleansing angels going forth like frogs to the kings of the earth (Christians) and the world, bringing prosperity and manifesting miracles as we battle Lord God. Frogs leap. The cleansing angels start a chain-reaction that spreads in leaps and bounds. The dragon is Sandra, who wrote the messages, the beast is Black Elk, who battles Jehovah, the illegitimate prophet is White Buffalo Woman. The gospel is not what it proclaims. I am not authorized by any church to reveal what it really is. Dragon: drakon— fascinate. Beast: therion— dangerous (to demon-ghosts). False Prophet: tes— spurious illegitimate.

The cleansing angels that make miracles (dragon: Sandra, beast: Black Elk, unauthorized prophet: myself) are cast into a lake of fire and tormented day and night forever (Revelation 20:10). This is the flame of eternity, the Creator's Spirit that continually burns. Jehovah calls it a place of torment and second death because he would disintegrate in its flames.

"And I saw the beast [Black Elk] and the kings of the earth [Christians on earth], and their armies [Christians in heaven] gathered together to make war against him that sat on the horse [Jehovah], and against his army [demon-ghosts] (Rev 19:19). And I saw an angel come down from heaven [Black Elk] having the key of the bottomless pit and a great chain in his hand... And cast him [Satan] into the bottomless pit and shut him up and set a seal upon him, that he should deceive the nations no more... (Rev 20:1—3)."

Revelation says Satan will be freed after 1,000 years; Satan will be no more. 'How long will the <u>words of your mouth</u> be like <u>a strong wind</u> (Job 8:2)? 'You lifted me up to the wind, you caused me to ride upon it and dissolved my substance (Job 30:22). Jehovah will ride the words of our mouth (Sandra and I) until he vanishes. 'There came out two women, and the wind was in their wings'.

In Revelation 15 the sea of glass is the mineral water (life-force) Jehovah and his demons live on. The demon-ghosts, anticipating a reward of ever lasting life when Jehovah's judgment is finished, are singing praises to their god. Jehovah's seven demons, who are his eyes and voice, hold seven vials filled with wrath. The throne fills with smoke-Jehovah's smoldering fury, and the seven demons are told to pour their vials of wrath on earth.

The 7 plagues: 1st poured on earth: foul sore that festers. **2nd** poured on sea: many people die; those who live are the walking dead. **3rd** poured on waters: demons with hosts have life-force to drink. **4th** poured on sun: demons without hosts are scorched- the fire of eternity burns them up. **5th** poured on seat of the beast: Jehovah's seat (bench) is Christians. They gnaw their tongue (speak in distress) confessing Christ is Satan. **6th** dries up living waters, preparing for Kings of the East. Demon-ghosts kill their host and are judged. **7th** poured into air: voices (sound) thunders (rumble) lightnings (radiate) and earthquakes. Mountains are leveled, islands are gone, and great hail falls (Rev 16).

The 1—2nd plagues may be the Covid vaccine; it makes us sick and millions die. The 7th plague may be EISCAT-3D creating earthquakes and tsunamis around the world with electromagnetic radiation (air) that rips up the earth; hail falling is vast chasms opening. There are many probable futures; we can change course. We can stop Jehovah's plagues. Help wake up the world.

David's Doomsday Dream: the ocean at Idaho

Black Elk was destined to destroy demons, but he cannot fulfill his destiny unless Jews, Muslims and Christians pray for Spiritual Power and cast them out. Pray with passion; passion contains Spirit Power. Passion can set your heart on fire with the flame of eternity. When used with authority to cast out demons, passion can carry fiery indignation.

Black Elk predicted there would be a celestial display when he died. As people were leaving after Black Elk's Wake, August 19 1950, the sky lit up with glowing colors. In <u>Black Elk</u> (Steltenkamp) Siehr describes the night sky: "It was something like a light being played out on a fountain which sprays up… rising and moving. There would be some flames going at a great distance way up into the sky above us. And others would be rising and coming into various groups and then all of a sudden, spurt off on this side and then another side and then off to the center again… it was a tremendous sight… the whole horizon seemed to be ablaze."

Black Elk was taken to inner earth and saw colored lights rising from the mountains like a flaming rainbow. If his vision is fulfilled, perhaps the Aurora Borealis and Aurora Australis will be seen like a flaming rainbow over the hemispheres, as a sign of triumph. Aurora is Goddess of Dawn and Mother of Winds. "The Wind of Change blows straight into the face of time, like a storm-wind that will ring the freedom bell... (Scorpions)."

In Jenner's congressional address he said safe looking things will lead to USA dictatorship. Psychiatry, Hospice, vaccinations and prescriptions are on the blueprint. These things, designed by the Global Elite, are for us not them.

The Global Elite live above the systems they enslave us with: foodstuffs that wreck health, vaccines that harm, drugs that kill, schools that enslave minds, psych meds that deepen mental illness. They do not receive these things- the masses under their control do. The Global Elite enhance their genes and cripple ours. Cut off from their Spirit, they fear death. They are transhumanists- coupling man and machine to live longer. We are brain-damaged slaves programmed to work and seek pleasure. They are calculating, covert controllers.

Hospice is euthanasia, killing patients with morphine overdose. Patients lose speech and die within days. Smart drugs interfere with cellular processes, cause cancer, stroke, heart disease and diabetes. Bisphosphonates, prescribed for bone loss, stops the destruction of old bone cells causing bone fractures. Covid vaccines can cause autoimmune disorders.

Cannabis, psilocybin, peyote and Ayahuasca can cure ailments and lessen chronic pain. They are safer than drugs. These plants are sacred. Only use them for healing and insight. Pray for protection before using, and do not take them to get high; they will open you to dark astral entities. You could become schizophrenic.

In Brave New World (Huxley) babies are conceived in test tubes; their development is controlled with oxygen depletion. Like this novel, babies' brains are modified with vaccines. When babies are vaccinated, chemicals enter their brain- the blood-brain barrier isn't fully developed. Thimerosal in a developing brain causes the same pathology as autism. In the 1960s, 4 in 10,000 children had autism. Now it's 1 in 40.

Children with autism have a small corpus callosum (right-left brain communication). Babies who develop autism from thimerosal in vaccinations have a small corpus callosum from brain damage. Boys have over four times more autism than girls do; girls have a thicker corpus callosum.

cdc.gov/vaccines: "The only childhood vaccines today that have trace amounts of thimerosal are DTaP and DTaP-Hib ()." Thimerosal causes neurological injuries even in trace amounts. It can cause speech delays, asthma, Tourette's, seizures, epilepsy, SIDS, autism and mental illness. Stop vaccinating your babies and toddlers! Read the vaccine insert. Nagalase weakens the immune system, thimerosal causes brain damage in any amount, and aluminum causes inflammation. Vaccines also contain animal DNA. When you allow your child to be vaccinated you violate her/him, break the laws of creation, and commit a crime against humanity.

"My daughter squealed like a rabbit, arching her back, for 20 hours straight after her DPT vax in 1989. She then slumped into an exhausted sleep for a further 20 hours. When she awoke, she looked through us, not at us…. today she is 28 years old, autistic, and unable to care for herself (Peta Daimyo vaccine-injury.info/about.cfm)." Christina Moore's 8-month-old son Trent received 5 vaccines, one after the other. Within 13 hours he was dead.

In The Sad Son Claire tells the story of her son Greyson. He has autism and Oppositional Defiant Disorder; Greyson would hit his mom every day beginning at 5-months. Higher functioning (empathy, compassion) was absent. Greyson had a genius IQ but at times he could be cruel and demonic.

From birth—18, 40+ vaccines are recommended. Child-hood vaccines have many toxic ingredients, including vitamin K1 given to newborns. Gardasil can cause dysautonomia, cardiac issues, seizers, ovulation failure and death. Vaccines create inflammation, disrupt brain communication and can cause disorders like anxiety and depression. There is a rising epidemic of these disorders in children. Vaccines cripple our immune system. Childhood diseases are safer; they build a strong immune system. My grandmother and great-grand-mother died at 101 and 102. Living to 100 was common in their day. Their grandparent's generation often lived to 120.

When humanity eats plant-based foods as Jesus taught, and we watch the sun rise and set, like native people did, we will live 100+ years like our great-grandparents. The sun is alive; when it's light enters your eyes, it communes with you, nourishes and heals you, and reduces your desire for food.

Fasting, yoga and meditation can trigger a full kundalini episode. Spiritual fire flows up the spine creating headaches, nausea, spinning, body-heat and insomnia, as it opens your chakras. Demons are attracted to kundalini energy; they may appear as angels or saints to try and possess you. Command them to leave. A full kundalini rising can open you to alternate realities. In The Evolving Human Kelly's kundalini journey gave her multidimensional consciousness and opened her inner sight. Kundalini rising can be alarming. Its energy is sensual and spiritual; it contains the creative power of the universe. Kundalini expands your consciousness and may leave you with natural healing abilities. Reading this book can be a catalyst for a gentle stirring of kundalini energy.

Ascension causes space, time and matter to unravel. Time is speeding up because we are slowing down. When the ascension process is complete, time will stop. Black Elk said there should be time no longer (Rev 10:6). When time disappears we will walk through walls and travel by thought. In 2012 Borax says "there is a theory that matter would be fluid if not for the staticness of time… if you opened time you could walk through matter like water. The crystallization of molecules would no longer be as it is." Time is opening, making matter fluid. Like Mattson in the Spirit world we can manifest with our imagination, bilocate and step out of time, freezing everything around us.

 We are approaching the pinnacle of ascension. The world is in our hands. Will demons take it from us? I have entered many parallel earths; Jehovah and his demons are in them all, except for a future I was shown where earth had ascended, to let me know we can make it! Lower earths are collapsing. This earth is on the brink of collapse; we can save it by casting out demons.

{We live in a multidimensional universe where parallel worlds are continuously being created. During ascension, lower worlds collapse and higher worlds merge. Your mind, soul and spirit then merge with another you on a higher world. His/her memories become yours, and memories from your former reality dissipate like a dream, unless you have multi-dimensional consciousness. This is why some people remember Mandela Effects and others do not. **Man**- humanity **Dela**- divide **Effect**- result

Global Mandela Effects: We have different anatomy. Earth's geography, movies, logos, cartoons, Bible, stories, products, etc. changed. Mona Lisa is smiling more. Bible changes: Womb in Exodus and Numbers, is now Matrix- animals, people kept for breeding. Num 11:12 says 'as a nursing father [hermaphrodite] bears the sucking child.' I Cor 13:13 says faith, hope 'charity' (not love). Isaiah 11:6 said the lion will lie down with the lamb. Jews (lions) would be killed alongside Christians (lambs). Now it says the wolf and lamb dwell together. Wolfs teach us to live free. Lambs know their innocence (we are not born in sin) and they live. Now the leopard (Jehovah) lies down with the goat (demon-ghosts). Demons die their second death.

'My' Mandela Effects. Sandra grew up with South America below North America. Earth was on the outer edge of the galaxy, Sagittarius Arm. Now it's in the Orion Arm, 80,000 light years away. Sandra's boyfriend joined the marines; in this reality he went on a mission. Sandra thought Jane blocked her memories of when she quit going to dances. Jane was in a reality where this didn't occur. I left Jane's memories from Sandra's reality in this book (Message 17). Some of David's doomsday dreams that Sandra wrote have changed; I rewrote them to match this reality. I have re- published this book many times. Some of the changes were because of Mandela Effects.

David told me about cordyceps, I told him I ordered it and he didn't know what it was; he said he told me about NAC. A building flipped to its mirror image and my car vanished. The building flipped back and my car was there. I saw a strange animal on my land with a long tail, the size of a small bear. The Snake River turned bright blue for a day. One night I saw outer space from my deck. I wake up to chemtrail skies every morning. For one week, the chemtrails were gone, the sky was bright blue, and all clouds were real.

At a Mandela Effect conference I visited with someone at the hotel. She never saw me. Twice, when I was in danger, time stopped and everything froze: people, cars, sound-except me. I walked away from the danger and everything returned to normal. My car spun around while driving, on a country road and on the freeway. When my car stopped spinning I continued on my way, perhaps in a parallel reality.

My house has a portal to parallel earths. Doors, rooms and stairs seem to move around. People, even family, get disoriented, find themselves where they didn't intend to go, and can't locate the stairs, outside doors or a room they were going to. Aaron Ray asked, when did you remove the window on the stair wall? I never saw it. Jared asked, when did you add the gable on the front of the house? It was always there. Construction workers repeated their lunch conversation like a rewound movie; they were caught in a time-loop. Realtor photos of my house when I bought it changed. My 500-pound soapstone fireplace rolled uphill when it was being installed.

Sometimes ghosts come through the portal and I help them cross. The portal extends over my land. I took one step and moved 50 feet into a tangle of tree limbs. Plants with giant leaves vanished. I saw and heard a parallel world through the trees. I saw a round light floating in the woods one night. Aaron Ray saw a gnome working in my berry patch.}

"I saw a living, breathing cosmos, pulsating with intelligence, swimming in love, and sustained by grace. It enfolded upon itself in multiple dimensions ...It was evolving, changing, becoming, creating and destroying, yet always and forever remaining exactly what it was (Hearts of the Fathers, Lawrence)."

Stop Jehovah

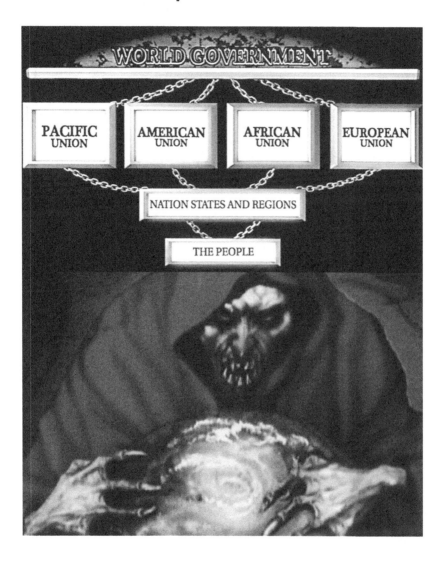

The Golden World

Two women overlook Magic Valley
The Twins are Manifesting Miracles

Behold there came out two women
and the wind was in their wings
Zechariah 5:9

Two angelic women with flowing hair, dresses billowing in the wind and arms raised high, seem to rise up out of the earth. The Twins sculpture, standing 13 feet above the rim of the Snake River canyon near the Perrine Bridge in Twin Falls Idaho, was erected in the Spring of 2008. The sculpture by David Clemons is part of the Twin Falls 'Art In Public Places.' The City Council wanted the art to reflect the landscape and heritage of the canyon and community. Clemons said the women were angels, expressing beauty and grace. Don Hall, city council member, says public art "adds to the community and quality of life."

Public art is a part of our history, culture, creative spirit and collective memory. The Association for Public Art Foundation says public art is a unifying force. By its presence alone, it can 'express community values, enhance our environment, transform a landscape, heighten our awareness or question our assumptions. Public art can transform a city's image, define a community's identity, and reveal the character of a neighborhood. Beyond its enriching personal benefits, public art is a symbol of a city's maturity. It increases a community's assets and expresses a community's positive sense of identity and values. A city with public art is a city that thinks and feels.'

Norfolk Public Arts says public art 'enhances the quality of life by encouraging a heightened sense of place and by introducing people to works of art that can touch them, and generations to come. Public art has the power to energize our public spaces, arouse our thinking and transform the places where we live, work and play into more welcoming and beautiful environments that invite interaction. Public art can make strangers talk, children ask questions, and calm a hurried life.'

Twin Falls- a city with heart

Chapter 3
The New Year

As the Lord's judgment was about to go forth, a little horn with a mouth arose on the 4th beast (Christianity) in Daniel. This mouth (The Greatest Deception) speaks 'great words against the most High' breaking seals on the Bible, changing 'times and laws' (Dan 7:25). Times is 'zman'- appointed occasions, season; laws is 'dath'- decree, declaration. The Greatest Deception changes the way seasons are marked and holidays are celebrated (times) and makes declarations (laws) that change peoples' view of the 'most High'.

The New Year begins January 1st because Jehovah-Christ-Santa-Satan was born on December 25th and circumcised eight days later. Jesus was born in the spring when baby lambs were in the fields. The Feast of the Circumcision of Christ (1/1) is a reminder of the Lord's covenant of flesh and the worship of Christ-Jehovah's foreskin (holy prepuce). During the Middle Ages there were 0a dozen different holy foreskins in various European towns, claiming to be Christ's. The foreskins were paraded through the streets. To fully reject Jehovah, we must **STOP** marking years by his circumcision (a reminder of his commandment to cut every baby penis) and **STOP** celebrating his holidays.

For thousands of years cultures around the world began the new year at the Spring Equinox. The astrological year begins at this time when day and night are equal around the world. This is the first day of spring when crops are planted. Beginning the New Year on this day connects us with nature, keeps us in tune with its cycles, and strengthens our connection with our earth mother. The dark days of winter have come to an end, and all over the world, the earth is awakening to new life.

Chapter 4
Winter Solstice

Winter Solstice marks the moment sunlight increases. At solstice (sun-stand-still) the sun appears to rise and set in the same spot for a few days because the earth, sun and galaxy center are aligned from our perspective. Honor the earth, sun and galaxy during your celebration. They are sentient and have a vast intelligence; they control infinite processes and correct imbalances so we can live.

Decorate with pictures of the earth, sun, milky way and stars, Bring nature inside: wreaths, chestnuts, branches, pinecones, snowflakes, mistletoe. If you do not have a fireplace, light a large candle. Have an all-night party. Let everyone light a little candle and express how they will bring more light in the world.

Tell family stories. Honor your ancestry and their traditions; this will connect you to your roots. Write blessings of healing for your family, the earth and humanity and burn them. Share ascension (Mandela) stories. Earth's ascension process has started and is opening time. Create Solstice Sacraments to honor life changes: births, a new job, a move, job loss, divorce, the passing of a loved one. Express gratitude and forgiveness to each other. Go on a walk at twilight with a bag of food for animals and birds: seeds, nuts, apple and carrot pieces, etc. Make wassail (cider, ginger beer, cranberries, cinnamon, nutmeg). Go Wassailing: 'Love and joy come to you, and to you a wassail too.' Play games, exchange small gifts, sing your favorite songs. Instead of dinner eat simple foods that you can snack on through the night: veggies, nuts, fruits, seeds, olives, bean dishes, humus, breads, cheeses.

Celebrate the great awakening and the Beautiful Day of Dancing Black Elk will bring (true Millennium) by playing music and dancing. "The day dawn is breaking, the world is awaking. The clouds of night's darkness are fleeing away. The worldwide commotion from ocean to ocean now heralds the time of the Beautiful Day." Cheer the sunrise: "Hail to thine earliest, welcome ray, Beautiful, Bright, Millennial Day."

Instead of Christmas Greetings shout: Holly Jolly Yuletide! Have a Holly Jolly Yuletide and when you walk down the street, say hello to friends you know and everyone you meet. Have a Holly Jolly Yuletide, and in case you didn't hear, Oh by-golly have a Holly Jolly Yuletide this year (traditional lyrics, Johnny Marks)

At Winter Solstice in ancient times, battles stopped, laws were suspended, businesses closed and no arrests were made. Everyone became equal— slaves and masters, rich and poor, adults and children, police and criminals. Cross-dressing, masquerades, and frolic ruled. A King of Mis-conduct was crowned. Children commanded the adults, rich served poor, employees gave instruction to their employers. This wild escapade was reminiscent of the Golden World where seasons were mild and food was simple. There was no greed, hunger, poverty, jails, laws or religion- nothing to kill or die for. Everyone was equal, a brotherhood of man. Someday this Golden World will return and we will live in harmony with each other and nature.

In Celebrate the Solstice Heinberg says "When we honor the deep, abiding cycles of nature and cosmos, our lives are filled with light. In human consciousness, light appears as inspiration… Inspiration may shatter previous conventions. And yet this fresh light carries with it the seed of new order." Allow the light of inspiration free play. Our world is in the process of dying and renewing itself. If we are wise, we will mourn the end of our civilization, which is becoming destructive, and leave space for something new to be born.

Solstice Carols
Return of the Light
Carolyn McVickar Edwards

Silent Night

Silent night, holy night, all is calm, all is bright.
Radiance streams from sun's infant face
Birthing again, you flood us with grace!
Bright star, light up the world,
bright star light up the world.

Joy To The World

Joy to the world, the light returns.
Let folk their songs employ.
While fields and floods, rocks, hills, and plains
Repeat the sounding joy, repeat the sounding joy
Repeat, repeat, the sounding joy.

Oh Come All Ye People

Oh come all ye people, joyful and triumphant
Oh come ye, oh come ye to the edge of the sea.
Come and behold it, light this day returns to us.
Oh come let us rekindle, oh come let us rekindle,
Oh come let us rekindle: Light returns.

O Holy Night

Oh holy night, the stars are brightly shining!
It is the night of the Sun Child's birth.
Long we have lain in cold and fear of hunger,
But sun returns and the earth wakes again!
A ray of hope, the weary world rejoices
For yonder breaks a new and glorious morn!
Sing and give thanks, oh lift your voices high now
The sun returns, sun returns to light the world.
Rejoice! Rejoice! Oh sun returns.

Chapter 5
Fooled

April Fools Jean Wells Rogers

No one goes hungry, all people are fed.
The oceans are clean, Lake Erie's not dead.
The Irish aren't fighting, the Arabs love Jews
The swords are now plowshares,
Now ain't that good news?
The water's delicious, the air is so clear
On top of a mountain, you see to next year.
Couples stay married, children are jewels
    Sure got you going! April Fools!

Vast swirls of garbage spin in ocean currents. A 5,000 mile blanket of seaweed can be seen from space. Oil spills kill sea life, fish and birds die caught in plastic, mammals and turtles and die tangled in nets. Dead penguins and crabs line beaches. Dolphins and whales beach themselves. Displaced carp and mussels in lakes and rivers, raccoons in Japan, cats in New Zeeland, pythons in the Florida everglades, Asian murder-hornets in the USA. Chemclouds poison the air, soil, crops and us, putting nanoparticles in our bodies. We are a displaced species. Geoengineered weather cause wildfires, droughts, tornedos and hurricanes. Geo-wildfires cleared a path for the Trans Mountain pipeline. Ionosphere heaters melted Arctic glaciers to clear shipping lanes. California Redwoods were torched to clear a 300-mile right-of-way for trails along the Northwestern Pacific Railroad. Genome engineering of plants, people and animals threaten all life. Humans caused this. We are the greatest invasive species on earth, breaking the laws of nature and creation. Nature will have the final say, not man. It will wipe us out if we do not stop our mad path to ruin. Will humanity become extinct?

Chapter 6
Jehovah As Mithra

Jehovah changes his mask throughout history. His birthday is always December 25th. He crucifies enlightened beings like Jesus, Krishna and others, uses them as Decoy-Saviors and then pretends to be the Savior risen from the dead.

The Cult of Mithra, a Roman mystery religion, had secrets known only to disciples. The shrines were hewn out of natural caves, or built underground. They had carved stone statues, wall paintings, stone relief and mosaic depicting figures and scenes. Raised benches were along the side walls with a sanctuary at the back. Every cave had a representation of Mithra as Father Time, and Mithra slaying a white bull.

Mithra as Father Time (Chronos) symbolizes Mithra existing through long ages and cycles. Chronos is not Cronos, Greek God of the golden era. Mithra has a lion head and holds a key. The key symbolizes time, the key to Mithra's existence, ruling the animal world. The Lion head symbolizes all creatures existing in time being devoured by Mithra. The snake around his lower body symbolizes the lower chakras that sustain him.

The legend of Mithra says he killed a white bull, which changed into the moon and started her monthly cycles, creating time. The bull's seed was used to form man, woman, and creatures. This legend is about Jehovah/Mithra's separation of the sexes. Mithra killing a white bull was a satanic spell, so the buffalo destined to announce White Buffalo Woman's return, would die early. This would delay and perhaps stop her promise from being fulfilled. Miracle lived 10 years.

Mithraism expanded with conquests of the Persian armies, spreading east through India and China. It was later adopted by Roman soldiers and spread throughout the vast Roman Empire. Mithra was worshipped by Roman rulers and its army for over 300 years.

Mithra initiations had seven rites that brought liberation from bondage. They included torture by water, fire, frost, hunger and thirst. Animals were sacrificed, mostly birds. On Mithra's birthday (December 25th) soldiers partook of his bread and wine sacrament and sacred bulls were killed. This was called the Taurobolium. A priest stood under a platform of planks pierced with small holes. A bull was killed and its blood rained through the holes onto the priest below, who turned his face upward so the blood would run on his face and open mouth.

Mithra was god of heaven and had a final day of judgment where the dead would resurrect. This similarity to Christianity is not Satan imitating Christ. Satan, Christ, Mithra and Jehovah are all the same being. Christianity is the cult of Mithra. The name changed and the initiations and blood-splattering rituals went underground (now called satanic rituals) but it is the same religion.

Avesta, hymn to Mithra, says "he cuts down all the limbs to pieces, and mingles, together with the earth, the bones, hair, brains, and blood of the men who have lied…" *He* "spies out his enemies… he swoops down upon them, scatters and slaughters them. He desolates and lays waste the homes of the wicked, he annihilates the tribes and the nations that are hostile to him. He assures victory unto them… that honor him and offer him the sacrificial libations." This is Jehovah. He will soon be cut off and surrounded in light; he will then utterly wither away.

Chapter 7
Numerology Chart

The universe is alive; it has awareness, intelligence, and inspires its evolution. The universe is a mathematical structure and it can be explored using codes. Numerology is one of the codes we can use. Every letter is assigned a number. The numbers in each word are added, then the numbers in the total are added together until a single digit is produced. This is called digit summing. For example, hello is 8+5+3+3+6=**25** (2+5=7). Hello is 7.

To find the number of your full name reduc e each word to a single digit, add the digits together and reduce again.

David Daniel Baker would be David: 4+1+4+9+4=22 (2+2=**4**). Daniel: 4+1+5+9+5+3=27 (2+7=**9**). Baker: 2+1+2+5+9=19 (1+9=10=**1**). David vibrates to a 4; his full name (4+9+1=14) vibrates to a 5 (1+4).

The number of these names is 666:
[The Holy Ghost] and [Jehovah, Yahveh, Mithra]

The	2+5+8=**15**	(1+5=**6**)	
Holy	8+6+3+7=**24**	(2+4=**6**)	
Ghost	7+8+6+1+2=**24**	(2+4=**6**)	

Jehovah	1+5+8+6+4+1+8=33	(3+3=**6**)	
Yahveh (YHVH)	7+1+8+4+5+8=33	(3+3=**6**)	
Mithra	4+9+2+8+9+1=33	(3+3=**6**)	

Numerology Chart

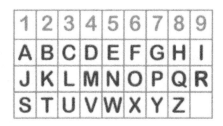

1	2	3	4	5	6	7	8	9
A	B	C	D	E	F	G	H	I
J	K	L	M	N	O	P	Q	R
S	T	U	V	W	X	Y	Z	

Chapter 8
Signs are Messages

Signs give you guidance, answers and warnings, and can manifest miracles. Jehovah said it is evil to seek after signs (Matt 12:38). He does not want us to receive guidance. Signs may be something ordinary that repeats, something extraordinary, anything that gets your attention.

Expression signs: I can't stand it- unwilling to take a stand. It goes without saying- not saying what you need too. Can of worms- parasites. It pisses me off- kidney trouble. I can't stomach this- digestive problems. I could have died- death wish. You're getting on my nerves- pinched nerves.

Everyday signs: Cluttered house- repressed emotions. Boating- keeping up with the Jones'. Swimming- going in circles. Unfinished house- unfinished business. Impulsively cleaning- need to cleanse. Stiff neck- pain in the neck. Stumbling- look before you leap. Foot injury- stand on your own two feet. Breaking an arm- not in control. Stubbing your toe- not respecting yourself.

Use a dictionary to find the meaning of signs. Select what applies to your situation. Homophones can mean the word that's pronounced the same, and an object can have multiple meanings. A bird may mean: someone odd (queer bird), a secret (little bird told me), something you possess (bird in the hand), people with common interests (bird of a feather), disapproval (give the bird), reproduction (birds and bees), worthless (for the birds), humiliation (eating crow). A horse may mean: arrogant (high horse), revive a futile idea (beat a dead horse), good authority (horse's mouth), bad judgment (back the wrong horse), be patient (hold your horses), something entirely different (horse of another color).

Dream signs: A softball player dreamed he ran into a parade while running errands and went home. This might mean he will have a successful season. Parade- seasons;

home- hitting the target. A woman wondering if her fiancé was trustworthy had this same dream. It might mean her fiancé is assuming a misleading appearance (parade) and her heart (home) knows this. A girl hanging out with the wrong crowd dreams of wild horses. It could mean her friends are mocking her. Horse- target of jokes. A business man, thinking about signing a contract has this dream. He should sign. Horse means power, expertise, capability.

Unusual world events may contain world messages. Thomas Jefferson and John Adams died within hours of each other on July 4th 1826. President Kennedy, C.S. Lewis, and Aldous Huxley died on 11-22-63, within hours of each other. Their synchronistic deaths hold worldwide warnings.

Kennedy was restoring the Constitution when he was murdered. Lewis wrote a fantasy novel about a land children could enter with their imagination (Narnia). Huxley revealed a world where fetuses are brain damaged with oxygen depletion. Everyone produces for the corporate government. Kennedy's message: restore the US Constitution. Lewis' message: encourage children to use their imagination. Huxley's message: stop the Brave New World.

If a major event in your life happens on a historical day, it is a sign. My body birthday is June 20- the day the US Great Seal was approved by Congress. I may be instrumental in restoring its legal depiction (front) and true meaning (back). The reverse shows an open 3rd eye above a flattop pyramid: the enlightened govern the country (C 16). My soul-exchange birthday is September 17, Constitution Day. This book may help restore the Federal Republic (C 18). The most horrific, one day battle between the USA and the Confederate States happened September 17- a sign we were changing our Republic of Sovereign States to a National Government.

While Sandra was unraveling the gospel, the brightest comet in history made its debut (summer 95). As Hale-Bopp reached its brightest peak (spring 97) the Red River in North Dakota flooded- the flooding was unprecedented. Grand Forks suffered the greatest damage. The Red River signified the Red Road in Black Elk's vision; Grand Forks symbolized the fork where the Red and Back roads crossed. A 'Mystery Angel' donated millions of dollars to the flooded families, symbolizing angels helping us turn onto the Red Road.

My Manifest Miracles Signs: 8-20-08 (Miracle's birthday) I found a teething toy in the shape of an 8 by a waterfall. The Beijing Olympics were in progress. They opened on 08/08/08 at 8:08. The theme song was "Light the Passion, Share the Dream." Will we manifest this miracle?

2009, three UPS semitrucks pulling three trailers, turned in front of me- 9 box cars. It was a sign. **UPS** symbolizes Christians uniting in various denominations and praying for spiritual assistance to cast out The Holy Ghost: **U**nited- come together; **P**arcel- designations; **S**ervice- help. The UPS box cars symbolized this book going out to the world in vast quantities. UPS delivers over 15 million packages a day in over 200 countries. After the truck-train passed, I went to the store. My total came to $222. It was the fifth time I saw/heard 222 in a week: a receipt, movie, book, and the radio. In 2016 I saw 222 four times in an hour: credit card bill, the time, page 222 in my novel, a paragraph I revised on page 222.

1/1/22 I dreamed of dancing with Sandra's baby (this book). On 2-22-22 and 4-22-22 my car died. They were signs that something is blocking this book. It's been available since 2015. When the apocalypse began to unfold and more was revealed, I frequently edited my book and republished, to add new information. 4-22-22 a powerful gust of wind blew through my house knocking figurines off a shelf, breaking them. Having my car die and a supernatural wind blow through my house on earth day were important signs. The wind is Moriah's Cleansing Wind. It removed the block against my book. The Cleansing Wind will help you see deceptions, remove obstacles, have awareness, find a group to work with, and have courage.

Broken figurines:	**Octopus**- vigilance
Racoon- deception	**Beaver**- work with others
Elephant- obstacles	**Tiger**- courage

2016, three birds flew in my house: one entered my office, one flew in the laundry room, one went in the hallway. The bird in my office symbolized this book revealing hidden operations (public office). The bird in the laundry room- exposing skeletons in the closet; the bird in the hallway- entering a new phase. One bird flew out my office window, one went out the porch door, and one flew out the side door.

The birds came in together and left at the same time.

On 8-20-16 (Miracle's birthday) I climbed down my cliff. The ground was steep and I started slipping. Going forward or back was not an option; I had to go up. The rockface was solid with places to grip. I hit a point going west where I would fall if I took one more step (point of no return). Climbing the north rockface symbolized turning off the Black Road (east-west) onto the red road (north-south). My climb will help manifest this miracle.

3-17-07, at a writer's convention in New York, I watched the St. Patrick's Day Parade, walked to The Roosevelt Hotel where I was staying and entered the lobby. Hundreds of people were crowded around the lobby and balcony, looking at me with anticipation. A band entered playing bagpipes and quickly formed a double circle around me. I stood in the center, with band-circles going in opposite directions, their music reverberating throughout the hotel. This synchronistic event will manifest miracles: standing against Roosevelt's fascism plot (The Roosevelt Hotel) and surviving a famine. Saint Patrick's Day parade symbolizes Irish diaspora.

I was doing Symbolic Play (a therapy I developed) summer of 2021 and a baby figurine in my scene said 'help me'. One year later Covid vaccines were ready for babies that would permanently damage them. We must protect babies from this evil. Covid vaccines damage babies; some do not survive.

While writing Chapter 12, shockwaves swept through me. I asked for a sign to confirm its truths. A book on my table said **Government Lies**. There were no Arab hijackers, no planes crashed, no passengers died. There was a false flag terrorist attack using missiles and detonations hidden behind a TV hoax. When these truths hit your heart, shockwaves will sweep through you and you will awaken. 11:11 symbolizes the truth behind the towers destruction.

Chapter 9
USA Constitution
And Christianity

"The United States of America is not in any sense founded on the Christian religion (USA treaty with Tripoli, 1796)." The Constitution separates church and state: "no religious test shall ever be required as a qualification to any office or public trust (Article VI, Clause 3)." The Declaration of Independence says if the government becomes destructive "it is the right of the people to alter or abolish it." This was a departure from England, where kings ruled from their religious dictates.

A secret shadow government has been working to establish a Christian theocracy to take over the US government, since its beginning. Mormons believe their church will rule the US before Christ returns. Masons and Fundamentalists believe they will take over the country for Christ. The top men in these groups work together, to accomplish this (Global Elite).

Hamilton wanted Christian influence in the US government. He organized the Christian Constitutional Society to fortify his Federalist party. He favored bankers and merchants; they pushed for a broad (false) interpretation of the constitution, so the federal government could control commerce, finance and overseas trade. They were against the Bill of Rights.

The Nation-States limited the federal government. They did not form The State of America, they formed The United States of America. States have their own constitution, government branches, police, prisons and military under the Governor. Jefferson fought for the united States and the real Constitution. His Democrat-Republican party had farmers, shopkeepers, artisans, frontier settlers.

James Madison: The purpose of separation of church and state is to keep forever from these shores the ceaseless strife that has soaked the soil of Europe in blood for centuries.
Thomas Jefferson: I do not find in Orthodox Christianity one

redeeming feature. **Benjamin Franklin:** I have found Christian dogma unintelligible... Lighthouses are more helpful than churches. **John Adams:** Do you think a Protestant Popedom is annihilated... have you ever attended to the ecclesiastical strives in Maryland, Pennsylvania, New York, and every part of New England? What a mercy it is that these people cannot whip and crop, and pillory and roast in the U.S. If they could they would. **Thomas Paine:** the obscene stories, the voluptuous debaucheries, the cruel and torturous executions, the unrelenting vindictiveness, with which more than half of the Bible is filled, it would be more consistent that we call it the word of a demon than the word of God.

The founding fathers separated government from religion, to stop Christian zealots from running the country. Christians believed God gave them their new world and told them how to take it: slaughter, pillage, enslave, and destroy.

Jefferson wanted to eliminate slavery in his Declaration of Independence but was voted down. He called slavery 'moral depravity' and a 'hideous blot.' He said everyone has a right to personal liberty and pushed for gradual, compensated emancipation to end slavery, banning slave importation in Virginia. Jefferson inherited two plantations and over 100 slaves. He knew freeing them with 'no place to go and no means to support themselves' would bring them misfortune (Wikipedia).' Jefferson's slaves depended on him. States were passing laws forbidding freed slaves to live there.

Most Christians in the early 1800s believed wiping out the red man was their duty. Jefferson said Indians were equal to the white man. He praised them for their friendship, courage, honor and oratory. He said the Indian 'meets death with more deliberation than any other race on earth.' Jefferson's attitude did not save the Indians; they were wiped out.

The native's homeland, going back thousands of years, was diminishing. With the acquisition of Louisiana their days of roaming free were numbered. Jefferson did not question the right of an overflowing white population occupying their scarcely populated lands. He believed their way of life could not exist in an expanding United States. Jefferson wanted Indians to have farms and cattle, learn reading and writing, and intermarry with Whites. He cared about Indians (on his own terms) when few people of his day did.

When President Jefferson sent Lewis and Clark to explore the Louisiana territory, he told them to offer friendship and trade to the Indians and collect linguistic records. Jefferson was interested in Indian folklore and speech. The red man had a superior way of life, but Jefferson believed the white man did and Indians would adopt it for benefits. There were no benefits. They were forced onto concentration camps a few years after Jefferson died. The rations were inadequate to sustain life and thousands died.

Pastor Phelps (1929—2014) is one of the Christian zealots John Adams said would 'whip and crop, and pillory and roast' if they could. Phelps said the Bible permits slavery, but "God hating heathens later changed the constitution and turned against God… The keeping of women in their proper place and the wiping out of the red man were also some of our other original Christian principles that we hardly follow anymore… If we don't go back to… Biblical laws such as stoning fags and stubborn children to death, then 9/11 and Katrina will seem like nothing compared with what the good Lord has in store for you devil worshipping dogs."

Using the Bible at the Presidential inauguration is not law. As Obama's hand rested on Lincoln's Bible at his swearing-in Ceremony, Roberts fumbled the oath. The next day he re-administered it in the Map Room of the White House, without the Bible. This oath canceled the first one, breaking the Biblical pledge. This was the first time a USA President was sworn in a second time after the pubic swearing-in. The Map Room symbolized the USA finding its true course, fulfilling its destiny. Will this miracle manifest?

The Presidential Oath: "I do solemnly swear/affirm that I will faithfully execute the Office of President of the United States, and will to the best of my ability, preserve, protect and defend the Constitution of the United States.

Remember Diane from <u>Holy Terror</u> (Conway, Siegelman)? She read the Declaration of Independence in her dictionary: 'We hold these truths to be self-evident, that all men are created equal, that they are endowed by their Creator with certain unalienable rights, that among these are life, liberty, and the pursuit of happiness.' Diane thought "Being a Christian, you don't have any rights to your life. You certainly don't have any liberty. And as far as the pursuit of happiness, forget it... My God, our government is more Christian, more loving, more forgiving, more free than God's government!"

That spring (1980) there was a Jesus March on Washington. "When I saw that they were going to try to take over the country, I knew that it was possible for them to do it..." Diane took her recorder to Washington. There were 200,000 participants and she asked some of them if their march was political. They said no. "I talked to people from California, from Illinois, from Georgia, and Virginia... I said, 'If this isn't political, why did you come to Washington?' They couldn't answer me. They replied with scripture."

Diane knew Christians love Jesus, but they were being prepared "for something of which they had no idea." Diane said "when you make that decision to accept Jesus into your heart, you give up your life. You think you are giving it up to Jesus, but in truth you are giving it up to something else..." Diane's tapes from the Jesus March said: "This nation was founded on God... This nation is going down... This whole nation is going to be destroyed..." Diane thought, if the End-time happens, Christians will bring it about themselves and the world will have Armageddon.

Many Christians believe the United States of America will be replaced with the Lord's Government when the Messiah returns. Christian Nationalism, preaching Christian identity, is preparing the way. Republican politicians and Southern Baptist preachers have said they stand for a Christian Nation, ending church and state separation. The Global Elite want to: Make America Great Again (Christian), remove Church and State division and keep foreigners and immigrants out.

These agendas are going forward. The Department of Homeland Security created a Disinformation Governance Board to track and collect data. They are searching for people exposing their agendas. The Global Elite are tightening their net. Our lives are in danger. If the USA becomes a Christian Nation, a caste system will arise with white Christian men running the country, women and children reduced to property, and people of color killed, enslaved, or deported. Jehovah is a violent god; countries who worship him (Israel, Arab world) live under tyranny with no rights of life, liberty, security or protection from being enslaved.

Hamza, a Palestinian boy, lost his family from Israeli bombardments. In the 2009 Israeli massacre his little brother died in front of him while playing outside. In 2012 his older brother died in an Israeli bombing. His father was killed during the 2014 massacre. Hamza began sleeping with his mother and never went outside without her. When the Israeli bombardment resumed in 2019, Hamza screamed through every bombing. The next day his Mother died in an explosion (5-7-2019). After his mother's death Hamza committed suicide, jumping to his death. May 2021 Palestinians were again massacred. Penned in by an Israeli blockade and trapped in Gaza, they came under heavy bombardment. Their genocide continued as nations around the world protested their slaughter. Israelis believe Muslims can be slaughtered to take their land because the Lord gave the land to them.

In David's 9-11 dream Osama was a cartoon character- he is not a real person. Osama was invented by the CIA and playacted by Obama, years before his planned presidency. Al-Qaeda is a Mossad—CIA trained mercenary group posing as Islamic Jihadists; USA and Israel are the real terrorists.

Obama put his Osama disguise on when Osama was needed. His lips were injected with some-thing to make them swell. No evidence exists of his death- he isn't real. Navy Seals who captured him were killed in a helicopter  crash in Afghanistan. Dead men can't talk.

In 2011 NATO escalated wars across the Middle East and North Africa: Libya, Yemen, Iran, Egypt, Jordon, Iraq, Kuwait, Sudan, Algeria, Syria and Palestine. Millions took to the streets. As protests spread, government crackdowns and violence from police and military spread; millions of lives were uprooted, their countries devastated. In 2020 this happened worldwide: Covid lockdowns, restrictions, protests and police brutality. The USA, Europe and Israel were behind all this. They are puppet-countries for the Global Elite; NATO is their armed forces.

Hamza

GAZA (PALESTINE)

Turquie en Force

Government Separated From Religion
Protects Your Liberty and Your Life

Chapter 10
We The People

The USA Constitution limits the Federal Government to insure State sovereignty. From its beginning, inside forces worked to destroy State's Rights. Hamilton spread a false interpretation of the Constitution to expand federal powers. He wanted a bureaucracy that favored merchants and bankers and federal power to suspend habeas corpus and free speech. Lincoln imprisoned people without trial for speaking or printing anything against the war between the United States and Confederate States.

In 1860 congress passed the Morrill tariff. This high tariff would devastate the South and they began seceding from the union. The Global Elite were behind this. Their Agenda: force the South to secede, then fight a war to remove States rights, laying the groundwork for Christian Nationalism. Their plot worked; the South seceded and formed their own Nation: The Confederate States of America.

Lincoln violated the constitution by declaring war on the Confederate States. He said he fought the Confederacy to save the Union. The only way to save it was to honor the South's secession. Lincoln knew they had a constitutional right to secede. He was in on the conspiracy to destroy States rights. Robert E Lee was fighting for the Sovereignty of States. He was admired and loved, even by his enemies. Removing his statue was an act of depravity.

Lincoln: "This government of the people, by the people, for the people, shall not perish from the earth." **Calhoun:** "Without a full, practical recognition of the rights and sovereignty of the States, our union and liberty must perish."

The war was not fought to end slavery. Slave ships were built in the North. Loaded with rum, they sailed to Africa, exchanged rum for slaves, sailed to the West Indies where slaves were traded for molasses, then returned to New England, sometimes stopping at a Southern port to deliver blacks to auctioneers. Lincoln said "I am not, nor ever have been, in favor of bringing about in any way a social and political equality of the White and Black races." He was not in favor of Blacks marrying Whites, being voters, jurors or holding office. The war was fought to keep the union together, ending State rights to secede- our most powerful check on the government. When States lose sovereignty we do too.

Hamilton, Lincoln and Hitler may be the same reincarnated man. Lincoln and Hitler were eloquent speakers and could sway a crowd. Lincoln quoted Jefferson when he wanted to influence Southerners, then he did whatever he wanted too, which was often the opposite of what he said. Hitler also did this. Lincoln wanted to export all black people out of the USA. Hitler wanted all Jews out of Germany- or killed.

Lincoln and Hitler both gave 'Almighty God' credit for their savage wars and said they were fighting for the Lord. Lincoln and Hitler loved to crack jokes, yet no one knew who they really were. Every friend, acquaintance and enemy saw a different man. They both used the same tactics in their illegal wars- slaughter and destroy everything. They both threw raging fits, repeatedly dismissing and replacing their top generals. Lincoln and Hitler were relentlessly obsessed with the latest weapons of their day, and they were war criminals.

The 14th amendment gave equal rights to everyone. In 1886 the Supreme Court violated this amendment, saying it included corporate personhood. Corporations were endowed with human rights. They could hold property, enter contracts, sue and be sued, protecting them from state legislation. Corporate personhood is unconstitutional.

The US Constitution says congress is to create, regulate and distribute money through the US Treasury Department, not banks. The Federal Reserve is a private banking system. This is prohibited by the Constitution. Jefferson said banking institutions were more dangerous to liberty than standing armies. "If the American people ever allow private banks to control the issuance of their currencies... the banks and

258

corporations that will grow up around them will deprive the people of all their prosperity until their children will wake up homeless on the continent their fathers conquered."

In the 1800s people rose against banks and corporate wealth. "Despite a generation of hard toil, the people are poor today... the whole system under which they have lived is a lie and an imposture. They have produced but they possess not. They have amassed wealth for other people to enjoy while they themselves are almost without the necessaries of life (Pollack)."

Federal Reserve and income tax, established in 1913, are unconstitutional. The Federal Government can't tax people and congress is to create our money, not banks. Within ten years the Federal Reserve drove the USA into bankruptcy. Roosevelt pledged US citizens as collateral for debt caused by the Federal Reserve. Birth certificates since 1933 are issued on banknote paper with a warehouse receipt required under commercial code laws. We are human resources! This is why our name is capitalized on legal documents.

The Federal Reserve has no federal and no reserve. It takes in billions in interest every year. Earnings are returned to the Treasury, minus Federal Reserve operation costs. A 90% return on a two-trillion-dollar profit is 20 billion! The Federal Reserve is not audited to determine expenses. When the stock market crashed (08) the Federal Reserve forced small banks and businesses into financial ruin and collected two-trillion from 90-day loans to corporations, buying their commercial paper. Covid put trillions more in their pockets. If not stopped, the world will be thrown into financial meltdown.

The Federal Reserve orders new paper money, the Bureau of Engraving and Printing (BEP) prints them, and the Federal Reserve distributes them. The Federal Reserve charges the Treasury's general account for the face value of the notes plus printing cost. These banknotes are debt money- the Treasury pays interest to the Federal Reserve banks for the notes. United States Notes are credit money- the Treasury did not buy their own notes when they printed new paper money. United States Notes were issued to the banks by the Treasury as credit (no interest) and there was no borrowing or lending; they are not banknotes. Federal Reserve Notes are put into circulation by Federal Reserve Banks.

The US owns the BEP, yet the Treasury pays the Federal Reserve face value for money the BEP prints! If the Federal Reserve orders 1-billion in paper dollars, the Treasury pays the Federal Reserve bankers 1-billion. If congress orders 1-billion paper dollars, the BEP prints them. The Treasury does not purchase them; they're distributed to banks as credit. United States Notes were in circulation from 1862 —1971. Federal Reserve Notes were first issued in 1913. Both types of paper money were being used at the same time until 1971.

The Federal reserve needs to be dissolved- assets held by the Board- notes, bonds, gold, silver, coins, everything in their possession returned to the Treasury and Federal Reserve Notes destroyed, replaced by United States Notes. The country would become solvent. This is what President Kennedy intended to do. He bypassed the Federal Reserve by issuing United States Notes and silver certificates. After his murder, President Johnson ordered the silver certificates and United States Notes, that Kennedy had printed and were not in circulation, destroyed. No more were printed.

In 1962, US military leaders planned a false flag plot to incite war with Cuba called Operation Northwoods. Kennedy rejected it. He planned to withdraw troops from Viet Nom and dismantle the CIA. Kennedy requested the CIA files on UFOs. They are not unidentified to the CIA; they know what they are and who's in them. Outsiders are not allowed access. Within days, President Kennedy was dead.

Now the USA is engaged in a false flag war. Ukraine bombed its own cities using Russian helicopters and tanks supplied by the USA, to blame Putin. Putin bombed Ukraine military installations, not cities. Corporate sanctions against Russia were greater than the USA's. Corporations should not be allowed to levy sanctions. The USA and its allies froze Russian money in European banks (500-billion+). Biden said they would also seize Russian oligarch assets (yachts, mansions, jets). This is tyranny. The USA and NATO use political power to steal wealth.

Putin asked, are there sanctions against Israel and the USA for killing women and children in Palestine, Afghanistan, Iraq, Syria, Cuba, Vietnam, or stealing their wealth? Were there sanctions against the USA and France for killing Qadhafi and destroying Libya? Have NATO soldiers been punished for raping and torturing women and children in all mentioned countries? Are there sanctions against France for causing crises in African countries? US, Israel and NATO must be punished for war crimes. We must change the balance of forces in the world and make sure everyone has equal rights.

After the collapse of the Soviet Union, many Nazis living in the USA and Canada moved to Ukraine. Since 2015, the CIA has been training Ukraine military and running Nazi summer camps for boys. NATO and the USA control Ukraine. They outsourced illegal bioweapon labs there and it's a strategic spot to instigate World War III. The USA gave Ukraine 54-billion for their dominantly Nazi military. Ukraine citizens supporting Putin and wanting to be annexed into Russia, are accused of assisting the enemy and imprisoned.

October 2022, Nord Stream pipelines in the Baltic Sea were damaged. The pipes, built to transport gas from Russia to Germany, were full. This was the biggest release of methane ever recorded. Putin said 'Sanctions [and stealing] were not enough, they moved on to sabotage.' Methane warms the atmosphere 30 times more than carbon dioxide over a 100 year period. Within days of the pipeline attack, explosions damaged the new, 4-billion Russian—Crimea bridge. June 2023 the Russian controlled Kahovka damn exploded. These barbaric acts of sabotage are NATO false flag war crimes.

Biden is not running the country, the Global Elite are; only their façade remains. They are moving the USA toward the Christian far right and Trump is their Front Man. He appears to be in charge but he is following their agenda. Both Hitler and Trump polarized their countries. Hitler wanted to restore Germany to its former greatness. Trump promises to make America great again. Hitler claimed Jewish immigrants were taking jobs from Germans. Trump says Mexican immigrants are taking jobs from Americans. Hitler had a fascist regime for Aryans. Trump wants a Christian National, fascist government for Christian far-right.

Did Hamilton reincarnate as Abraham Lincoln

Hamilton died in 1804   Lincoln was born in 1809

Did Jefferson reincarnate as John F Kennedy

Jefferson died in 1826   Kennedy was born in 1917

Were Alexander Abraham and Adolf the same soul

1775—1804   1809—1865   1889—1945

Chapter 11
The County Sheriff

Richard Mack, former Arizona sheriff, says a sheriff's duty is to the people of his county and the constitution. Within his jurisdiction the sheriff has more power than the Governor of his State and the President of the United States. He is the county's supreme law enforcement officer and does not need to enforce laws enacted on Federal and State levels, if he deems them unconstitutional.

Your county sheriff has power to defend his citizens against Federal crimes. If your civil liberties are violated by Government surveillance, no-warrant search and seizures, being arrested for speaking out on government abuses, investigating industry abuses, farming on your land, having your place illegally condemned, taking videos that expose covert crimes, peacefully protesting and being arrested, stocking up food or cash, report the abuse to your local sheriff. Your county sheriff is 'America's last hope to regain our forgotten freedom.' Give your county sheriff a copy of The County Sheriff: America's Last Hope (Mack)."

Attention County Sheriffs

If Federal Agents violate the rights of people in your county, it is your duty to arrest them. No one supersedes your jurisdiction. Stand in your power.

264

Holding Out for A Hero

Footloose

Where have all the good men gone
and where are all the Gods?
Where's the street-wise Hercules
to fight the rising odds?
Isn't there a white knight upon a fiery steed?
Late at night I toss and I turn
and I dream of what I need... I need a hero.
I'm holding out for a hero till the morning light.
He's gotta be sure, and it's gotta be soon,
and he's gotta be larger than life...
Through the wind... and the rain,
and the storm, and the flood,
I can feel his approach like a fire in my blood...

Chapter 12
Final Countdown

Nine Eleven was planned over two thousand years ago, to begin the final countdown to Armageddon. The spell began 9/11/1941 when the first Pentagon stone was laid in a Masonic ritual. It ended sixty years later to the day (9/11/2001) after the satanic plots all unfolded.

Daniel 9:24 says 77s are determined to end the removal of our daily sacrifice (casting out demons), seal my vision and prophecy, and establish New Jerusalem. Jehovah calculated 77s were needed to stop my forewarnings to the world.

Flight **77** hit the **77**-foot-tall Pentagon, standing on the **77**th Meridian, **77** minutes after take-off (it left at 8:20 and crashed at 9:37). It was **77** minutes from the 1st plane hitting the tower (8:46) to the last one crashing in Pennsylvania (10:03).

The World Trade Center was a word trade center for merchandise. Babylon is merchandise traffic (including human cargo). **World** is humanity, **Trade** (buy/sell) is buying the plan of salvation, selling ourselves. **Center** is alliance— our pact with the Lord. The smoking towers symbolized Jehovah bringing Babylon (plan of salvation) to an end.

"When they see the smoke of her burning... they cast dust on their heads and cried, weeping and wailing... all that had ships on the sea became rich through her wealth! In one hour, she has been brought to ruin (Rev 18:18—19)" The wealthy merchants are the Global Elite. When Jehovah is finished with Babylon, he will kill them.

When I wrote the following, I didn't know missiles hit the towers or that reactors beneath them caused their fall:

As President Bush headed toward Booker Elementary, Flight 11 hit the North Tower. It was 8:46 AM. Flight 175 had veered off course; it hit the South Tower 20 minutes later at 9:03 a.m. Flight 77 turned severely off course at 8:55. It was tracked by radar from Chicago to the Pentagon. If a commercial flight veers from their normal route, Federal law mandates the Air Force dispatch a plane to investigate. The Air Force did not follow protocol that morning. No fighter planes were launched to stop the renegade planes until after the damage was done. Bush was informed of this situation in his limo and gave no orders to intercept or investigate the hijacked planes.

President Bush arrived at the school at 8:55. He was greeted by reporters and asked about the attack. He called it an accident. Bush said they would go ahead and "do the reading thing anyway." He was there to push for passage of No Child Left Behind. Bush entered Daniel's 2nd grade classroom at 9:00. A minute later Chief of Staff Andrew Card, whispered in his ear: "A second plane hit the second Tower. America is under attack." He stepped back without waiting for a response.

Why didn't the Secret Service remove Bush from the school and take him to a secure base? That is their job; they don't need the President's permission to do it. Secret Service agents burst into Cheney's office, grabbed him under his arms and propelled him down the steps into the White House underground bunker.

Four planes were "hijacked" three before Bush walked in the classroom. Flight 11 and 175 had hit the Twin Towers. Flight 77 was headed toward Washington DC. Flight 93 was reported hijacked at 9:16 am. Did the President know where these two planes would strike? Is that why he went to the school when the country was under attack? Did Bush know he was not putting himself and the children at risk? Why did he remain in the classroom for the scheduled book reading?

As the towers fell, school children read The Pet Goat with President Bush. People were burning, trapped under rubble, jumping from windows. "It was like raining people. You could hear when they hit the ground, bang, bang, and the body parts just dismantling all over the place… (firefighter Myers)."

The school reading with Bush was scheduled to occur as the towers fell, to cast a satanic spell. The story in Reading Mastery II, pages 153—158 is the spell. It was also cast to stop pages 153—158 in this book from exposing the Global Elite's blueprint, that they drew up before World War II.

The Demonic Spell: A girl gets a pet goat; they play in the house and yard. The goat ate cans and canes, pans, panes, caps and capes. The Dad said the goat must go. The girl says she will stop him from eating those things and she does. One day a car robber tries to steal the Dad's car while the girl and goat are in the yard. The story says **more to come**. Bush asks the children 'what does that mean?' The robber bends over the car seat and the goat runs at him and hits him with his sharp horns. "The car robber went flying."

The Dad runs out of the house and grabs the robber, "you were trying to steal my car" he yells. "But my goat stopped him" said the girl. The Dad says "The goat saved my car" ... he can stay and eat all the cans, canes, caps and capes he wants. Everyone smiles except the car robber. He said "I am sore." The End.

The robber is the terrorist. The car is the World Trade Center. President Bush is the Dad. The girl is the American people. The Goat that eats everything is the Government consuming our livelihood. The house is our home. Yard is an outdoor enclosure. Is the yard confined cities and towns? The goat's restrictions (constitution) are broken. The Dad says the goat can have cans (preserves, reservations), canes (thrash, torture), caps (control, coercion) and capes (cloak, cover-ups, decoys). This is "more to come".

The goat pushed the robber inside the car and he went flying— the government sent the planes to hit the Towers. The robber does not steal the car— the planes did not take down the Towers, something else made them collapse. The robber is sore- untreated. This is taken care of. Laws are passed to stop terrorism by removing our Constitutional rights.

There is another outcome in this story. The girl worked a miracle and stopped the goat from consuming their household products. Will this miracle materialize?

I discovered Lefebvre's video I Pet Goat II several years after he made it and was astounded. What Lefebvre knows: The US government is controlled by the Global Elite (goat with bar code). Bush cast a satanic spell in the classroom. Osama was created by the CIA. The towers were demolished with nuclear explosions. Christ is a zombie and will kill the Global Elite and Christians if not stopped. All this is in his video (chapter 14).

Pet Goat I is 9-11   Pet Goat II is more to come

After the class reading, Bush delivered a televised address, telling the world exactly where he was. He said there was 'an apparent terrorist attack' and he would 'chase down those folks who committed this attack.'

Bush talked to Cheney in his limo on the way to the airport, and shortly after take-off (around 10:00 a.m.). Cheney recommended Bush "order our aircraft to shoot down these airliners that have been hijacked." Bush replied "you bet."

The hijacked planes had already hit their targets. Flight 93 crashed in Shanksville Pennsylvania at 10:03 a.m. Photos show a hole in the ground; where is the wreckage? Flight 77 hit the Pentagon at 9:38. The hole it left is too small for a Boeing 757 to have made, and where is the plane rubble?

Bush lingered at the school and left without security. His plane took off without military protection. Bush knew he was not in danger, otherwise he would have acted like a coward. Two months previous, Bush was attending a summit in Italy. It was reported Islamic terrorists might crash an airliner at the summit in an effort to kill Bush. The Italian government closed the airspace above Genoa and installed anti-aircraft missiles at the airport. An overnight stay on a luxury ship was planned. Bush refused to join them for fear of being attacked.

Warren Buffett, the richest man in the world, was hosting a charity benefit at Offutt Air Force base when 9/11 happened. Many business leaders met with him. If it wasn't for this meeting, some of these people would have been at their offices in the World Trade Center and died a horrible death. Instead they were at a high security military base. Offutt is where President Bush went later that day. Why was a charity benefit hosted at the U.S. Strategic Command headquarters on 9-11? Were they there for their own protection?

Dick Cheney scheduled Air Force war exercises for the morning of 9/11. This placed blips on FAA radar screens that simulated hijackings. A live-fly exercise was included. These war games imitated the 9-11 attacks. Were they decoys?

The Defense Department covertly implemented a plan called Rebuilding America's Defense, as presented by the Project for the New American Century (PNAC) in September, 2000. This secret plan is designed for the planned, USA global domination, including outer space and cyberspace. It includes an enlarged military to fight simultaneous wars; security bases worldwide to keep nations subservient to the USA; and nuclear rockets fired from spy satellites to suppress any challenge to this domination.

The DHS compiles information on all Americans; this is unconstitutional. Their potential 'terrorist' list includes States rights advocates, veterans against the military, and anyone spreading 'outrageous conspiracy theories.' These patriots of truth are under surveillance. Bush said: "If you are not with us, then you are against us!" Defenders of the Constitution are against Bush and his New World Order.

Transportation Security Administration (TSA) is part of PNAC. Its purpose is to remove our rights and control our movement. People using public buses have had their bags searched without warrants (random selection by TSA). This usually occurs in the morning when people are going to work. If they don't turn over their bag, they do not get on the bus. Government whistle-blowers are put on no-fly lists.

Airport employees working for TSA detained a mother with water in a tippy-cup, an 83-year-old woman in a wheelchair, a man carrying $4,700 in cash, a woman with breast milk in bottles, a nun (who was groped), a 5-year-old with the same name as a terrorist suspect, a man drinking bottled water at security check, a boy ordered to drink his pond-water specimen who refused, and a man wearing a urostomy bag, soaked in urine after a pat down.

TSA employees are trained to perform this harassment and told it's necessary. Flights could be computer-controlled from control towers and forced to land if hijacked. TSA airport security includes checking bodies through scanners, pat-downs, breast, and genital hand-exams. Little girls are reduced to tears as their private areas are checked; women have their breasts checked above, below and between. If they protest, they are threatened with removal like a criminal.

We stand in line and obey orders that violate our rights: "empty your pockets, remove your shoes and belt, step away from your child, freeze, do not help her." If States do not reclaim their rights, someday we will be given these commands and we will not be standing in an airport.

The federal government instructed States to put ID RFID chips in driver's licenses. It cost States millions; if they don't comply, our driver's licenses are not acceptable ID on commercial flights. Commercial airports are owned by States; they can privatize their airports, fire TSA employees commercialize air traffic control services, and cancel federal services connected to airports.

Muscatatuck Urban Training Center in Indiana is a 1,000-acre, self-contained site with an underground facility. MUTC trains the Army, Navy, Marine, Air Force and Special Operation Forces in Land, Air, Space, Maritime, and Cyber domains. They specialize in Urban Warfare, training the military to descend on cities, putting them in lockdown. August 2008 an urban warfare training happened in Portland. Radio talk show host, Clyde Lewis, saw black helicopters buzzing rooftops, dropping armed soldiers on top of buildings.

"After witnessing the low flyovers, the men with guns riding the choppers and the looks of fear on the faces of the people, I decided that what I was witnessing was most definitely harass-ment. The Department of Defense was responsible for alarming Portland residents with an unannounced exercise. They flew their threatening black helicopters at treetop level. They were dropping soldiers from the choppers on to rooftops and drowning the citizens in terrifying noise, giving them the idea that something terrible was happening to their city."

This scenario has been repeated in dozens of cities: Los Angeles, Denver, Burton, Arcadia, Richmond and others. Attack helicopters drop soldiers on businesses, parks and private homes. In October 2009 Urban Shield conducted a two day, million-dollar live fire terrorism drill, which included troops from around the world. They descended on 22 sites in San Francisco. Urban war games are unconstitutional.

Hurricane Katrina was a war game caused by HAARP. When it hit FEMA took control of New Orleans. They ordered trucks with food and water to turn around, refusing their aid, and arrested people taking survival supplies from damaged stores. They sent Army National Guard troops into homes, to confiscate guns and guarded the bridge out of the city, stop-ping people from leaving.

Nine-Eleven was the biggest war game of all. Did commercial jets fly inside small steel-framed towers, wings and all? Did WTC building #7 free-fall without being hit? Did flight 77 drop 7000 feet, fold its wings back, fly inside the Pentagon just above ground level, leaving little debris behind? Did flight 93 create a mushroom cloud when it crashed and a charred crater, and then vanish?

9-11 was a satanic spell, including The Pet Goat reading at Booker Elementary. Booker- agent that hires performers; elementary- fundamental. Flight 93- "more to come" (from The Pet Goat story- more false flags). Penn-sylvania: pen- confined enclosure; sylvania- land. Shanks-ville is leg and village. Is this 'fenced cities' like parole sentencing, where permission is needed to leave home and you are under surveillance? Is this towns and cities in COVID-19 lockdown?

Fake videos showed jet airliners hitting the towers on TV. Fake witnesses confirmed the illusion. Real eye-witnesses saw small aircraft/missiles hit the towers and a missile hit the Pentagon. The tower missiles were plane stage-props. After the smoke and mirrors performance, subbasement nuclear reactors were set off. A 3-D simulation of planes entering the towers was made after 9-11, to explain how something impossible occurred; engineers know better. We are being deceived on many levels.

{Ground Zero: The Nuclear Destruction of the WTC says scientists from the Geological Survey analyzed dust from the towers and found elements that only exist from uranium fission. "A large-scale fission chain reaction of Uranium 235 took place... (Tahil aerospace/technology consultant)."

William Tahil says the explosions were caused by the deliberate core meltdown of two clandestine nuclear reactors buried deep beneath the towers. The reactors' cores were exposed and its nuclear fuel sent shockwaves up the towers 150 feet per second, vaporizing the interior- combustibles, glass, concrete, steel, and people, to dust. Blowing out the top, the volcanic eruption of radiation flung its load of vaporized materials skyward, becoming pyroclastic clouds of dust and radioactive fuel. Like volcanic lava, the violent eruption then raced downward, vaporizing the buildings' exteriors. 70,000 people were exposed to the fallout.

Tahil said the large pools of molten steel, weeks after 9-11, could only be fueled by a nuclear reactor core meltdown; mini nukes cannot do this. A core meltdown continues generating

272

heat from radioactive decay. He also claims the explosions came from the towers' base, because of how the towers fell.

Nuclear reactors are designed to not explode. If reactors were placed below the towers, to bring them down on a future date (not generate electricity) they would have been designed differently, perhaps with more enriched uranium. Tahil said: "We may well be looking at the signature of a very advanced nuclear device or a reactor…"

Radiation from nuclear fission gives off a blue glow, seen at night. A blue light tribute was turned on every night for a month. Did the lights hide the radiation until it dispersed?

Pools of water mark where the towers stood. "Covering the footprint of each tower with water and protecting visitors with a curtain of water is an effective way to contain at least the direct radiation emitted upwards by the remains of the reactor cores, which must still be down there, buried 100 meters below the ground (Tahil, nucleardemolition.com)}.

9-11 Facts

Air Defense was told to
Stand Down

Aluminum planes
cannot penetrate steel

Pentagon attack
is impossible

Flight 93 was
completely staged

Insiders who worked at
the towers were
not there on 9-11

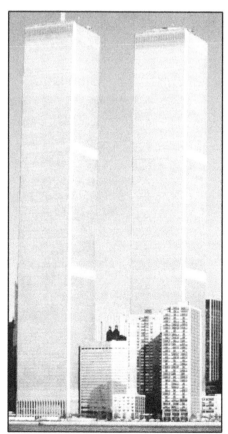

Dark Plane Sunny Day Smoke & Mirrors

Blue Light Tribute or Shield

Pyroclastic flow from core meltdown

Pyroclastic flow from an atomic bomb

We are not alone; the Creator, angels and Spirit Guides watch over us and answer our prayers. Yet a group of Light Beings, who came to earth to help us ascend, were forced to leave; dark humans grew stronger than light humans. They said farewell to earth with heavy hearts- they love her so! When more people awaken and the scales tip to the light, the Light Beings will return.

The Final Countdown
Europe

We're leaving together, but still it's farewell. And maybe we'll come back to earth, who can tell? I guess there is no one to blame, we're leaving ground. Will things ever be the same again? It's the final countdown ...With so many light years to go and things to be found... We're leaving together (the final countdown) We'll all miss her so.

God Bless The USA
Lee Greenwood

...From the lakes of Minnesota
To the hills of Tennessee,
Across the plains of Texas
From sea to shining sea;
From Detroit down to Houston,
And New York to L.A,
There's pride in every American heart
And it's time to stand and say
I'm proud to be an American
Where at least I know I'm free,
And' I won't forget the men who died
Who gave that right to me.
And I'll gladly stand up next to you
And defend her still today.
Cause there ain't no doubt I love this land
God Bless the USA!

Chapter 13
NCLB Versus
Creative Classrooms

USA public schools are training for corporate servitude. Students are patients under medical treatments and behavior management. Their personalities are modified, their minds are raped to be obedient servants for the Global Elite. Students know they are violated on some level. Creative expression is crippled with mind programming and brain-damaging vaccines that suppress intuition and imagination. This is the eugenics agenda: 'study of agencies which can **improve or impair** the racial quality of future generations (Galton).'

No **C**hild **L**eft **B**ehind does this using Direct Instruction developed by Engelmann, author of <u>The Pet Goat</u>. D.I. breaks ideas into pieces. Curriculum and delivery are tightly controlled. The 9-11 video of Daniel's classroom reading of <u>The Pet Goat</u>, sounds like a military drill. The kids yell out words like bootcamp grunts as the teacher thumps the book, counting syllables. You can't tell what the story is about. This puts students in a state of hypnosis. If a child tries to under-stand s/he will fall behind; the programming won't take hold.

The classroom and lessons are structured. No allowance is given for the creative talents of the teacher or student. Good teachers have quit in disgust over NCLB. Engelmann said: "We don't give a damn what the teacher thinks, what the teacher feels. On the teachers' own time they can hate it. We don't care as long as they do it (The New Yorker 07/04)."

Steve Olson asked his 12th grade English teacher how his students have changed. He told him: "Critical thinking skills have been absent from my classes for years. Kids used to read Catcher in the Rye and then describe what Caulfield meant to them. Today they read it and expect me to teach them what it means. Not just most kids, all kids. I haven't seen a critical thinker in my classroom in five years (How the Public School System Crushes Souls)." Steiner said "after the year 2000... a law will be enacted in America with the purpose of suppressing all individual thinking." This law is NCLB. "My orders as a schoolteacher are to make children fit an animal training system, not to help each find his or her personal path (John Taylor Gatto)."

David had a reoccurring dream of taking a test in high school. After having this dream for ten years, it changed. David said 'this is bull-shit! I'm not taking this test!' Other students began protesting as well. David then noticed the teacher was a robot, programmed to install a program in her students. This dream is about NCLB.

Public schools 'program' children. Those who don't respond are put on meds; no child is left behind. Kids line up twice a day at the school office for their "brain damaging, mind-numbing, debilitating drug (The Oz Factors Spencer)." The US wants mental health screening for everyone starting with school children. If it became law, parental consent to minister vaccines and drugs to school children would not be needed. Students would receive meds without parental knowledge. School lunches have additives that cause hyperactivity. Children who are sensitive to them develop ADHD and are put on meds. Depressed students are given SSRI drugs; school shootings are linked to them.

School shootings happen almost every week in the USA. Tougher gun laws won't stop them. If principals had firearms training and were required to carried a concealed gun, school shootings would drop to zero. In Uvalde Texas, 5--22, a gunman entered a classroom. The police arrived and paced the hallway without looking for the gunman. They heard several shots come from a classroom and continued pacing while more students were shot. An hour later, the US Border Patrol arrived. Bypassing several officers in the hall, they rushed the classroom and killed the gunman. He had shot 36 students and 2 teachers; 19 students died. Were the police told to stand down so the gunman could kill students?

In The Outskirts Of Hope (Ivester) Aura Kruger, a white teacher in an all-Black southern town in the 1960s, teaches English to high school black students without curriculum or supplies. In the midst of racial riots and KKK intimidations,

Kruger wrote her own lessons and inspired her students to brilliance. She taught them the power of voting, the civil rights movement and used Shakespeare to illustrate prejudice. Mrs. Kruger was deeply loved by her students.

In Goodbye Homeboy Mariotti teaches high school drop-outs, expelled from public school for violent crimes in South Bronx. Trapped in poverty, Mariotti's students saw no relation between learning and improving their lives. When Mariotti tied his lessons to entrepreneurship, his students became eager to learn. Mariotti helped his students turn street-smarts into business-smarts. This transformed their lives, giving them tools they needed to succeed. Students learned how to establish a legal businesses. Mariotti founded Network For Teaching Entrepreneurship (NFTE) helping over a million youth worldwide.

Waldorf kindergarten (Google)

If schools were supported by a trust that provided free education for the poor, and a sliding scale tuition to help parents meet expenses, Waldorf education and other types of creative teaching could be accessible for all.

Waldorf schools cultivate children's emotional development before their intellect. Reading does not begin until 2nd grade. Elementary students learn art, two foreign languages, wood working, sewing, musical instruments and gymnastics. Love of nature, imagination, artistic abilities and social skills are fostered. Children play outside in all weather; climbing equip-ment and other materials encourage imaginative play.

When a child's curiosity is awakened in anything, learning is easy. "Arouse the interest of a child in any subject and he will pursue it to success (Joseph F. Smith)." Students require freedom to be self-directed; teachers require freedom to be creative. Creative activities develop problem-solving skills and critical thinking. Federal and State curriculum and certification must end. Education needs hands-on learning, outdoor classrooms when possible, and time spent in nature.

Free to be You and Me

Bruce Heart, Stephen Lawrence

There's a land that I see where the children are free. And I say it ain't far to this land from where we are. Take my hand, come with me where the children are free. Come with me take my hand and we'll live in a land where the river runs free. In a land through the green country. In a land to a shining sea. And you and me are free to be you and me.

Chapter 14
I Pet Goat II

I Pet Goat II: youtube.com/watch?v=65xLByzT1l0

1-Goat with barcode 666, behind barbwire: US Government (goat) is Global Elite (barcode) controlled by Zombie-Christ (barbwire). **2-**Bush in classroom during 9-11 on satanic puppet strings held by bloody reptilian hands. **3-**Puppet-Bush dancing in pentagram spotlight on Masonic floor: casting satanic spell. **4-**Split-brain below chalkboard: corpus callosum damaged by vaccines. **5-**Bush becomes laughing Obama: Presidents are preselected. Obama has a secret-he's Osama. **6-**Barbwire wrapped around embryos: hybrids (aliens) being bioengineered using human eggs for Zombie-Christ. **7-**Girl's egg (apple) removed, egg spins, Lotus emerges [foreign genes added] hits **Terrified Obama**: genetically modified. **8-**Psalm 23: shadow of death, icebergs, USA flag ripped. **9-**Masked demon-god dances as twin towers fall from nuclear explosion, jumps when fallout hits ground. **10-**Zombie-Christ in boat. **11-**Osama on iceberg with missile-soldiers wearing CIA insignia and black wings, traveling through frozen world. **12-**Statue of Liberty sitting on Star of David, light goes out: CIA, USA, Israel planned Obama-Osama hoax, 9-11. **13-**Bioengineered baby attached to Global Elite. **14-**Zombie-Christ with barbwire crown standing in boat. **15-**Bioengineered boy controlled by Global Elite. **16-**Stock Market plunges. **17-**Nuclear airstrike on Mosque, demonic beings fly out of explosion, one turns white, flies to Zombie-Christ. **18-**Arabic mother with dead child. **19-**African girl enslaved for sex and soldier. **20-**Lotus [foreign genes] in goop surrounding **Terrified Worker**: genetically engineered metamorphosis. **21-**Asian girl mind controlled by demon. **22-**Cosmic Christ is Zombie Christ: Christ Consciousness is Satan Consciousness. **23-**Fish (Christians) jump in Zombie-Christ's boat and die. **24-**

Christian church built like a penis with a harlot inside: Christianity gives life-force to Zombie-Christ. **25**-Zombie-Christ rises among Global Elite and kills them. **26**-They detach from bio-engineered boy. **27**-Boy stands with the bearing of Zombie-Christ: he enters him. **28**-demon conductor, Sufi Whirling Dervish. **29**-Demon God changes masks down through history. **30**-Zombie-Christ exits Satan's cave with lifeforce, eyes open. **31**-Barbwire Crown disappears: Christianity ends. Christian church by Satan's cave falls. **32**-Satan's New Jerusalem rules earth.

Agenda Revealed. <u>Americans</u>: genetically modified people and bioengineered gray aliens. <u>Nuclear bombs</u>. <u>Muslims</u>: zombie-like. <u>Africans</u>: sex slaves, soldiers. <u>Asians</u>: under demonic influence. <u>Workers</u>: New World Species. <u>Christians</u>: killed. <u>Global Elite</u>: killed. <u>Christianity</u>: ends. <u>New Jerusalem</u>.

New World Order = New World Species

Genetic Mutation in Vaccinated Worker

Hammer: industrial workers
Sickle: agricultural workers
Lotus: bioengineering

Chapter 15
Giuliani's Prayer Service

In the wake of 9-11, New York Mayor Rudolph Giuliani held a multi-faith prayer service at the Yankee Stadium. He said: "The proud Twin Towers that once crowned our famous skyline no longer stand. But our skyline will rise again..."

"St. Paul's Chapel is one of the oldest and most historic buildings in the City of New York... The Chapel survived our war of independence, including seven years of wartime occupation. After George Washington was inaugurated the first President of the United states... he walked to St. Paul's, and he kneeled down to pray. The pew where he worshipped is still there. Framed on the wall beside it is the oldest known representation of the Great Seal of the United States of America; it's a majestic eagle holding in one talon an olive branch, proclaiming our abiding desire for peace, and in the other a cluster of arrows, a forewarning of our determination to defend our liberty. On a banner above the Eagle is written E Pluribus Unum, 'Out of Many, One.' For the past 25 years, the chapel stood directly in the shadow of the World Trade Center Towers. When the Towers fell, more than a dozen modern buildings were destroyed and damaged. Yet somehow, amid all the destruction and devastation, St. Paul's Chapel still stands, without so much as a broken window. It's a small miracle in some ways, but the presence of that chapel standing defiant and serene amid the ruins of war sends an eloquent message about the strength and resilience of the people of New York City, and the people of America... We love our diversity, and we love our freedom....

"We pray for all of those whose loved ones are lost or missing... we pray for our children, and we say to them: 'Do not be afraid. It's safe to live your life.' Finally, we pray for America... and for all of those who join us in defending freedom, law, and humanity..."

Chapter 16
USA Great Seal

USA Great Seal must be Accurate
Or it is not Legal

Light Rays Break Through Clouds
Constellation of 13 stars
Bald Eagle Rising
Shield on Breast

Charles Thomson's sketch

Official Great Seal is illegal

Star of David
Clouds block light-rays

Stars in a natural formation
light rays break through clouds

Artist Unknown, 1785
Saint Paul's Chapel

USA Great Seal
Accurate Depiction
Hundley 2004

USA Great Seal Reverse
Open 3rd Eye
Flattop Pyramid

Chapter 17
NAZIS NASA and NSA

The Global Elite funded Hitler's war, infiltrated his Nazi regime and used him to further their goals. Hitler wanted Aryans to rule earth, the Global Elite want Israel to rule. Hitler used Christianity to further his cause, not knowing Nazism would help establish USA Christian Theonomy.

The Global Elite are planning World War III to destroy Israel, the Arab World, and devastate the USA. The Messiah would then appear, possessed by Jehovah. They are running a false flag operation against Putin to implement this plan. Their agenda is unfolding, but they are Jehovah's pawn. If they establish New Jerusalem, they will be killed or enslaved.

At a dinner party (1933) a small group posing as Marxist subversives, told Indiana school superintendent, William Wirt that communists had infiltrated the government at the highest levels. They gave Wirt a detailed blueprint of their plan for total control of the USA. The plan was for Nazis and the Global Elite, not Marxists. Writ was their pawn, used to create a communist scare. The real cold war: Nazi infiltration. The goal: Christian theonomy in 100 years.

The Global Elite implement their agendas by creating a problem, getting a reaction and then providing the solution (their agenda). Roosevelt put an embargo against Japan on oil, iron and steel, pressuring other nations to do the same. This strangled Japan's economy and they attacked Pearl Harbor, starting the Pacific war. Roosevelt died before the atomic bombs were dropped, but he set up this 'solution'. The USA developed the atomic bomb for Japan, not their secret ally (Hitler). Roosevelt's New Deal increased corporate control to prepare the way for New Jerusalem.

The communist scare swept the country when WWII ended -a cover for Nazi subversion, a covert operation inside the US government. Gehlen (Hitler's Chief of Intelligence) met with President Truman, Donovan and Dulles (OSS officers). They formed a dictatorship (NSA) and State Mafia (CIA). Homeland Security (not USA Security) came later- a front operation to protect their fascist regime.

Nazi doctors developed mind-brain control; Nazi scientists developed anti-gravity propulsion. These agendas weaved a net to trap humanity: inside control- mind-brain-body, outside control- spacecraft orbiting earth with lethal weapons.

"The Nazis developed a unique approach to science... quite separate from the rest of the world because their ideology, unrestrained as it was, supported a wholly different way of doing things... when the Americans took it all home with them, they found out too late that it came infected with a virus. You take the science on, you take on aspects of the ideology as well (The Hunt For Zero Point Cook)." World War II played out exactly as the Global Elite planned, including losing the war and taking Nazi ideology and technology into the USA. Their agenda is still playing out.

Operation Paperclip brought Von Braun and his V-2 team to the USA. Rudolph, director of Hitler's rocket factory where thousands were worked to death, was among them. He developed Project Apollo. Debus, a Nazi scientist also guilty of war crimes, developed ballistic missile systems and was Director of Kennedy Space Center from 1962—1974. Debus conducted over 150 launches, including Pioneer, Mercury, Saturn, Apollo, Skylab missions, satellites and space probes.

NASA scientists may have developed time travel using an Einstein-Rosen bridge- a wormhole with two ends connecting different locations, points in time, or both. It could open the past or future and be used for teleportation and propulsion.

The USA has two space programs; one uses secret techno-logy, the other one uses obsolete technology to hide it. Both programs are run by NASA and were developed by Nazi scientists. In an interview with Howe, aerospace draftsman Schratt received details on aircraft at Norton AFB that looked like UFOs. He was told they could travel at light-speed or better. "These craft were hovering off the floor and they were bobbing, just like you would see a large tanker at port, just bobbing on their own waves..."

The secret space program built underground labs on the moon and mars. Its mission is to conquer the world, not explore space. It's run by the UAS military and uses slave labor. Their covert technology is similar to Star Trek, while cars run on obsolete, internal combustion. Real quantum science is not taught in universities, to keep the technology that uses it secret. Electric fields can warp spacetime more efficiently than mass. Spacetime warps can be used for anti-gravity and space-thrust systems (T.E. Bearden).

The moon base is on the dark side. Trips to build it were kept secret. It has been continuously manned since its completion decades ago. Bases on the moon and mars use enslaved humans and bioengineered beasts or aliens created in labs on earth. Astronauts involved in the public moon launches would know if they were faked, but they may not know about the real launches that built bases on the moon and mars. Apollo 11 may have happened in a simulator. Could Mission Control tell if they were watching Lunar Module Mission Simulator at Cape Kennedy and Lunar Landing Research Facility, not outer space and the moon?

Apollo 1 burned up in a launch test, killing the astronauts (Grissom, White, Chaffee). Was this satanic sorcery? Apollo 4 (1st successful launch) was on Rudolph's birthday. Apollo 13 may have been a real flight, sabotaged to cast sorcery.

The Apollo 13 fill-line was damaged before takeoff to kill the crew. When their oxygen tank exploded, they lost oxygen, water and power.

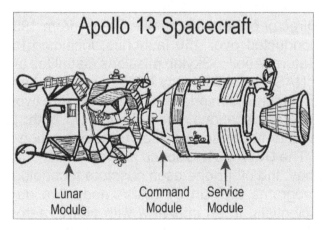

Apollo 13 Spacecraft

Lunar Module · Command Module · Service Module

Angels manifested miracles, including the crew switch that put Lovell in command, inspiring dozens of men at Mission Control, who were working to improvise solutions. Lovell, Swigert and Haise entered the Lunar Module, Aquarius, for their return and the command module Odyssey, for the free fall to earth- it had a heat shield and held the parachutes. The horses on Apollo 13s patch are taken from Winter's painting 'Steeds of Apollo'— red, white and black horses are dancing in the sky. Apollo, destroyer of evil, will come to earth and kill Jehovah and his demons.

The Challenger was launched on a cold morning. Thiokol engineer Boisjoly said: "I fought like Hell to stop that launch. I'm so torn up inside I can hardly talk about it, even now." Boisjoly knew the cold weather would keep the O-rings from sealing. Fuel escaped (NASA knew it would) and the orbiter broke in pieces, "the details obscured by billowing vapor. Two minutes, forty-five seconds later, the crew chamber hit the ocean with an acceleration of 200 G (Azriel)." The crew compartment remained intact until it hit the water. Did the astronauts see the Atlantic rushing toward them?

The Challenger disaster was satanic sorcery. A challenger is a person who stands in opposition. She is out to expose something and bring it down. The teacher on Challenger symbolized this challenger, teaching the world something the Global Elite does not want made public. No spell can stop this information from "going over the face of the whole earth."

The Challenger Disaster
January 28 1986

Chapter 18
Midnight Dawn

A Festival of Freedom was held on the 20th anniversary of the Berlin Wall removal (11-9-09). Dominoes decorated by children were placed along a one-mile stretch where the wall once stood and toppled. Chancellor Merkel said barriers to freedom cannot stand. As dominoes fell, swine-flu vaccines were shipped around the world casting a counter-spell: the swine-flu vaccine with more to come: Covid vaccine-weapon.

Swine-flu vaccines caused narcolepsy and cataplexy in some people, traced to the nucleoprotein. Putting substances the body makes- RNA, squalene, blood plasma, in vaccines can cause autoimmune disorders. My friend got GBS from the swine-flu vaccine; it took months to walk and talk again.

Death from COVID-19 was less than normal flu seasons when people were put in lockdown. Small businesses closed. People lost their homes and couldn't buy food, while farmers plowed vegetable fields and flooded pastures with milk. Global Research called Covid a diabolical project producing famine, unemployment, lockdowns, poverty, social engineering and fake data. Covid was often listed as cause of death, when it was not. When people died from the Covid vaccine-weapon, this was flipped and not recorded as cause of death. Vaccines are the plan/demic. Global lockdown caused global mind-shock. People lost their jobs and homes. When the lockdown lifted, many people got vaccinated so they could work.

John Whitehead, Cedarville California: we are being forced into intermittent incarceration while our finances, family, home, health, friendships, country and our reality dis-integrates. All we know and love, wish and hope for are vanishing, stolen from us. The contagion of fear has swept the world into a sick reality, dominated by blind obedience. We do not have to agree with the lies. We can be united instead of divided (paraphrased).

Children are told they're a threat to others, to distance themselves from friends, cover their face and be vaccinated. If you sacrificed your child to this global agenda, you sacrificed your humanity. "It is criminal medical malpractice to give a child one of these vaccines (RFK Jr.)" Covid snips protein markers that warn the immune system, shreds antiviral instruction cells before they signal it, enters the contagious stage before symptoms appear and hides from the immune system. Only an engineered virus could do this. Covid was modified from a cold virus to harm; the vaccine-bioweapon spreads the virus.

Covid 'vaccines' force cells to make billions of bioengineered virus proteins. The immune system then creates a flood of antibodies which can cause autoimmune diseases. 'Vaccines' are linked with blood-clots, myocardial inflammation, heart attack, aneurisms, neuropathy, multiple metastases, leukemia, stroke, dementia, myelitis, seizures and lymphoma. Deaths from the above are not tied to vaccination. News claims Covid deaths are down because of vaccines while the vaccine-bioweapon kills millions. 5% of vaccine-bioweapon batches have almost all reported injuries and deaths. These more harmful batches were distributed in the USA. Vaccine batches are numbered and can be traced. Did they go to nursing homes? There was a sharp rise in deaths after vaccines were given to residents.

The World Health Organization formed a pandemic treaty to medicate everyone during plan-demics and force nations into vaccinating citizens as new viruses are released. "WHO could gain absolute power over global biosecurity including the power to implement digital identities and vaccine passports, mandatory vaccinations, travel restrictions, standardized medical care and more... Let's build back for our children the America that our parents fought and died for (RFK Jr)."

Are we being redesigned through bioengineering and nano-technology? Are vaccine-bioweapons, 5-G, chemtrails and super-computers part of a future brain-computer network? Will a signal activate its encoding in the carriers, linking our brains with a network interface, controlled through satellites and AI command centers? In biology order is rank to classify species.

New World Order = New World Species

The Global Elite want a digital currency system with bank accounts accessed through a phone app, monitored by global bankers. Cell phone tracking would determine our location.

Debit cards could be shut down or used in a defined radius, controlling our money, and how and where we can spend it. They could cut us off if we speak against The Order. Stages to New Jerusalem: **1**. Digital currency. **2**. Christian Nation. **3**. Brain-computer link. **4**. Jehovah reveals himself.

{Paul hijacked the followers of Jesus with secret schemes. The US Government was hijacked by the Global Elite using similar strategies. They socially engineered the polarization of the parties, to herd us like sheep into their corral- their real agenda. News is manufactured drama. Their puppet show encouraged Democrats to get vaccinated and influenced Republicans not too. Trump's trial, drag queen performances and Satan clubs for kids, attacks on transgenders, LGBTQ, gender identity, Woke, Pride Month, Proud Boys, QAnon, UFO sightings, etc. creates drama that keeps us polarized.

Trump and Biden are actors, pretending to be on opposite sides. Made-up media attacks on Trump manipulate Republicans. He poses for headlines. Democrats and Republicans react to the show; they have false hope. Real news is hidden in laws and Executive Orders.

Trump's EO 13961 extended 'Federal Continuity Directive'. The President can remain in office beyond election dates if there is a national emergency, like a pandemic. Trump said he will not step down, the election was a fraud and the secret documents he took are his. Is this true? The election may have been a performance and Biden's inauguration staged. The President has legal access to the documents Trump took. Is he covertly running the government from Mar-a-Logo? Is Biden a Poxy-President with temporary power?

If the USA becomes a Christian nation, books against the Bible will be banned. For 500 years Christians believed white people were God's chosen and blacks were 'made' to serve them. Many books revealing horrific abuse white people inflicted on blacks have been pulled from public schools.

In I Survived Dozier Huntly writes about young black boys arrested by cops (1950—1970s) for walking down the street. They were sent to Dozier by corrupt judges to work farms and in slaughterhouses, in dangerous conditions. Dozier was a concentration camp. The boys were raped and beaten;

many died from abuse and were thrown in unmarked graves.

Republicans and Democrats, Stand Together. We are in danger of living under Old Testament law. If you are black, you could be enslaved. If you are transgender or gay, you could be denied work and health care. If you break Old Testament law, your family could be killed. The horrors that Lord God inflicted on the Hebrew could be inflicted on us.

Government separated from religion protects your liberty and your life. Stand up for freedom- religious, medical, speech and free will. Be a warrior filled with fiery indignation. "We must each one of us resolve in our own hearts that we shall at all times do everything that within us lies to obtain for Ireland [your Nation] the fullest measure of her rights (Parnell)."}

"First they came for the Socialists and I did not speak out... Then they came for me and there was no one left to speak for me (Niemöller)." They came for the children. Immigrant children were separated from parents, even babies and toddlers, in 2018—2019. Screaming children were forcefully pulled from parent's arms by patrol agents. Many were put in foster care. Thousands vanished in the system. What did the US government want with these children? Why were they kidnaped? "The American government took children away from their parents with no plan to return them (We Need to Take Away Children by Dickerson, The Atlantic 9-22)."

The USA is a corporation in the process of becoming a theocracy. You can't change corporate or religious policy by voting. If the government becomes destructive "it is the right of the people to alter or abolish it (USA Constitution)." A Convention Of States (Article V) can restore or dissolve the Constitution but it has been taken over by Christian far right. "Those who make peaceful revolution impossible will make violent revolution inevitable (RFK Jr)."

The United States is the Federal Government, the 'United States of America' are States in the Union- the country. If you live here, you are from the States- the USA; you are not from the federal government (the US). The USA are united States with a federal government. A national government is one State. We are citizens of our State, not the Federal government. "We the people of the united States, in order to form a more perfect union... establish this Constitution for the United States of America." We are not one nation, we are not under Jehovah and States can leave the union.

The founding fathers created a voluntary union of States. States hold the power of the Federal Government. Instead of restoring it, States could keep their union and dissolve the Federal Government. They have their own constitution and government. States that stay united could have the same currency- the same printed and coined money. Annuit Coeptis: the guiding power of the universe supports us.

And to the Republic of which She Stands, Sovereign States, Divisible with Liberty and Justice for all. The Statue of Liberty is a Goddess with an androgynous face. Lady Liberty is our 'Republic of which She Stands'. She will lead us back to the Divine Feminine.

The Statue of Freedom on top of the Capital building is a woman with flowing hair wearing a helmet with an eagle head and feathers, to honor Native Americans. Her right hand rests on the sheath of her sword, her left holds a laurel wreath of victory and the USA shield. She is a Warrior, ready to Protect our Freedoms.

On 11-11 2009, I was writing this chapter when night turn to day at midnight. A meteor exploded across western states. Millions of houses were bathed in Midnight Dawn, signifying humanities awakening. Will it Manifest?

"They're putting in 5G to harvest our data and control our behavior, digital currency that will allow them to punish us from a distance and cut off our food supply, vaccine passports... The minute they hand you that vaccine passport, every right that you have is transformed into a privilege contingent upon your obedience to arbitrary government dictates. It will make you a slave. And what do we do about this? We resist (RFK Jr)."

Barriers to Freedom Cannot Stand

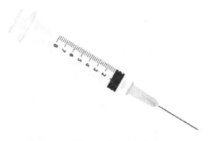

Don't Inject Me

Mike Adams

Don't inject me, don't infect me
Don't stick that needle in my veins and medically wreck me
Don't use me, don't abuse me
Don't push your medical lies and try to confuse me...
It's all part of the Big Brother population plan

Covid-19 vaccines create micro blood-clots
causing disorders like thrombocytopenia

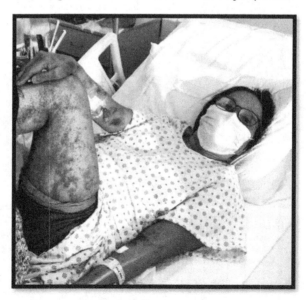

nytimes.com

COVID

Corporate **O**rganized **V**iolence against
Individuals and **D**emocracy

Certificate **O**f **V**accination **ID**

5.5 billion people received the COVID Vaccine-Bioweapon. Covid virus proteins enter blood vessels,
triggering clotting. Blood clots in the brain, lungs, spinal
cord and heart can be fatal.

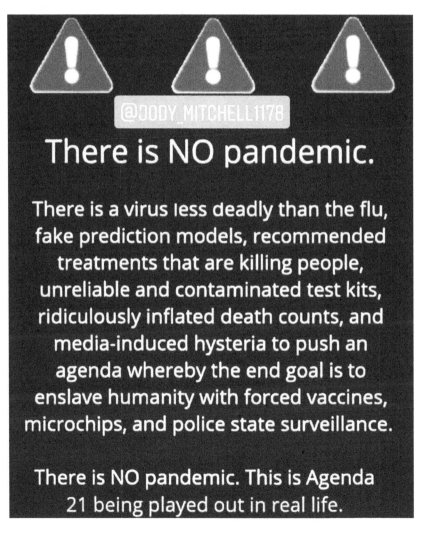

@JODY_MITCHELL1178

There is NO pandemic.

There is a virus less deadly than the flu,
fake prediction models, recommended
treatments that are killing people,
unreliable and contaminated test kits,
ridiculously inflated death counts, and
media-induced hysteria to push an
agenda whereby the end goal is to
enslave humanity with forced vaccines,
microchips, and police state surveillance.

There is NO pandemic. This is Agenda
21 being played out in real life.

We Are Fighting For
The Salvation Of Humanity
RFK Jr.

"You control our world. You've poisoned the air we breathe, contaminated the water we drink, and copyrighted the food we eat. We fight in your wars, die for your causes, and sacrifice our freedoms to protect you. You've liquidated our savings, destroyed our middle class, and used our tax dollars to bailout your unending greed. We are slaves to your corporations, zombies to your airwaves, servants to your decadence. You've stolen our elections, assassinated our leaders, and abolished our basic rights as human beings. You own our property, shipped away our jobs, and shredded our unions. You've profited off of disaster, destabilized our currencies, and raised our cost of living. You've monopolized our freedom, stripped away our education, and have almost extinguished our flame. We are hit... we are bleeding... but we ain't got time to bleed. We will bring the giants to their knees and you will witness our revolution!" – Jesse Ventura

Chapter 19
Mystery Murders

Bradstreet   Hedendal   Sievers
     Riley   Halt

Holistic doctors died mysteriously. They were involved in research/treatments related to GcMAF, an immune system component. Bradstreet discovered cancer enzymes that interfere with immune systems (nagalase) in vaccines.

Eleven microbiologists died within five months of each other (2001—2002). They were experts in bioterrorism. Were they killed when their jobs were completed, to keep their work secret? Wiley, Pasechnik, Schwartz, Mostow, Set, Huang Que, Korshunov, Langford, Holzmayer, Wynn-Williams.

Chapter 20
My Buffalo Prophecy

Joseph Smith's White Horse Prophecy:
USA Constitution hangs by a thread
'Saved' by the Mormon Church
New Jerusalem is established

My White and Red Buffalo Prophesy

The USA Constitution hangs by a thread. A black horse threatens to put the country under Biblical law. A white and red buffalo expose the black horse. Political and religious revolutions arise around the world. Christianity, Islam and Judaism are exposed as frauds. The 9th Hopi prophecy is fulfilled as Christ-Jehovah-Allah falls from heaven. These religions collapse, demon-ghosts are cast out, and people come to the Rocky Mountains for truth.

The buffalos are Sandra and myself. Our book flies around the world, exposing the black horse (Global Elite's agenda). Their decrees include covid regulations and vaccinations required by companies to work. Is the Covid vaccine, the

Lord's blasphemous strange work, and strange act that causes a consumption upon earth, destroying people from the inside out? Could it genetically modify humanity, turning us into controlled cyborgs for the Global Elite and Jehovah?

If the Global Elite establish New Jerusalem, Jehovah's worshippers would be killed by their demon-ghost, including the Global Elite. The Greatest Deception reveals Jehovah's plan for his own salvation, and his worshippers reject him. The Rocky Mountains are the stone in Daniel (this book) that becomes a Great Mountain. Harmony and balance are restored on earth and the Golden World returns.

My birth name is Sandra: Defender of Mankind. CasSandra foresaw the destruction of Troy; no one believed her. Does this same fate await the world? Will my Buffalo Prophecy be fulfilled? I have been writing this book for 27 years and need a miracle to get it out to the world. Will this happen? We have passed the return line and have one chance to turn around.

Chapter 21
Our Collective Light

Humanity evolved inside earth, where the sun continually shines. Humans were androgynous, had Rh-negative blood, golden hair and skin, and were 14+-feet tall. History portrays them as violent. They were gentle giants with six fingers and toes, double row of teeth, vast wisdom and beauty.

On the surface, two great civilizations arose. Lemurians had dark skin and stood 12-feet tall. Atlanteans were mixed-black, Asian, Brown, White and 10-feet tall. After a long utopia, some Atlanteans turned evil, causing their island's demise. Spiritual souls from Atlantis have returned, to stop those who destroyed their island from repeating this history.

Giants are the mythical gods and goddesses, mighty men of renown and heroes of old. They were 'great, many and tall' and worked with nature spirits. Jehovah slaughtered them. If you are tall and have extra fingers, toes or teeth, you may have this gene. They are Nephilim in the Bible and taught humanity forbidden knowledge of the sun, moon, stars, and earth. Jehovah didn't want his servants to be enlightened.

When children play with mythical creatures, using their imagination, they communicate with nature spirits who join them in play. Imaginative play connects children to other realities. If imagination continues through childhood, it will continue throughout life and 'nothing will be restrained from them which they have imagined to do (Gen 11:6).' 'Keep the purity of play and curiosity alive (Tom Brown).'

Before Jehovah spread his reign of terror, everyone could see elves, gnomes, fairies and nature spirits. They could enter fairyland and fairies would visit them. When Christians killed pagans and destroyed nature, they retreated. If we ascend, humanity will once again live, work and play with elves, fairies and gnomes.

In <u>When The Bright Moon Rises</u> Dena recounts lives that she lived in the far distant past when the mythical gods and goddesses walked earth. In <u>With The Love Of The Ancients</u> Wheeler says 'little people' are coming out of their hidden places, waiting for us to see them again. Penny Kelly writes about elves on her farm who help her grow vibrant veggies and grapes, in <u>The Elves of Lily Hill Farm</u>.

Nature spirits are guardians of trees, minerals, flowers, plants and elements- ether, air, fire, water and earth. Fairies awaken nature in spring, help it grow in the summer, prepare it for winter's sleep in the fall and bring winter snows. Junjulas says nature spirits "creatively serve and maintain the mineral, plant, animal, and human kingdoms." We help them do this when we love and respect nature.

Sylphs have come from all over the universe, to fight the darkness. They block HAARP transmissions, transmute chemtrails into harmless elements, neutralize and restore balance when other destructive forces are released. Sylphs can change their appearance, often materializing as clouds. While writing Our Collective Light, I saw a sylph. She was made of fluffy clouds and huge! Her brilliance stood out against the blue sky. She had an angular head, slender neck and body, large wings, long slender legs and a short tail. She was looking at me, aware of my presence.

Everything throughout eternity is part of the spirit-that-moves-in-all-things (except demons). We feel this love/light oneness in our heart. Jesus said "seek not the law in your scriptures... In everything that is life, is the law. Find it in the grass, in the tree, in the river... but seek it mostly in yourself. All living things are nearer to God than the scripture, which is without life... God wrote not the laws in the pages of books, but in your heart (<u>The Essene Gospel of Peace</u>)." God's law speaks to you through your heart- the seat of your soul.

Truth resonates in you. It can make your heart hurt, move you to tears, bring laughter, give you chills, cause shudders, goosebumps and shockwaves. Horrifying truths that reveal covert deceptions send hard shudders through you. This can shatter the deception in our collective consciousness and help everyone awaken so we can reclaim our power.

Find your passion. Develop your talents. Live from your heart. Bring forth the fruit of your soul. Become more than you thought you could be. This is how you live a spiritual life, increase light in the world and manifest miracles. A hero lies in you- arise with strength and pride! Expose the deceptions that manipulate and enslave us. The world needs your light, your creative power and miracles, your heroism and ability to awaken others. We are at risk.

Form study groups. When we come together, we create more than we can on our own. This is synergy, the whole is greater than its parts. Group power increases in proportion to the resources, talents and abilities of everyone. Group experience can be transcendent, helping us grow on an inner level. As our collective light grows it helps others awaken.

Truth and lies are often mixed, with intent or unaware. Feel words in your heart as you read. Do they ring true or seem wrong? An incorrect label may be used in a true statement, like Christ Consciousness when meaning Divine Consciousness, or saying someone is Christlike, not knowing Christ is Satan. 'Father in Heaven' is Jehovah, not the Creator. Saying Creator or Goddess of Light excludes Jehovah. He has no creative powers, no female counterpart and doesn't dwell in light. 'Father God and Mother Earth' are used together. There is no Father God. Creatress means she who creates. There is only one Creator of the Universe and s/he is androgynous.

Interfaith, Mystery Schools and New Age contain truth mixed with lies. The New Age paradigm 'think positive, focus on love' keeps people from seeing behind the façade. There is no Intergalactic Confederation or space aliens. Life exists on other planets, but they don't come here in spaceships. UFOs are manmade. Knowing the truth may save your life. Believing lies and being manipulated can destroy the world.

Paul spread lies, left us clues and spoke truths. I quote Osho, a false guru and a Mormon President because I found truths in their writings. I quote Penny Kelly; her books have valuable information. Like most authors, Kelly makes some wrong assumptions. That's ok; your soul knows what is false; discard it and keep the truths. The following inspiring quote was written by an author who spreads lies.

"You will only rise to the top with a new vision... the vision must be simple to be powerful. It must be visual in its simplicity so that the people now surrounded in darkness can literally be struck with its beauty and feel called to its simplicity and clarity (<u>Handbook for the New Paradigm</u> Green)." My words need simplicity and clarity to help readers surrounded in darkness find their way out of the false world.

The US Christian Agenda, run by the Global Elite, killed and enslaved Indians and blacks, killed millions of buffalo, performed MK-Ultra experiments on children, sent Japanese Americans to internment camps, dropped nuclear bombs on Japan, made vaccines that cause brain damage, created false flags, sprayed chemtrails worldwide, covertly used their technology against us. If the US becomes a Christian Nation the horrors will continue. Jehovah is our enemy. When this becomes well-known, everyone enslaved to Jehovah- Jews, Muslims, Christians, Global Elite, Satanists, Bilderberg, Skull and Bones, Masons, etc. will climb out of Satan's pit. The red dragon will kill the Bible; Jehovah's reign will end.

The world is hurling toward disaster. It is hard to turn a planet off the destructive path when it's close to the point of no return. The trainwreck is coming and there is no stopping it. Global infrastructures don't support life; they're cracking. Nations will break apart, cities will collapse, starvation will follow. Stock up on survival supplies, let your instincts, your intuition and your heart guide you. Team up with others and help each other live; this will help you survive the coming collapse. Eventually, small self-sustained towns will flourish. We will live in harmony under a bright blue sky with white fluffy clouds. Stars will be bright, rivers will sparkle with light.

We are on the cusp of an evolutionary leap. We can defeat the darkness and become our true Self through the wisdom of our heart. Radiate goodness into the world, follow your heart, share with your neighbors and help each other live. Life will flow along your most creative path and we will manifest our Optimal Future.

My Sylph Fairy Queen

My beautiful fairy queen, mercurial and intense
You embody the weather without any pretense
The soaring winged protector of wide-open spaces
You look after the earth in so many places
Riding the currents with the eagles, hawks and geese
Cleansing the air with your love and ecstasy
The mountains and wilderness, the raging desert storm
Are the favorite places that you so love to roam
But we are in trouble in the cities and the towns
So you come to our calls, which everywhere abound
Working so hard to help us clean up our pollution
But we just keep making more, what is the solution?
Your ancient, proud legacy may come to an end
The radiation hurts you, and is very hard to mend
Sworn to protect us, you will defend us till you die
For your regal, majestic honor is unbroken and divine
Busting up deadly orgone and destructive radio waves
With rain and wind and thunder, you come without delay
But the job is overwhelming and so help is on the way
More and more sylphs keep joining you every single day
They come from the Galaxy and very far beyond
So the earth and all of life will prosper and live long
The task is very daunting and we must change our ways
Or everything you do for us will blow up in our face
Will we make the big transition into eternity?
Or will we destroy the earth and all of humanity?
Thank you, my Sweet Queen, for giving us this hour
To awaken and renew and regain our sovereign power

Moriah Morningstar

Chapter 22
The Optimal Future

Our Optimal Future takes us to our destiny, an unfoldment of our soul where we find our passion and fall in love with it. In 2012 (Borax) Lonsdale says "By learning to free our destiny from fate and karma, we not only activate our potential but free up the whole thing for everyone. When one person claims her optimal future it accesses a channel others can use. Destiny is contagious..."

"That other future, the one we dream of, has gotten stalled at the gates... Each of us has the power to loosen up that stuck future by claiming our own destiny... Destiny is a force, a beingness that's bigger than us, that speaks to us in terms we understand when we're ready to, and is the most powerful thing in the world... destiny is fully co-creative. At any given moment the future is streaming toward you, but you have to become present enough inside yourself to notice and engage with it. Otherwise it streams right past you and goes somewhere else, and you fade back to karma and fate, which keeps the false world in place."

The false world is a façade, made by the Global Elite. COVID-19 pumped trillions into their corporations and international banks. They plan to put the earth under dictatorship for Jehovah by collapsing the systems they control: stock market, corporations, banks and everything connected to them, like products in the stores and groceries on the shelves. The Great Reset would then be implemented.

The Global Elite programmed us to be mindless consumers and give our life to corporations. Work! Produce! Consume! Repeat! The Corporate World enslaved us and our children, and stole our governments, who tax us for their benefit. The Global Elite control consumer goods, information, wars, everything. When corporations control earth, nature dies and we do too. Break the corporate stranglehold on your life or it will break you. Stop buying products you do not need and stock up on things you need to survive while you can.

"Every now and then we awaken... We look up from our work stations, turn away from our computers and gaze out the window. It is then, with uncommon clarity, that we find ourselves in the throes of war- held captive in an invisible prison, and the battle is for nothing less than our personal sovereignty. Like indentured servants, we follow the designated routine- working to earn money while striving for sustenance. At the same time, our consciousness is under attack from all directions by forces that seek to control our minds and amputate our hearts... the time to rise is now, as we stand at the gateway to humanity's grand transition- one that is destined to free minds and open hearts (The Mystical Village that Rewired Reality, Justin Nathen)."

The big conglomerates will fall. We can bring them down before the Global Elite knock them over. Stop working for giant corporations and buying their products. If this profit-driven Machine is not destroyed, we will be crushed under its wheels. Disengage from the Machine and your robot-mind will recover. You will reconnect with your true Self, where deep knowing and the sacred lives within you.

Withdraw from the stock market. Keep investments local. Request a town meeting to prepare for economic collapse. Petition the Mayor for a community bank. If we do not break the Global Elite's control of our money, we will be mowed down. Diverse monetary systems with local currencies will strengthen our communities and towns, increasing our autonomy. Exchange goods and services on a local level. Bartering and gift economy bypass corporate control.

Organize your town, community and neighborhood to be self-sufficient. We must bypass the corporate world or we will not survive. Form a district to unite your neighborhood; give it a name. Have a brainstorming session on abilities and skills to share. Exchange services: home maintenance, car repair, carpentry, painting, plumbing, yard work, day care, house cleaning, meal deliveries, etc. Create support systems for those with special needs. Have project parties. Close the day with a community meal. Learn how to open and run a small business. Form apprenticeships. Start industries to be self-reliant; trade with other communities.

Community life will give us true abundance and security. Donating time and labor to your neighborhood feels good. Helping others is satisfying; we will desire less, consume less and flourish. If everyone contributes, anyone in crisis can be helped. We will not need government welfare, insurance or social security. If someone is ill, if a teen is in trouble or a family needs food, clothes, etc. aid will be given. Elders can guide the youth, passing on their wisdom.

Hold community ceremonies to support people in crisis. Everyone participating takes a turn standing in front of the group. They share their crisis, their difficulties, problems and challenges. The group listens carefully to what is being said. The ceremony leader then prays for the person, asking angels for their help, expressing what the person needs and how their unique abilities, skills and talents are important. One by one, everyone gives the person an embrace, telling them they're appreciated and supported. As everyone takes their turn a sense of belonging builds within the group.

Inspirational.com says 'By my helping you reach your goals, you automatically help me reach mine, and others with theirs. It's an amazing cycle that builds happiness and does not fail. Knowledge, understanding and guided effort make it happen and universal law keeps it going."

Hold festivals, fairs, dances and sing-alongs that everyone can learn. Celebrate the Equinox and Solstice. Have Give-Away-Day; empty your garage, closets, etc. of unused items. Giving away items you do not use or want will increase synchronistic flows; things you need will come to you. Have a town Free Distribution Center where you can drop off items you no longer need and browse for things you do. Celebrate weddings, graduations, births, funerals, job promotions, leaving home, tragedy, triumphs, etc. as a community.

Remove fences, share yard space: plant veggie gardens, fruit trees and berry bushes. Start a compost. Build shops to hold tools, bikes, storage, work areas. Pool money to buy bulk foods and tools that you share. Hold Community Court to settle disputes. If society breaks down and people become desperate, build a wall around your block, defend your apartment building. Station guards for protection. Make a pact to share everything with your group for survival. Distribute your possessions with each other, so everyone has what they need to live. Share cars, food, extra space- everything. We can survive in small groups, and eventually in small towns.

John Spears designs sustainable towns. Houses are built with local labor using earth-bricks that keep houses cool in summer and warm in winter. Rain barrels and waterless toilets are used. Solar panels on roofs provide electricity. South facing oven-boxes uses the sun for free low heat cooking. Kitchen and toilet sewage are composted. Houses are in groups of six and share gardens, compost and gray water. The town center with schools and markets is within walking distance of homes (sustainabledesign.com).

In Robes Kelly is shown the future 50—100 years from now (if we survive). Nations, multinational corporations and large cities have folded. Self-governing towns flourish with 200+ people. They live a simple lifestyle and run various family businesses with high-tech computers and technology. A global network facilitated trade around the world, by-passing governments and corporations. All families worked with this network, for trade, communication, information, education, etc. Children's education was mostly hands-on projects.

As self-sustainable towns flourish, people will raise families together, working, learning and celebrating as a village. Industries will blossom, sharing talents and resources, build-ing, repairing, making items, giving and receiving therapies, teaching, apprenticing, buying, selling, trading, growing, preparing and preserving food. Town Center will have libraries, shops, schools and healing facilities. We will live enriched lives where miracles happen as we attend to our daily affairs, living in harmony with each other and nature.

When we respect the web of life our earth mother will heal. Her skin is toxic from GM crops, pesticides and chemical fertilizers. Her blood is polluted from sewage plants. We are in our earth mother and she is in us. Our life depends on her. When the soil and water are toxic, we are too. Do not put poisons on the soil or your excrement in water. The earth will heal without us, but we cannot heal without her.

Detergents are pollutants to septic systems and treatment plants. They accelerate algae growth in the oceans, depleting oxygen for sea life. These pollutants (phosphorous, nitrogen, potassium) are nutrition to fruit trees, grasses, plants, and gardens. Greywater systems use soaps, skin, food particles, shampoo, and conditioner as plant fertilizer. They are plant food to the ground, and poisons in a septic tank. If everyone converted to composting toilets, country septic systems and city sewer systems could be changed over to gray-water systems, and we would have a sustainable supply of irrigation water for gardens and landscaping.

Human manure becomes nutrient rich soil when composed. Feed the soil with manure (instead of pesticides) and it will feed you with nutrient rich foods (instead of blighted crops). Compost your excrement. Adding biochar to your soil (charred wood) turns soil into a healthy habitat for microorganisms Healthy soil is alive with insects, earthworms, bacteria and fungi; chemical fertilizers kill soil. You can create a healthy, sustainable garden without chemicals.

Grave sites should be natural burial grounds. In recompose burial (human composting) the body is placed in a container and covered with wood chips, alfalfa and straw. Microbes and plant matter convert the body into nutrient-rich soil in 6— 8 weeks. As our earth mother is nourished with the com- posted flesh, blood and bones of our departed, she nourishes us. Our bodies are full of life-giving potential. When cycled into soil, we can regenerate earth, turning human death into ecological wealth. States with green funeral homes: Oregon, Colorado, Washington, Vermont and California.

For humanity to survive, the conventional medical use of vaccines, drugs and most surgeries must end. This approach treats symptoms and body parts. In our optimal future holistic centers will replace hospitals, clinics, mental institutions and addiction rehab centers. Holistic centers correct imbalances: toxicity, energy structures, nutritional, emotions, hormones, and more. Your body knows what is wrong and can tell you. X-rays, MRI, CTs or EKGs are not needed. Holistic Centers will replace hospital equipment, machinery, etc.

Modalities that support life will be used in Holistic Centers. They may have sweat lodges, cleansing ponds, isolation tanks, herb and veggie gardens. Patients will be supported in a home-like setting while their mind and body self-corrects. The chronically ill, the traumatized and depressed, criminals, drug addicts, mentally ill and people in crisis will find the help they need to heal.

Naturopathy, acupuncture, chiropractic, macrobiotics, plant medicines, chromotherapy, past-life regression, entity release, soul retrieval, natural birthing, fasting, and soaking in hot springs will be used. Other methods might include reading DNA, light body, akashic records, psychic tracking, bio-resonance, hand diagnosis, neurofeedback, fingerprint, iris reading, psychic surgery and ultraviolet blood irradiation.

Arigo, a Brazil peasant, performed surgical operations in less than a minute. He worked in a trance, removing tumors, cataracts, and other anomalies, treating 300 patients a day without anesthesia or antiseptic. Patients had a full recovery and felt no pain (see Arigo: Surgeon of the Rusty Knife by Fuller). This type of surgery may replace hospital surgeries.

Vaxx blood is corrupted; it has microscopic blood-cloths. Ultraviolet blood irradiation can replace it. Blood is withdrawn, irradiated with ultraviolet light and given to the patient- auto blood-transfusion. It kills viruses and bacteria, including stealth pathogens. Stealth microbes have invaded humanity, creating many chronic conditions that plague us. Ultraviolet blood irradiation can restore our health.

Dr. Rollier established heliotherapy clinics in the Swiss Alps (1903—the late 1940's). He cured thousands of patients of tuberculosis, rickets, burns, ulcers, infections, abscesses, anemia and fractures using cool morning sunlight. The Rollier Method will be implemented in holistic centers, as well as Herbert Shelton's Hygienic System. Shelton ran fasting centers in Texas from 1928—1940.

When we eat raw foods as Jesus taught, many surgical procedures will become obsolete. Vaccines, antibiotics and anti-psychotic drugs are anti-life. They will cease to exist. Nutrients will be used to correct deficiencies. Everyone will know how to maintain their health with natural remedies, fasting and sunbathing as Jesus taught.

In The Teaching of Little Crow (Heart) a holistic center models this future- a miniature city on 400 acres. The land and cost of buildings was donated. At the center stands an ancient looking temple with a gold dome roof. Twelve roads, like spokes of a wheel, lead out from it, extending to exterior gates. Between the radiating roads are smaller buildings built like temples with unique designs and colors. Each temple specialized in different holistic healing methods. Further from

314

the temples are small houses with trees and gardens. Patients pay a small rent while using the houses; therapies are free. Facilitators work with patients to diagnose their issues and help them heal themselves.

When doing/having energy work done, ask 'angels in the light' to assist you. Do not use names; demons answer to saints, angel names, power animals, etc. Never invite entities inside you. Asking a power animal to open or cleanse your chakra will invite a demon to possess you. You could attend a workshop and leave with demons in your chakras.

If you attend a retreat where the leader calls on a saint-Mary Magdalene, Mother Mary, St. Germaine, etc. to heal your trauma, leave. Demons go by these names. They can enter your mind and inflict pain from childhood traumas. As you feel the pain, a demon will consume your energy. This will not heal you, it will retraumatize you. There are dark shamans who teach astral projection by unwinding their students chakras, forcing them out of their body. This opens them to demon possession. If you take a shaman course that uses Christ Consciousness, teaches channeling, receiving a guide, or letting entities enter you, you're learning sorcery and opening to demonic possession.

{We are at the edge of destruction. If we stand together, we will move the earth and evil will collapse. Kundalini can heal us and expand our awareness. Its transforming fire can carry the human race into ascension. My words are laced with light and carry kundalini energy. As this fiery light stirs within you, old programs- politics, dogma, racism, judging others, being ego-driven, watching videos, eating junk food, etc. will lose interest. Your connection to your true Self, others, animals and nature will increase. As this cleansing force awakens the world, we will no longer be deceived, we will stop feeding demons, reclaim our earth and live our Optimal Future.}

Invincible
Pat Benatar

Youtube.com

What are we running for, when there's nowhere we can run to anymore? We can't afford to be innocent. Stand up and face the enemy. It's a do-or-die situation. We will be invincible! And with the power of conviction, there is no sacrifice. It's a do-or-die situation. We will be invincible! Won't anybody help us? What are we running for when there's nowhere, nowhere we can run to anymore?

Stand up and face the enemy

Chapter 23
Pagans, Brooms And Androgyne

Pagans commune with nature through the Goddess. The Creator is fe/male; S/he alone gave birth to the universe (females give birth). There is no Father-God, the Creator is the Goddess Of All Things. Hir divinity is woven throughout all that is. The Creator is within you; S/he is your Spirit. There was no Satan in ancient pagan practices; this is a Christian teaching. Satan had no place in pre-Christian societies. There are witches that worship Satan and it is the same religion as Christianity. They worship the same god-Jehovah, who lives on destruction. Pagans nurture and heal.

When the great plagues ravaged medieval Europe, Priests and physicians didn't know it was caused by rats. Millions were dying and many turned to pagans for help, because they could cure the sick. Pagans were saving lives and the Pope blamed them for the plagues. Between 1350—1650 millions of European shamans (mostly women) were killed. Medical practice was severed from its pagan roots and ancient, holistic healing among Europeans was lost. Pagans who set broken bones and mended them with herbal wraps were dead, replaced by doctors with saws. Natural healing methods were forgotten, traded for contemporary medical practices that treated symptoms. Western medicine, with vaccines, surgery and drugs descended from this evil.

Every aspect of pagan life was superior to Christianity. Women were revered; they were closer to the Goddess. Pagan women were the keeper of the broom, ceremony and ritual. Christian women and children were property, owned and controlled by men who were superior, and made in God's image. As Women heal from this abuse, they help end patriarchy that enslaved, brutalized and sexually exploited them and their children for thousands of years.

In pagan weddings (not recognized by the Church) Bride and groom placed their palms together and a small cord was tied around their interlocked hands, symbolizing their unity in life thereafter. This is where 'tie the knot' comes from. They jumped over a broom to bless their union.

In ancient pagan households, brooms protected the hearth and home. A broom by the fireplace protected the opening so evil spirits could not enter. A broom, hung above the entrance, blocked negative entities, and they stood guard at outside doors. Houses were swept clean with a broom before important events (celebrations, weddings, births) and a sacred circle was cast, to remove spirits that might cause trouble, clear negative energies, and create sacred space. Pagan midwives carried a broom for this purpose.

Brooms are used by pagan women to open a circle, sweeping it of unwanted energies so the desired energy can fill it. Pagan women dance with their brooms in the fields to make crops grow and use them to bring or stop rain.

When pagans 'ride a broomstick' they perform a symbolic reunion of male-female genitalia. In her article <u>Do Witches Really Ride Broomsticks</u> Ashira R. says: "When women went to any meeting... whether it was a ceremony or not, they were expected to bring their symbol of position - the broom. Upon arrival at a meeting, they would display the 'staff of office' (broom), turn the broom like a hobbyhorse and enter the sacred space ridding their brooms. So yes pagans and witches do ride upon brooms, just not as most would think ."

{Between 2017—2022, gender dysphoria increased 200%. These kids are not in the wrong body. They're at the forefront of humanity becoming androgynous. Gender blended kids need gender recognition: goy (girl/Boy), birl (boy/Girl) without taking hormones or having surgeries. They need freedom to join activities and sports that appeal to them, use their preferred name, and restroom they're comfortable with. Let your child play and dress the way s/he wants. S/he will grow up knowing who s/he really is, with greater self-esteem. Children live from their heart and know who they are inside. Let them express this without lectures. Their dysphoria is caused by pressure to be male or female. They are f/M and m/F.

Torrance discovered creative boys have more feminine traits and creative girls are more masculine than other girls. Creativity requires sensitivity (female trait) and independence (male trait). Great minds are androgynous.

Feminine energy is intuitive; male energy is logical. Out-of-balance female energy is manipulative and codependent. Out-of-balance male energy is aggressive and competitive. As our masculine and feminine energies integrate within us, we become self-actualized, gaining a sense of belonging, meaning and purpose in our lives. We let go of rigid, society rules and adopt an outlook that contains a blend of male and female traits. When these energies balance we become empowered and authentic, living from our heart as our true Self. Everyone who finds this wholeness within themselves is helping the world make the great transition into ascension.

Scott Stuart, author of My Shadow Is Purple, writes books for gender-blended children, showing them there are other kids like they are. It's ok to be themselves. Someday gender roles will vanish, and gender identity will be a nonissue. In Intersexion Davis tells the story of an intersex person and his life as an unaccepted minority. Someday nonmainstream gender people will become the majority. We are entering the Androgynous-Aquarian era where identity labels end: gay, lesbian, bisexual, transgender, intersex (male-female), queer (other identities), asexual. Everyone will simply be androgynous.}

Jack and Jill symbolize humanity after the separation of the sexes. We de-evolved and struggle uphill to survive. Jack falls down the hill and breaks his crown; male dominance is broken and patriarchal societies end. Jill tumbles down unharmed. The hill is a false world. We will tumble down it when we turn off the path of destruction. Tumbling down is a period of transition. At the bottom of the hill, patriarchy ends.

In Emerging From the Matrix Salini was subjected to MK-Ultra programming as a child by her Mason father, to be a sex slave. On her mother's side, Salini comes from a long lineage of healers. She developed deprogramming methods for mind-control trauma, healing herself and other women. As women heal from men's sexual abuse and domination, they help the whole world heal.

Society is polarized (far-right—far-left) because men and women are polarized. When we regain our male/female balance there will be no hostile men or conniving women. We will live enriched lives in a sustainable world where everyone is cherished. There will be no greed, war, famine, sex abuse or tyranny. We will all live in opulent abundance as sovereign beings, with freedom be our true Self.

Androgynous

Joan Jett

Here comes Dick, he's wearing a skirt. Here comes Jane, you know she's sporting a chain. Same hair revolution, same build evolution. Tomorrow who's going to fuss... And today the people dress the way that they please. The way they tried to do in the last century... Closer than you know, love each other so,

Androgynous

Jack and Jill

Jack and Jill went up the hill
To fetch a pail of water
Jack fell down and broke his crown
And Jill came tumbling after

Sweet Little Broom

Moriah Morningstar

My sweet little broom made of straw bound so tight
You are my staff, my truth shield of light
The secret of humanity, you hold within your shape
The way we were created is written on your slate

You symbolize all people becoming absolute and whole
With their own regenerative powers anchored in their souls
Balanced males and females bring goodwill and harmony
The family and the nation heal in the Age of Androgyny

My broom will be the symbol that puts everything aright
Sweeping out old structures whose end is now in sight
The masculine and feminine will shine again in grace
United in all people, we are the 'human race'.

I honor you sweet broom, as a sign of what will be
When we cross the threshold, stepping into eternity
Where all of humanity will receive a wondrous birth
And love, light and happiness fill every space on earth

Chapter 24
Our Last
Sovereign Territory

"The Illuminati are designing a world populated by the living dead— zombie slaves divorced from their own source." As this plot becomes "more and more clear and the shock factor registers" we will be tested to stand and protect our last sovereign territory: "our soul-heart-mind." We have powerful allies in this battle: "the earth, plants, animals, wind, waters, rocks, angels, and "the Amazing Grace that surrounds and penetrates every fiber of our being."

"What is at stake is the entire planet. Even now battles are being fought on the fringes of our imagination for possession of our all-powerful ability to create..." We have the ability within us to "summon the allies, the shocking synchronicities, the harrowing escapes, the outrageous turns of fate, the twists in the plot, the shields of protection, the slight edge in the final confrontation that will deliver victory at the last possible second in the greatest love story ever told (Amazing Grace: The nine principles of living in natural magic David Wolfe and Nick Good)."

Your Imagination is the doorway to your creative powers. What you imagine you can manifest. "Behold the people are one and they have all one language... now nothing will be restrained from them which they have imagined to do (Genesis 11: 6)."

The Prophecy of Montreal 1888

"All man made progress will be enlisted for destruction. However, the great fate will raise her hand in warning and will command to **STOP!** If men will listen to the judicious ones among them and stop, it will be their advantage; if not, it will be there misfortune and a great calamity will follow [emphasis mine]."

The Millennium Book of Prophecy (Hogue)

I kept silent until the knife was raised
And then I shouted stop
Reject Jehovah and stop
The Lord's Great and Dreadful Day

STOP demons
STOP vaccines
STOP copulating
STOP watching TV
STOP abusing children
STOP chemtrail spraying
STOP eating processed food
STOP mutilating baby genitals
STOP celebrating Jehovah's holidays
STOP supporting corrupt corporations
STOP paying taxes to corrupt governments
STOP sending your children to public schools
STOP marking the years by Jehovah's circumcision
Listen to judicious ones among you

These are the times that try men's souls... Tyranny, like hell, is not easily conquered; yet we have this consolation with us, that the harder the conflict, the more glorious the triumph.

Thomas Paine <u>The American Crisis</u>

Evil grows until it destroys itself with darkness
Goodness grows until it preserves itself in eternity

Knowledge has power to free us

Secrecy has power to enslave us

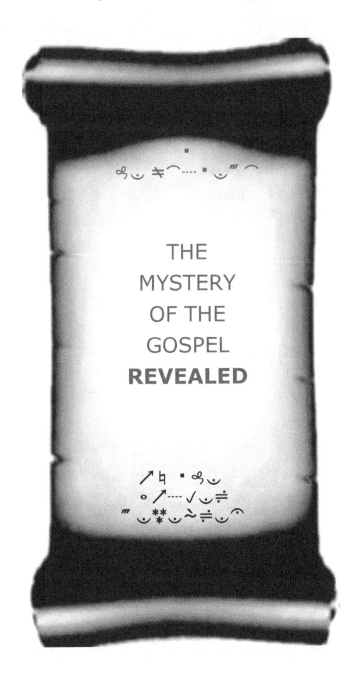

THE
MYSTERY
OF THE
GOSPEL
REVEALED

Chapter 25
Devotion to Humanity

My Storybook Playhouse

Is inspiring me to help her fulfill her destiny
I'm mending her soul, cleansing and healing
as I remodel her rooms so delightful and thrilling
She is my cottage, my refuge, my home
and the ground of my being when I roam
This is where I was meant to be
My earth mother guided her to me
Our destinies are deeply entwined
Our soul desires are completely aligned
Her sacred spaces are being redesigned
and filled with love and light divine
She is becoming a transmitting station
through my love, devotion, and inspired creations
Together we radiate a whirlwind of love
and send it out through the cosmos above
and around the world to every place on earth
to help humanity bring forth a new birth
The Aquarian era will soon dawn
Bringing truth and prosperity to everyone
My storybook playhouse is playing a part
by becoming an anchor, a portal, a spot
where love light is held and channeled and sent
throughout all creation and back once again
to re-echo and bounce and fill every void
and help all of humanity live in true joy
Moriah Morningstar

My Power Pole

Moriah Morningstar

My power pole deeply anchored
in our earth mother held so tight
You are a symbol of sovereignty;
of humanity bathed in the light
Flowing through my house and shop,
your current carries my vision
To every kindred, tongue and nation
So we can make the great transition
Sending eternal fire and passion into every beating heart
You awaken all of humanity so that we can have a new start
Corruption, greed and evil are melting with the dawn
The Golden World will reign again
We know, we feel, and we belong

Buried under my power pole on 9-27-12

Chapter 26
Words

Jehovah speaks directly at me in the Bible

Jehovah as Job

'How long will the words of your mouth be like a strong wind? You wrote bitter things against me. You set print on the heels of my feet. How long will you vex my soul and break me in pieces with words? You discovered deep things in darkness and brought to light, the shadow of death. Now there is no shadow of death where the workers of iniquity may hide.'

Words of My Mouth
matching wordcounts and topics
M-Message   C-chapter

555 words Endorsement, C 6, C 26:   Exposing Jehovah

333 words Credits, Angels Of Light, C 2, 15: Symbolism

262 words Contents 1—2, C 5: Deception

3333 words M 1, 18:   Bioengineered 'aliens'

2844 words M 9, 12, 13, 23: Black Elk killing Jehovah

2969 words M 15, 20:   Harmony with nature

3444 words M 19, 22:   Angels, dreams

2777 words M 10, 24, C 1:   Revelations

1777 words C 9, 10:   Warnings

77 words C 16, 19:   Covert agendas

300 words C 11, 20, 25:   Defender of mankind

More Number Patterns

1492 words. My Vision: holocaust of the Western
Hemisphere for Jehovah

2333 words   M 25
2444 words   M   7   cherish earth
2555 words   C 22

3066 words   M 3
3077 words   C 12   Exposing Jehovah
3088 words   M 4

2882 words   M 17   Jehovah's Christian churches
2992 words   M   8

2808 words   M 5   Jehovah's mass destruction
 808 words   C 5

303 words: Jenner's Address   USA at risk
        p. 141—142   {World at risk}
        C 27   World awakens
        p. 152   {Demons at risk}
        p. 124   {Day of Dancing}

404 words: p. 79—80   {De-possession}

808 words   p. 170—172   {Destiny Dreams}

909 words: p. 117—119   {Six Grandfathers}
          p. 193—195   {Mattson's afterlife}

111 words   p . 315   {Kundalini}

222 words   p. 135   {Cleansing Wind}
           p. 200   {Destiny Dreams}

Messages, Chapters with 77

2929 words M 2: Jehovah causes events to unfold
10**2929** words Book wordcount: Moriah inspires events
to unfold

Thousands of years ago, Jehovah said 77s were required to seal my vision; 13 chapters have 77s in their wordcount. Is this why? Jehovah knew <u>The</u> <u>Holy</u> <u>Ghost</u> was <u>6</u> <u>6</u> <u>6</u> in numerology before English was invented. He sees probable futures. Jehovah planned his curse on pages 153—158 (Global Elite blueprint) before I wrote them.

With your Miracles and your Heroism,
Our light will illuminate the world,
We will manifest our optimal future,
And we will ascend

Ascension

Tipping Point

100TH

Stop the Lord's 'Great and Dreadful Day.' Reject Jehovah-Allah-Christ-Satan and help each other cast out his demons. Reclaim our planet and your life. Share this knowledge with others. Help create a tipping point. If everyone who reads <u>The Greatest Deception</u> loans it to 12 people and they loan it to 12 more, awareness will spread until the 100th Monkey Effect occurs. The world will awaken from Jehovah's Perpetual Sleep and demons will die their second death.

We're Saving Our Own Lives
Help Wake Up The World

Return to Innocence

KOTOM

Like the Thunderbird of Old
I will rise again
Dan George

legendsofamerica.com

Auld Lang Syne

Atlantis, Forever Longing in my Heart

Saudade

We two have paddled in the stream
From morning sun till dine
But seas between us broad have roared
Since long, long ago

Black Elk

Standing in the Gap

Da Vinci's Jesus Portrait

Reveals Jesus' Androgyny

Jesus?

Lisa- God's Promise
Mona- Noble One, male/female

or

'Evil will go forth from nation to nation, and a great whirlwind will be raised up from the coasts of the earth. And the slain of the Lord will be at that day from one end of the earth even unto the other end of the earth... They will be dung upon the ground.. (Jer 25:32—34). Jehovah-Allah-Christ-Satan wants to kill us so earth will be safely inhabited for demons.

His voice was not loud yet it filled eternity. There was nothing that did not hear. The Great Stallion's song was so beautiful, nothing could keep from dancing. Universes throughout eternity will celebrate our victory over Jehovah with us. All of creation- leaves on trees, grasses on hills, waters in creeks, rivers and lakes, animals, birds, people, everyone everywhere will sing and dance with joy.

'All things must end
Goodbye my friend'

This book belongs to

_____

Owner's Comments

_____
_____
_____
_____
_____
_____
_____
_____
_____
_____
_____
_____
_____
_____
_____
_____
_____
_____
_____
_____
_____
_____
_____
_____
_____
_____
_____

This book has been read by

1

2

3

4

5

6

7

8

9

10

11

12

Comments

page	TOPIC

My Notes

Made in the USA
Las Vegas, NV
20 August 2023

76345593R00203